# Crisis and Neoliberal Reforms in Africa

Langaa &
African Studies Centre

# Crisis and Neoliberal Reforms in Africa

## Civil Society and Agro-Industry in Anglophone Cameroon's Plantation Economy

Piet Konings

Langaa Research and Publishing Common Initiative Group
PO Box 902 Mankon
Bamenda
North West Region
Cameroon
Phone +237 33 07 34 69 / 33 36 14 02
LangaaGrp@gmail.com
http://www.langaa-rpcig.net
www.africanbookscollective.com/publishers/langaa-rpcig

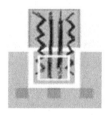

African Studies Centre
P.O. Box 9555
2300 RB Leiden
The Netherlands
asc@ascleiden.nl
http://www.ascleiden.nl

ISBN: 9956-578-03-7

# Contents

# Acknowledgements

This volume is the result of extensive research I have done over many years on the most important agro-industrial enterprises in Anglophone Cameroon's plantation economy. From the very start, I was able to benefit from previous studies on these enterprises, notably the outstanding work of Edwin and Shirley Ardener on the Cameroon Development Corporation (CDC) and Georges Courade on Pamol.

During my fieldwork, I became indebted to a great number of people and, unfortunately, there is only room to mention a few of them here. I am particularly grateful to old colleagues at the former Institute of Human Sciences in Yaoundé, in particular Nantang Jua, Joseph Ngu, Cyprian Fisiy and the late N'Sangou Arouna who all helped me to feel at home in Cameroon and who were always prepared to give me advice.

I am also grateful for the hospitality and assistance I received from various institutions in Anglophone Cameroon, including the Head Offices of the CDC and Pamol, the Buea National Archives, the provincial and divisional offices of the Ministry of Labour and Social Insurance, and the divisional unions of agricultural workers. My greatest debt in Cameroon, however, is to the members and leaders of the regional civil-society groups and associations who were always willing to answer my numerous questions.

I would also like to express my gratitude to the African Studies Centre in Leiden that funded the entire project. Two ASC members have been particularly helpful. I wish to thank Ann Reeves for copy-editing the text and Dick Foeken for his advice and assistance in the production process.

Finally, I would like to acknowledge the invaluable role played by Peter Geschiere and Francis Nyamnjoh in my research projects in Cameroon over the years. They have been a constant source of friendship and intellectual stimulation and I thank them for this.

# List of Tables

# Abbreviations

| | |
|---|---|
| AAC | All Anglophone Congress |
| BAT | British American Tobacco |
| BCCI | Bank of Credit and Commerce International |
| BCUF | Bakweri Co-operative Union of Farmers |
| BLC | Bakweri Land Committee |
| BLCC | Bakweri Land Claims Committee |
| BNA | Buea National Archives |
| CAM | Cameroon Anglophone Movement |
| CAMAGRIC | Cameroon Agro-Industrial Company Ltd |
| CCCE | *Caisse Centrale de Coopération Économique* |
| CDC | Cameroon Development Corporation |
| CDCWU | Cameroon Development Corporation Workers' Union |
| CNU | Cameroon National Union |
| COMDEV | Commonwealth Development Corporation |
| CPDM | Cameroon People's Democratic Movement |
| CTE | Cameroon Tea Estates |
| CTUC | Cameroon Trade Union Congress |
| CYL | Cameroon Youth League |
| DO | District Officer |
| DUAW D/M | Divisional Union of Agricultural Workers of Donga-Mantung |
| EAC | Estates and Agency Company Ltd |

| | |
|---|---|
| EKOSCOOP | Ekondo Titi Oil Palm Smallholder Cooperative Society |
| FED | *Fonds Européen de Développement* |
| FONADER | *Fonds National de Développement Rural* |
| ESAP | Enhanced Structural Adjustment Programme |
| ECOSOC | (United Nations) Economic and Social Council |
| FAWU | Fako Agricultural Workers' Union |
| FCFA | *Franc de la Communauté Financière Africaine* |
| FFB | Fresh Fruit Bunches |
| IDA | International Development Association |
| IMF | International Monetary Fund |
| JCC | Joint Consultative Committee |
| KTDA | Kenya Tea Development Authority |
| MAWU | Meme Agricultural Workers' Union |
| NAWU | Ndian Agricultural Workers' Union |
| NEC | National Executive Committee |
| NGO | Non-Governmental Organisation |
| NUCW | National Union of Cameroon Workers |
| ONCPB | *Office National de Commercialisation des Produits de Base* |
| PCWU | Pamol Cameroon Workers' Union |
| SAP | Structural Adjustment Programme |
| SCNC | Southern Cameroons National Council |
| SDA | Smallholder Development Authority |
| SDF | Social Democratic Front |
| SDO | Senior Divisional Officer |

| | |
|---|---|
| SOCAPALM | *Société Camerounaise de Palmeraies* |
| SODECOTON | *Société de Développement du Coton* |
| SONEL | *Société Nationale d'Électricité* |
| SOSUCAM | *Société Sucrière du Cameroun* |
| SWECC | South West Chiefs' Conference |
| SWELA | South West Elites Association |
| UAC | United Africa Company |
| UN | United Nations |
| WCTUC | West Cameroon Trades Union Congress |

# Map of the Republic of Cameroon

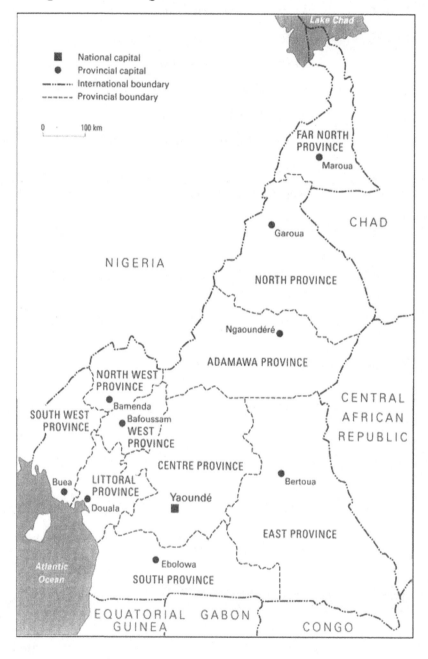

# Civil society and Anglophone Cameroon's agro-industrial crisis and reforms

## Introduction

Anglophone Cameroon is somewhat exceptional in the West and Central African region in the sense that a plantation economy was established there during the German colonial era (1884-1916) and has remained as a dominant feature of the regional economy ever since. Two agro-industrial enterprises have dominated the plantation sector: one is a huge parastatal enterprise, the Cameroon Development Corporation (CDC), and the other is a private company, Plantations Pamol du Cameroun Ltd, or Pamol as it is popularly known, a subsidiary of Unilever.

Most of the estates are located in the present South West Province of Anglophone Cameroon. Since 1977, however, the CDC has extended its activities beyond the South West Province to other provinces by creating four additional estates. It took over the Ndu Tea Estate from a Lipton subsidiary, Estates and Agency Company Ltd, in the Anglophone North West Province, and acquired land to set up three new estates in the Francophone area, namely the Kompina and Penda Mboko Rubber Estates in the Littoral Province and the Djuttitsa Tea Estate near Dschang in the West Province. The acquisition of these new estates demonstrated not only the Cameroonian government's persistent faith in the CDC management and its development potential but also its intention to transform the corporation from a regional into a national agro-industrial enterprise.

There are different theories on plantation agriculture but all seem to agree that this form of production is more likely to meet the imperatives of increased agricultural output and capital accumulation than smallholder production can. Existing studies on the CDC and Pamol mostly maintain that such agro-industrial enterprises have contributed greatly to regional development. They are seen as the lifeline of the Anglophone region in general, and the South West Province in particular.

The economic and financial crisis that befell the Cameroonian agro-industrial sector in the 1980s has however brought both companies to the verge of collapse. This crisis, which caused great commotion in Anglophone Cameroon, presented a serious challenge to existing theories on plantation production and capital accumulation and led to the implementation of a number of neoliberal economic reforms in an attempt to revive Anglophone Cameroon's ailing plantation economy and set it on the road to renewed capital accumulation. Such reform measures included the withdrawal of state intervention and state subsidies from the regional agro-industrial sector and the restructuring, liquidation and privatisation of existing agro-industrial enterprises with a view to enhancing their efficiency, cost effectiveness and international competitiveness as well as to attracting foreign investment. The Cameroonian state refused to assist Pamol during its deep crisis and, as a result, the company was put into voluntary liquidation in October 1987 and has been up for sale ever since. The CDC was first denied public grants and subsidies, then restructured, and set for privatisation in 1994.

The neoliberal reform measures had severe consequences for civil-society groups that had a direct stake in these agro-industrial enterprises, notably the ethno-regional elite and their associations, regional chiefs and their organisations, plantation workers and their trade unions, and contract farmers and their cooperatives. This study shows that these civil-society groups have never resigned themselves to their fate but have been actively involved in a variety of formal and informal methods of resistance. In this connection, it is important to observe that the introduction of various neoliberal political reforms in the early 1990s, as in other African states, created more political space for civil-society organisations (Bratton 1989, 1994; van de Walle 1993; Konings 2009b). Following political liberalisation, several associations of the regional elite and chiefs emerged (Nyamnjoh & Rowlands 1998), and older organisations like trade unions and smallholder cooperatives regained a large measure of autonomy, allowing them to represent their members' interests more effectively against management and the state.

In the first section of this introductory chapter, I discuss some of the major theories on plantation production that have influenced previous studies on the CDC and Pamol. In the second section, I first show how the regional agro-industrial crisis and reforms have seriously threatened the interests of various civil-society groups and organisations and then introduce the prominent ones.

## Major theories on plantation production

A review of the literature reveals an apparent lack of consensus among specialists on the essence of plantation production. A number of definitions are in circulation (cf. Pryor 1982; Graham & Floering 1984; Rote 1986; Kurian 1989), yet they are little more than attempts to describe some of the specific characteristics of plantation production. One of the most frequently quoted definitions is the following:

> A plantation is an economic unit producing agricultural commodities (field-crops or horticultural products but not livestock) for sale and employing relatively large numbers of unskilled labourers whose activities are closely supervised. Plantations usually employ a year-round labour crew of some size and they usually specialise in the production of only one or two marketable products. They differ from other kinds of farms in the way in which factors of production, primarily management and labour are combined. (Jones 1968)

What this definition has in common with some of the others is that it identifies the establishment of managerial control over a large labour force as a basic element in plantation production. Beckford (1972: 9) and Wolf (1982: 315), following Thompson (1975), went as far as comparing rigid managerial control in plantation production with military regimentation and, therefore, refer to plantation production as 'military' agriculture. Other specialists, on the contrary, tend to underline the similarities in managerial control between modern plantations and industrial enterprises and thus speak of 'industrial' plantations (cf. Courtenay 1965).

3

Such descriptive definitions undoubtedly have a certain merit but also some fundamental weaknesses. First, they appear unable to include all the existing types of plantations. For instance, Jones's definition quoted above does not account for the emergence of modern, highly capitalised sugar plantations that only employ a relatively small number of (skilled) workers (cf. Graves & Richardson 1980). Secondly, they lack analytical rigour as they do not allow differentiation between the varied relations of production in plantation agriculture, e.g. slave labour, indentured labour, squatter labour, free wage-labour, and so on (cf. Bernstein & Pritt 1974). And thirdly, they are essentially timeless definitions because they do not reflect the constant changes that occur in plantation production as a result of modifications in the conditions of land and capital ownership, labour supplies and control, technology and market structures.

In the absence of any satisfactory definition, Kurian suggests studying plantations in their specific social and historical context:

> In many ways, therefore, generalisation on the nature of plantations appears problematic and perhaps unwarranted. The range of literature casts no doubts on the existence of the phenomenon of plantations, nor on the rigid character of their labour-management relations and their historical significance in many Third World countries. Yet comparisons give rise to strong differences which only underscore the importance of a specific social and historical context (Kurian 1989: 4)

Close study of the existing literature reveals that the major theories on plantation production, such as modernisation, dependency and the articulation of modes of production schools, have tried to evaluate the role of plantation production in processes of capital accumulation as well as its relationship with peasant production and societies. A short discussion of these theories might contribute to our understanding of the dominant role of the agro-industrial sector in Cameroon's political economy.

The *modernisation school* has always advocated the diffusion of western capital, know-how, technology and values as a necessary prerequisite for development and capital accumulation in developing countries (Long 1977; Varma 1980). It claims that plantations are economically efficient units of production that benefit from considerable economies of scale and technical progress, and should be seen as significant agents of development and capital accumulation (cf. Courtenay 1965; Jones 1968; Graham & Floering 1984; Goldthorpe 1985). It should be noted that these claims have often been disputed. For example, de Silva (1982) and Rote (1986) have convincingly demonstrated that most plantations have barely undergone any technological innovations and have largely preserved their labour-intensive production techniques to date.

Of considerable importance to the study of plantations was the so-called *dual society and dual economy theory,* a well-known variant of the modernisation theory (cf. Boeke 1953; Lewis 1954). It defends the near absence of any linkages between a dynamic/western/capitalist sector and a backward/domestic/pre-capitalist sector. Some of these theorists did not, however, exclude the possibility of a 'demonstration effect' of the modern plantation sector on the traditional peasant sector. This theory has been severely attacked by the dependency and articulation of modes of production schools (see below).

Most studies of the Anglophone Cameroon's plantations have been either implicitly or explicitly written from a modernisation point of view (cf. Bederman 1968; DeLancey 1973; Epale 1985). Epale's book on the history of plantation production and the CDC in Anglophone Cameroon was clearly inspired by the dual economy theory:

> It will be shown in this study that in the special circumstances of Western Cameroon, the introduction of a modern plantation enclave in the relatively backward and inarticulate economy of the region at the turn of the last century and the development of that enclave to its present-day state, had, in balance, a salutary effect on the economy. (Epale 1985: 7)

Unlike the modernisation theory, the *dependency theory* argues that the promotion of capitalist plantation production in the 'periphery' inevitably leads to growing underdevelopment and dependency on western 'metropoles' (cf. Frank 1967, 1969; Amin 1974, 1976; Leys 1975). This dependency perspective of plantations as agents of underdevelopment and exploitation has been elaborated on in specialist studies of plantation production in Latin America (cf. Oxaal 1975; Benn 1974), Asia (cf. de Silva 1982; Bagchi 1982) and Africa (cf. Brett 1973; van Zwanenberg 1975; Leys 1975). The most influential work in this school of thought has undoubtedly been Beckford's *Persistent Poverty: Underdevelopment in Plantation Economies of the Third World* (1972). He characterises plantations as 'enclaves' due to:

- their domination by external forces – metropolitan capital and management – interested in the drain of capital from the periphery to the metropole;
- their exclusive specialisation in export commodities, resulting in monocultural cropping patterns, neglected food production and a dangerous dependence on world market prices;
- their lack of linkages with other sectors of the economy as exemplified by their dependence on the import of various inputs and machinery; and
- their calling into being of societies of their own, alien and inward-looking, and cut off from the outside world, societies marked by 'total' management control over labour inside and outside the labour process, cultural and racial differences, and large income inequalities.

According to Beckford (1972: 215), this enclave nature of plantations causes a number of underdevelopment biases in the domestic economy and society and also creates a 'chronic dependency syndrome' that manifests itself as a value system characterised by dependency and low motivation as well as by strong authoritarian traditions. Strikingly, several studies of plantation production in Anglophone Cameroon have tended to support his negative assessment of the consequences of plantation systems for local societies and economies and the development of a chronic dependency syndrome among the local population (cf. Ardener 1970; Epale 1978, 1985; Courade 1978, 1981/82; Molua 1985).

The dependency school's perspective on plantations seems to be able to overcome some of the shortcomings of the modernisation theory. It helps us to situate the study of plantation production in a historical and international context, with its introduction during the colonial period as an important locus of metropolitan capital accumulation, its (former) domination by foreign capital and management, and its vulnerable dependence on world market commodity prices. However, the dependency theory has not paid sufficient attention to the changes that have occurred in plantation production in the wake of transformations in the world capitalist system and the independence of colonial states. On the one hand, multinational corporations now control the capitalist world market and trade in plantation products. They also control much of the necessary processing, though they have tended to disinvest in the (risky) production of plantation crops *per se* (cf. Dinham & Hines 1983; Barker 1984; Marcussen & Torp 1982; Kemp & Little 1987). On the other hand, post-colonial states have attempted to establish a larger measure of control over their national economies. They increasingly intervene in the control, regulation and stimulation of plantations and are trying to integrate smallholders further into the plantation system, thus challenging the dependency school's thesis of the existence of a comprador political class in newly independent states and the impossibility of a more autonomous capitalist development on the periphery (cf. von Muralt & Sajhau 1987; Sajhau & von Muralt 1987). In some cases, post-colonial states have taken measures that have led to either complete or partial nationalisation (cf. Bolton 1985), while in other cases, they have acted as partners in joint ventures with foreign or local private capital.

A third school of thought that has made a significant contribution to the study of the role of plantation production in capital accumulation and its relationship to peasant production and societies has been the so-called *theory of the articulation of modes of production* as propagated by scholars such as Laclau (1971), Meillassoux (1972, 1975, 1977), Rey (1971, 1973, 1976, 1979), Terray (1969, 1975, 1979), Wolpe (1972, 1980) and van Binsbergen & Geschiere (1985). They do not accept the dependency view that pre-capitalist societies have been destroyed or fully transformed following incorporation into the world capitalist system. Instead they argue that pre-capitalist modes of production have at least been partially preserved since colonial rule, albeit in subordination to the dominant capitalist mode of production. Some of them, particularly Meillassoux (1975) and Wolpe (1972, 1980), have emphasised that this (partial) preservation of pre-capitalist modes of production might be functional to dominant capitalist sectors such as mining and plantations. Capital accumulation by plantations is dependent on, and safeguarded by, the domestic community's supply of cheap land, labour and commodities. Plantation owners can shift the costs of reproducing their labour force onto domestic communities and in this way lower their costs of production.

Most of these scholars claim that the establishment of capitalist domination and the subordination of pre-capitalist modes of production have not always been easy or automatic processes in African social formations. Rey in particular asserts that the 'lineage mode of production' may offer (initial) resistance to capitalist domination in defence of its own autonomy and that capitalism may face considerable obstacles in its attempt to take root in pre-capitalist modes of production. He tries to demonstrate the existence of a variety of mechanisms for integrating pre-capitalist modes of production into the capitalist system, mechanisms that may occur in different forms and combinations and account for the huge variations in the processes of articulation in Africa: (initial) state violence, class contradictions within pre-capitalist mode(s) of production, the establishment of alliances between the dominant classes within the capitalist and pre-capitalist sectors, and the (gradual) operation of market forces (cf. Geschiere 1978, 1985).

Of particular importance to the 'freeing of labour' from the non-capitalist sector to the capitalist sector is, according to Rey, the existence of specific relations of exploitation between the elders and young men and women within the 'lineage mode of production'. The dominant position of the elders and their control over the labour power of the young is usually based on their control of processes of reproduction and bridal goods. Rey claims that the monetarisation of bride wealth in lineage societies after capitalist penetration had effects similar to those of the transformation of feudal land rent in Europe: both developments helped solve the capitalist labour problem, as they forced producers to leave their communities and work as wage labourers on the capitalist market.

Contrary to the modernisation and dependency schools, the articulation of modes of production school has been able to demonstrate the problems that accompany the subordination of autonomous pre-capitalist societies to the imperatives of capital accumulation and to provide a more detailed picture of the varied impact of capitalist plantation production on the surrounding domestic communities. By moving from the level of exchange to that of production, it has been able to explain the continuing existence of pre-capitalist modes of production which, rather than being destroyed, are reshaped and subordinated to capitalist modes of production. By exploring pre-capitalist mode(s) of production, it has been able to show that beneath the apparently socially integrative façade of kinship there are relations of exploitation and dominance that serve in the aftermath of capitalist penetration as major mechanisms of regular labour supplies to dominant capitalist sectors, like plantations. Such regular supplies of labour have always been an essential prerequisite for capital accumulation. Although they appear to disagree with a number of the tenets of the articulation of modes of production school, studies of Anglophone Cameroon's plantation labour by Ardener *et al.* (1960) and Konings (1993a, 1995a, 1996c, 1998a) still reflect some of its insights.

These three schools of thought provide a useful starting point for explaining the continuing interest of some post-colonial states in plantation production. The agro-industrial sector in Cameroon has become one of the main pillars of the post-colonial state's agricultural policies. Courade (1984) and Konings (1993a) have convincingly demonstrated that the Cameroonian post-colonial state has continued to allocate a substantial proportion of its agricultural budget to the expansion of the agro-industrial sector, in particular to the creation and expansion of agro-industrial parastatals, which accounted for nearly 60% of its agricultural budget during the country's third and fourth five-year plans (1971-1981).

Modernisation theorists see the Cameroonian post-colonial state's support of agro-industrial expansion as a clear expression of the political elite's selfless and detached commitment to the modernisation of agricultural production. The latter's promotion of plantation production is more likely to contribute to increased output and capital accumulation than 'archaic' peasant production. The dependency theorists, on the contrary, argue that the Cameroonian post-colonial state's encouragement of agro-industrial expansion reflects the political elite's class interests. They allege that the ruling class is collaborating closely with foreign capital in stimulating agro-industrial expansion as it has its own stake in a project that will inevitably lead to deepening dependency and underdevelopment.

The theory of the articulation of modes of production is also potentially able to help explain the Cameroonian post-colonial state's interest in agro-industrial expansion. This school has often assumed that state intervention was only required in the *initial* process of the articulation of modes of production (cf. Rey 1971, 1973; Meillassoux 1972, 1975). Initial state intervention would help to establish the supremacy of the capitalist mode of production and the ultimate subordination of pre-capitalist modes to the imperatives of colonial capital accumulation: the supply of land, labour and agricultural commodities to the capitalist sectors, especially the plantation sector. It seems to have overlooked the possibility that the post-colonial state's interest in expanded production and capital accumulation might lead to renewed state intervention so as to incorporate the relatively autonomous domestic communities further into the capitalist mode of production (cf. Hyden 1980; Konings 1986a).

From the point of view of the political elite (and their interests), an extension of the modern agro-industrial sector into the rural areas is of utmost importance to national development: agro-industrial expansion seems to be not only a more reliable trajectory for maximising capital accumulation in the short term than peasant agriculture but also a major tool in integrating the relatively autonomous domestic communities further into the capitalist system. Agro-industry is capable of playing a significant intermediary role in these efforts at incorporation. Of late, it has become increasingly evident that agro-industrial expansion in Cameroon is oriented towards two ways of proletarianising the domestic communities' labour power (Konings 1986b):

- the transformation of domestic communities into suppliers of a regular and adequate wage-labour force to the plantations. This has become the most common form of proletarianisation in Cameroon.
- the introduction of contract farming schemes into villages close to agro-industrial plantations. This is a new way of subsuming domestic communities' labour power to the agro-industrial imperatives of increased output and capital accumulation. These schemes entrust agro-industrial enterprises with the responsibility of modernising and

10

supervising participants' production as well as processing and marketing their output. They usually aim at a virtually total destruction of the local peasantry's autonomy and its subordination to management authority over the labour process: its substantial loss of control over the means of production and the processes of production and exchange tends to result in a peculiar form of proletarianisation (cf. Amin & Vergopoulos 1974; Banaji 1977; Bernstein 1979; Boesen 1979). These and similar schemes are becoming increasingly popular in developing countries as they appear to have the potential to raise the local peasantry's productivity and improve its standard of living (cf. Glover 1984; Barker 1984; Goldsmith 1985; Konings 1986a). The growing importance that governments in developing countries are attaching to this peculiar form of proletarianisation constitutes a serious challenge to unilinear models of agrarian transition in developing countries that predict that increased capitalist penetration into the rural areas will result in a progressive transformation of the local peasantry into a wage-labour force (cf. Goodman & Redclift 1981).

These three major theories help to explain the role of plantation production in processes of capital accumulation, its relationship with pre-capitalist societies and the continuing interest of some post-colonial states, like Cameroon, in its expansion. However, they also have shortcomings, and I have criticised them elsewhere in some detail on both empirical and theoretical terms (Konings 1993a). One of their main limitations is their failure to explore what Marx strikingly called the 'hidden abode of [capitalist] production'. That is why they have never been able to underscore the economic and political significance of the continuous struggles between labour and management regarding control over the labour process. It is evident that the subordination of labour to management authority in the labour process is one of the most essential preconditions for capital accumulation in plantation production.

Studies of the labour process in western capitalist countries provide substantial evidence that the constantly renewed managerial strategies of labour control have failed to eliminate labour autonomy

11

completely within the labour process and fully subordinate labour to the commands of capital (cf. Braverman 1974; Friedman 1977; Edwards 1979; Burawoy 1979, 1985; Thompson 1983). In the case of Africa, the chances of controlling labour would seem to be even more reduced in view of the incomplete character of capitalist penetration, workers' close links with non-capitalist social organisation and value systems, and the remaining (though probably declining) possibilities of workers' withdrawal from the capitalist mode of production to non-capitalist modes of production (cf. Hyden 1980; Cooper 1981). African labour is, therefore, inclined to defy management's authority within the labour process and to assert the autonomy of the worker.

In previous studies on plantation labour in Anglophone Cameroon (Konings 1993a, 1995a, 1998a), I have shown that the establishment of control over the labour process was a persistent source of worry to the Cameroonian state and plantation management. Anglophone plantation workers have always tried to preserve a certain degree of autonomy within the labour process and studies covering the early period of regional agro-industrial enterprises show that the CDC and Pamol management experienced difficulties controlling their workers, who often preserved close links with pre-capitalist modes of production. Workers tended to accept only short spells of work and to return to their home communities once they had achieved their 'targets' (cf. Ardener *et al.* 1960; Wells & Warmington 1962). Temporary work and target work were, in fact, significant manifestations of labour autonomy since they enabled workers to earn money according to the rhythms they themselves chose (cf. Cooper 1986). It is therefore not surprising that the CDC and Pamol management soon became keen to stabilise labour as stability helps to reduce labour autonomy and also raises productivity. CDC and Pamol workers have always felt exploited in the labour process and, like other African plantation workers, have continued to receive relatively low remuneration for their hard labour (cf. Ardener *et al.* 1960; Konings 1993a, 1995a, 1998a; Leitner 1976; Clarke 1977; Vail & White 1980; Bolton 1985; Sajhau 1986; Collier & Lal 1986). And their feelings of exploitation have been reinforced as a result of being confronted with the unequal distribution of income at the workplace on a daily basis.

From the outset, the CDC and Pamol management and the state devised a number of strategies to subordinate labour to management authority. These included the establishment of a hierarchical and military style of organisation of production (Konings 1993a, 1998a; Courade 1978), disciplinary measures, incentive schemes and social welfare services, the propagation of ideologies such as paternalism and 'national interest', attempts to form alliances with certain groups of workers and especially the educated and better paid workers, the prohibition of labour engagement in (disruptive) political activities and, as a last resort, the use of the forces of law and order. It is striking that these strategies of labour control have intensified since independence. There was growing intervention by the post-colonial state in the labour process, which is reflected in the political elite's efforts to regulate and centralise almost every aspect of industrial relations, including strikes and union activities (cf. Kendrick 1979). This intervention stems not only from the political elite's interest in achieving harmonious relations between employers and workers and in the maximisation of capital accumulation but is also, as Bayart (1979) rightly observed, a clear expression of the total control that the Cameroonian post-colonial state is trying to establish over civil society as part of its hegemonic project. And secondly, the CDC's management could only acquire substantial loans for its post-colonial expansion programme from international financial institutions, such as the World Bank, if labour control and labour productivity were enhanced.

Remarkably, CDC and Pamol workers have continued to oppose public and managerial efforts at control and have engaged in several, often hidden, forms of resistance against control and exploitation in the labour process (cf. Cohen 1980). Crisp (1984: 5-7) identified three broad types of labour resistance that are relevant to labour action in the CDC and Pamol. On the basis of three main criteria, namely visibility, inclusiveness or scale of resistance, and duration, he distinguishes between:

1. *Informal modes of resistance.* Informal action is usually pursued on an individual or small-scale basis, intermittently and in a covert manner. 'It is not normally part of a deliberate strategy to remedy the source of grievance; indeed it may well derive from a generalised sense of dissatisfaction rather than consciousness of a specific grievance, and so may not be

conceived as industrial conflict at all.' Since the publication of van Onselen's 1976 book on labour protest in the mining compounds of Rhodesia, there has been growing attention in African labour studies to the wide variety of informal modes of labour resistance within and outside the labour process. These range from desertion, absenteeism, malingering, sabotage, theft, the smoking of hemp and the excessive use of alcohol to more positive examples such as the creation of individual, anti-employer work cultures and the adoption of religious beliefs as forms of resistance to the demands of the capitalist mode (cf. Gordon 1977; Perrings 1979; Cohen 1980; Crisp 1984; Lubeck 1986; Cooper 1986; Agier *et al.* 1987).

2. *Collective modes of resistance.* Collective action, such as strikes, riots, demonstrations and go-slows, is more inclusive, overt and of specific duration. It 'normally involves a deliberate attempt to change the situation which gives rise to conflict; it is purposeful activity designed to achieve some concrete improvement'. Collective actions such as strikes often give workers a feeling of power and control over their own lives (Shadeed 1979) and the history (and often the myths) of past militant collective action may shape the consciousness and actions of current workers.

3. *Institutional modes of labour resistance.* Institutional action such as union action is collective, normally overt and requires continuous commitment. Trade unions are supposed to be organisations that defend and protect their members' interests against the employers and the state. However, one should not overlook the contradictory tendencies within the unions (cf. Hyman 1971; Sandbrook 1982; Southall 1988). On the one hand, they articulate their members' common grievances and coordinate their actions, while on the other, they can control their members' activities and assist in their integration into the capitalist mode of production. State and management have, in fact, always tried to emasculate the threat inherent in trade unionism, especially by co-opting union leaders into the control structures over labour. The state's efforts to control organised labour in Africa go back to the latter's origins during the colonial period. Almost all post-colonial regimes tried to extend and refine the existing panoply of labour controls and

sanctions within a few years of independence and to incorporate trade unions into the state structure (cf. Sandbrook 1982; Freund 1984, 1988).

Like the Ghanaian miners (Crisp 1984), CDC and Pamol workers have constantly taken the initiative against management and the state, shifting between informal, collective and institutional modes of resistance according to the perceived economic and political environment, forcing management and the state to respond with new strategies of control.

Although these various forms of resistance are often motivated by industrial and economic objectives, especially an improvement in workers' conditions of service, they inevitably become political struggles in the process. They tend to challenge the unequal distribution of power and income within the labour process as well as the determined efforts of the political elite to accumulate capital in the agro-industrial sector. In this respect, Burawoy's attempt (1985) to link 'politics in production' with 'global politics' is relevant here. Of course, collective and institutional modes of labour resistance are more serious threats to post-colonial regimes than informal modes of labour resistance but Bayart (1979, 1981) points out that even the most elusive forms of popular action tend to acquire political meaning in Cameroon. 'Overpoliticisation' is a characteristic feature of Cameroonian society and is obviously a direct consequence of the Cameroonian post-colonial state's pursuit of hegemony in all spheres of civil society.

The analysis in this book extends from labour and trade unions to other civil-society groups and organisations. Some have had a long-standing role in agro-industrial development while others started or intensified their activities during the crisis and reforms in Anglophone Cameroon's agro-industrial sector.

## Civil society, the agro-industrial crisis and reforms

The serious economic and financial crisis in the Anglophone Cameroonian plantation economy since the early 1980s has threatened not only capital accumulation by agro-industrial enterprises but also the interests of regional civil-society groups.

The latter started organising and mobilising their members during the crisis and the subsequent neoliberal reforms. Political liberalisation in the early 1990s enhanced the capacity of these groups to organise. Legislative changes permitted more freedom of expression and association, which led to the emergence of new organisations and a larger measure of autonomy for already-existing state-controlled organisations.

Civil society and empowerment have become buzz words in neoliberal development discourse. Typically, neoliberals perceive civil-society groups as a vital intermediary channel between the citizens and the state for the successful implementation of economic and political reforms. I have recently criticised such neoliberal views in some detail (Konings 2009b) and so will mention here only two major shortcomings that are relevant to the discussion in this book.

First, as in some previous studies (cf. Abrahamsen 2000; Konings 2004b), this book offers evidence that the prescribed empowerment of civil society could constitute an important means not only of realising neoliberal reforms but also of challenging neoliberal orthodoxies. Second, neoliberals tend to base their argumentation on western notions of civil society and have been inclined to define civil society in terms that are too narrow for the African context, and to demand too much of it. Although there may be differences of opinion on the exact definition of civil society, they usually agree that the core of civil society consists of modern, largely urban middle-class professional associations, organisations of workers, women, students and churches and non-governmental organisations with external links, such as groups advocating human rights and civil liberties. Strikingly, they often exclude ethno-regional groups and associations from their definitions of civil society, mainly because they are thought not to function according to neoliberal norms and to present an obstacle to democracy.

In sharp contrast to such neoliberal definitions, I have argued that ethno-regional associations may be of even greater significance to the ordinary people in Africa than conventional civil-society organisations that are based on horizontal bonds and solidarities. This is due not only to the largely underdeveloped nature of most African economies, which have delayed the crystallisation of class differentiation and professional groups, but to an even larger extent to the power of ethno-regional identity in Africa too.

Both ethno-regional and conventional civil-society groups have played a prominent role during the crisis and reforms in the Anglophone Cameroonian agro-industrial enterprises. I will now briefly discuss the most important ones.

## Ethno-regional elite associations

The Pamol estates and most of those of the CDC are in the present South West Province. The history of these estates is closely connected to the complicated political developments in this region since European occupation (cf. Mbuagbaw *et al.* 1987). What is even more significant for this study, however, is that the crisis and reforms on these estates took place in an era of both growing regionalism and divide between the South West and North West elites in Anglophone Cameroon (Konings & Nyamnjoh 2003).

The region where the Pamol and CDC estates are located belonged to the German Kamerun Protectorate (1884-1916). After the First World War, this erstwhile German Kamerun Protectorate was divided between the French and the British, and the region first became a British Mandate and subsequently a British Trust Territory until it gained independence in 1961. Being part of what was variously called the 'Cameroons Province' or 'Southern Cameroons' during the British era, it was then integrated into the administrative system of Nigeria. The 1954 Nigerian Constitution, which outlined the framework for a Federal Nigeria, gave it a quasi-regional status and a limited degree of self-government within the Federation of Nigeria (Chiabi 1982). It obtained full regional status in 1958, which placed it on a par with the other regions in the federation. It is beyond doubt that the administration of the Southern Cameroons as an appendage of Nigeria (which led to the blatant neglect of the region's development) and the dominant position of Nigerian (mainly Igbo and Efik-Ibibio) migrants in the Southern Cameroons economy were key factors in the decision of the majority of the Southern Cameroons population to vote for reunification with Francophone Cameroon rather than for integration into Nigeria in the 1961 United Nations plebiscite (Chem-Langhëë 1976, 1995; Konings 2005). At the same time, it is clear that the British-Nigerian colonial experience has had a lasting role in the construction of an Anglophone identity among the Southern Cameroons elite.

Reunification on 1 October 1961 signalled the start of a unique experiment in Africa whereby the political elites of two regions with different colonial legacies – one French, the other British – agreed to form a federal state (Ardener 1967; Johnson 1970; Le Vine 1971; Benjamin 1972; Forge 1981). With the creation of the Federal Republic of Cameroon, the Southern Cameroons was renamed the Federated State of West Cameroon and French Cameroon was renamed the Federated State of East Cameroon.

Stark (1976) convincingly argued that from its inception, federalism in Cameroon was 'more shadow than reality'. During negotiations on the federal constitution, notably at the Foumban Conference from 17 to 22 July 1961, it was already evident that the bargaining power of the Francophone delegation was far greater than that of the Anglophones. Compared to the Francophone region, the size and population of the Anglophone region was small, comprising only 9% of the area and about 25% of the federation's total population. Even more importantly, the former French Trust Territory of Cameroon was already an independent state, the Republic of Cameroon, by the time negotiations were held. The British Trust Territory of Southern Cameroons was, under the terms of the 1961 United Nations plebiscite, still to achieve independence by joining the sovereign Republic of Cameroon.

Capitalising on his territory's 'senior' status, Ahmadou Ahidjo, the then prime minister of the Republic of Cameroon and leader of the Francophone delegation, was able to dictate the terms of federation. Although John Ngu Foncha, prime minister of Southern Cameroons and the leader of the Anglophone delegation, had proposed a loose form of federalism that he regarded as guaranteeing the preservation of the cultural heritage and identity of the Anglophone minority, Ahidjo eventually forced him to accept a highly centralised form of federalism. Ahidjo, who would become the president of the Federal Republic of Cameroon, saw federalism as no more than an unavoidable but transitory phase in the total integration of the Anglophone minority into a strongly centralised unitary state. He employed several tactics to achieve this objective (DeLancey 1989: 52-65; Bayart 1979). One was to play off Anglophone political factions against each other and eventually integrate them into a single party, the Cameroon National Union

(CNU). Another was to remove any Anglophone leaders who remained committed to federalism from their positions of power, replacing them with others who favoured a unitary state. Yet another tactic was to create 'clients' among the Anglophone elite. By granting top posts in federal institutions and in the single party to representatives of significant ethnic and regional groups in the Anglophone region, Ahidjo tried to control these groups. Finally, he did not shrink from repressing opposition. Through these and other tactics, he succeeded in abolishing the federation on 20 May 1972. His justification for this 'glorious revolution' was that federalism fostered regionalism and impeded economic development (Stark 1976).

A growing number of the Anglophone elite, however, were inclined to attribute the emergence of regionalism and lack of economic development not to federalism *per se* but to the hegemonic tendencies of the Francophone-dominated state. They began complaining about the loss of regional autonomy and the subordinate position of the Anglophone minority in the unitary state. Their numerous grievances were mainly political, economic and cultural, particularly concerning their under-representation and inferior role in national decision-making councils, their region's neglected infrastructure and the exploitation of its rich economic resources, especially oil, and attempts at 'Frenchification'.[1]

To reduce any danger of united Anglophone action against the Francophone-dominated state, Ahidjo decided to divide the Anglophone territory into two provinces, the South West and the North West Provinces, after the glorious revolution in May 1972. This decision, masterfully informed by the internal contradictions within the Anglophone community between the coastal/forest people (South West Province) and the Grassfields people (North West Province), exacerbated divisions that would later be the Achilles heel in most attempts at Anglophone identity and organisation.

One of the major reasons for these internal conflicts was the loss of hegemony by the South West elite. The coastal population had been exposed to early contact with Western trade, religion and education, giving it a head start over the Grassfields population. An intelligentsia had subsequently emerged in the coastal area, notably among the Bakweri, and it quickly rose to the forefront in the nationalist struggle and continued to dominate the Anglophone political scene until the end of the 1950s. The transfer of power from the South Westerner, Emmanuel Endeley, to the North Westerner, John Ngu Foncha, was a political event that had significant repercussions for South West-North West relations.

Following this transfer, the North West elite began to assert itself and soon became ubiquitous in the higher levels of government and in senior non-governmental positions. By keeping the top jobs as well as the best lands in the South West for its members, it provoked strong resentment among South Westerners to North West domination (Kofele-Kale 1981). South West sentiments were intensified because the entrepreneurial North Westerners gradually succeeded in dominating most sectors of the South West economy, particularly trade, transport and housing (Rowlands 1993). Another reason for the South West-North West divide was the 1961 United Nations plebiscite in which the South West had shown considerable sympathy for alignment with Nigeria, although the choice for Cameroon prevailed, mainly on the strength of North West votes. A final source of tension was the massive migration from the North West to southwestern plantations and the subsequent settlement of northwestern workers in the South West (Konings 1993a, 2001).

Political liberalisation in the early 1990s not only created political space for organisational efforts in Anglophone Cameroon but also fanned the rivalry between the South West and North West elites in their struggle for power at the regional and national level. The South West elite became alarmed when political liberalisation resulted in the rapid growth of both the North West-based opposition party, the Social Democratic Front (SDF), and several Anglophone associations operating under an umbrella organisation, the Southern Cameroons National Council (SCNC), which contested Francophone domination and demanded first a return to the federal state and later outright secession (Konings & Nyamnjoh 2003; Takougang & Krieger 1998). The growing popularity of these organisations immediately raised suspicions of renewed North West domination.

From a South West point of view, such suspicions were not without foundation. The SDF was clearly a party organised and controlled by the North West elite and although the party enjoyed less popularity among the autochthonous population in the South West Province than in the North West Province, it could nevertheless count on massive support from northwestern workers and settlers in the region. In addition, it soon became clear that the SDF's frequent, and often violent, confrontations with the regime, which were turning the Anglophone region into a veritable hotbed of rebellion, were having the paradoxical effect of advancing the political careers of northwestern politicians. The year 1992 witnessed first the appointment of a North Westerner, Simon Achidi Achu, as prime minister in an apparently desperate attempt by the regime to contain the enormous popularity of the SDF in the North West, and later an impressive performance by the charismatic SDF chairman, John Fru Ndi, in the presidential elections (Konings 2004a).

Understandably, southwestern memories of northwestern domination in the Federated State of West Cameroon created resistance among the South West elite to the Anglophone movements' advocacy for a return to a two-state (Anglophone/Francophone) federal arrangement. They were therefore inclined to champion a ten-state federal system based on the existing ten provinces in Cameroon, which would retain the separation between the South West and the North West Provinces, thus safeguarding the former's autonomy. Furthermore, although South Westerners dominated the leadership of the most important Anglophone associations, the vast majority of the members appeared to be SDF members. Little wonder then that the South-West elite was inclined to perceive Anglophone associations as auxiliary organisations of the SDF.

Given their repeated failure to form a party of the same standing as the SDF, the South West elite started to create regional associations to represent and defend South West interests. The most prominent were the South West Elites Association (SWELA) and the South West Chiefs' Conference (SWECC). There is some overlap between these organisations, with some of the important South West chiefs also being members of SWELA (Nyamnjoh & Rowlands 1998; Eyoh 1998; Konings 2001; Nkwi 2006).

SWELA was an attempt to unite all the existing elite associations in the South West into one single organisation. Its leadership continually claimed that it was a non-political pressure group whose main objective was to promote the socio-economic development and cultural revival of the South West Province. The South West was to be restored to its former glory after having been marginalised by the Francophone-dominated state and subjected to Grassfields imperialism. Although SWELA supported most of the Anglophone grievances about Francophone domination, it equally claimed that the South West had been more disadvantaged than the North West in the post-colonial state. Clearly, fear of renewed North West domination was one of the underlying motives for its foundation as it came into existence after the launch of the SDF and the latter's subsequent expansion into the South West Province. On several occasions, SWELA leaders, especially those closely allied to the ruling regime, issued public statements blaming the SDF for acts of violence and anti-government activities in the South West (Nyamnjoh & Rowlands 1998; Nkwi 2006).

Given the intensification of the power struggle between the South West and North West elites during the political liberalisation process, the Biya government felt it increasingly lucrative and politically expedient to tempt the peaceful and conciliatory South West elite away from Anglophone solidarity with strategic appointments and the idea that their real enemy was the unpatriotic, ungrateful and power-mongering North West elite. Government divide-and-rule tactics culminated in the 1996 Constitution. While the previous (1972) constitution had emphasised national integration and equal rights for all citizens, including the right 'to settle in any place and to move about freely', the new constitution promised special state protection for autochthonous minorities (Geschiere & Nyamnjoh 2000; Konings 2001). Not unexpectedly, the new constitution boosted South West feelings of identity and fuelled existing tensions between South Westerners and North Westerners. The South West elite immediately demanded state protection for the autochthonous southwestern minority against the dominant and exploitative Grassfielders. Appeals to the state for protection were often accompanied by threats of ethnic cleansing and the removal of Grassfields 'strangers' (Konings 2009b).

The crisis and reforms on the Pamol and CDC estates quickly sparked regional sentiments. They brought to the fore existing contradictions not only between the Francophone-dominated state and the Anglophone community but also between the South West and North West elite. The Anglophones' great fear was that their regional agro-industrial enterprises would be sold to Francophone or French business interests. Although the South West elite entertained similar fears, they were equally opposed to a North West takeover as this might result in renewed North West domination over the South West.

## Chiefs and their organisations

As elsewhere in Africa, chieftaincy in Anglophone Cameroon has played a varied role in agro-industrial development. One of the most significant has been mediation between capital and labour in the realisation of two major prerequisites for capital accumulation in agro-industrial enterprises, namely the procurement of a regular and adequate supply of labour and the establishment of managerial control over the labour process in order to raise labour productivity. Realising these objectives may be particularly problematic in areas where the capitalist mode of production has not yet deeply penetrated and where the majority of the population has not been completely severed from the means of production and have not internalised the norms and values of capitalism (Konings 1996c).

Regarding the establishment of capitalist control over labour supplies, there is now abundant literature on the intermediary role of chiefs in the supply of local male labour to capitalist enterprises, particularly in the early colonial period. Despite some initial resistance, the chiefs were soon forced to assist in meeting the growing capitalist demand for male labour, and many eventually capitalised on their intermediary role. Unfortunately, far less attention has been paid to the chiefs' concomitant widespread opposition to female migration and proletarianisation. They opposed migration by women on the grounds of their vital productive and reproductive labour and their subordination to 'patriarchal' controls in many African societies (Stichter & Parpart 1988).

Chiefs in Africa have frequently tried to safeguard male control over women's productive and reproductive labour in their local communities, arguing that it is an essential part of African tradition. Women who succeeded in escaping from patriarchal controls and migrated to towns had to endure social ostracism as alleged prostitutes for the rest of their lives (Obbo 1980). The chiefs repeatedly appealed to the colonial authorities to use state power to help keep women under control and because they relied on the chiefs to maintain order in the rural areas, the authorities were inclined to side with them, taking legislative and administrative measures to strengthen patriarchal dominance (Chauncey 1981). From time to time, single women living in colonial towns were rounded up by the police and forcibly returned to their villages (Obbo 1980; Ruel 1960; Walker 1982).

Articulation theorists, like Meillassoux (1975) and Wolpe (1980), have argued that the supply of exclusively male labour to capitalist enterprises was functional to capital accumulation as women's continual productive and reproductive responsibilities in the non-capitalist sector served to lower labour costs in the capitalist sector. While these theories often assume the joint interest of chiefs and employers in keeping women confined to the non-capitalist sector, the actual situation may have been more complex, and it was certainly more dynamic. Studies on the copper mines in Zambia (Chauncey 1981; Parpart 1986) and the plantations in Anglophone Cameroon (Konings 1993a) note that employers initially favoured the employment of single men but gradually came to agree that married men's greater stability and productivity more than compensated for the extra costs of housing and feeding their wives and children. They therefore became increasingly committed to married labour.

In this book I argue that tea estates were among the rare capitalist enterprises during colonial rule that gave preference to female labour over male labour. Managerial attempts to recruit female pluckers on the newly created Ndu Tea Estate in the Bamenda Grassfields immediately gave rise to serious confrontations with the local chief, who feared female employment on the estate would endanger traditional patriarchal control and insisted on recruiting local male labour exclusively.

Concerning the establishment of capitalist control over the labour process, it would appear that attempts by management and the state to co-opt chiefs, tribal elders and representatives into the hierarchy and grant them authority over the labour process have been insufficiently studied.

The first such attempt in the British African colonies was apparently made in the early 1930s. It must, however, be situated in the context of growing concern at the British Colonial Office regarding massive labour migration, poor working and living conditions among labourers, and the first waves of strikes in Africa. Various solutions to the 'labour problem' were put forward including the institutionalisation of channels of communication between workers, management and the colonial administration. On 17 September 1930, Sydney Webb (Lord Passfield) circulated a dispatch to all colonial governors urging the legalisation of 'sympathetically supervised and guided' trade unions and the creation of labour departments in the different colonies (Meebelo 1986: 191-92; Freund 1981: 174). Most colonial officials and employers were, however, openly opposed to the development of trade unions and postponed their introduction. They argued that the necessary conditions for their emergence were not in place: most workers were illiterate and were still firmly encapsulated in their tribal organisations and cultures. It was therefore believed that traditional, ethnically based channels of communication would be more suitable in the African context than modern, class-based channels of communication such as trade unions.

Epstein (1958) and Crisp (1984), among others, described the tribal elders or heads who played a key role in the Zambian and Ghanaian mines as brokers between workers, management and (local) government. However unlike Epstein and Crisp, who viewed the role of these tribal elders as manifestations of control strategies by corporate capital and the colonial administration, Lentz & Erlmann (1989) stressed the ambiguous position of brokers in the relationship between workers and management. On the one hand, tribal heads tended to be part of the mine management and as such functioned as controllers of labour but on the other hand, they often defended the interests of members of their own ethnic group and provided them with a wide range of services: accommodation and job opportunities for new migrants; the settlement of internal disputes; support in emergencies such as sickness, accident and death; and mediation in conflicts with management, local authorities and other ethnic groups.

The tribal elders, representatives or heads in the Zambian and Ghanaian mines were more or less managerial creations. Their authority had no basis in tradition and their mediating role between labour and capital rested ultimately on managerial recognition. Interestingly, both Epstein and Lentz & Erlmann note that most of them tried to establish or claimed already to have close relationships with the royal families in the rural areas. In fact, they owed their prestige to the fact that they were often close kinsmen of the chiefs, and often described themselves as chiefs. To legitimise their authority among the people, they tried to traditionalise their appointment by adopting chiefly ceremonies, rituals and attributes. All this indicates the persistence of traditional political values among ethnic communities in industrial milieus.

The strategy by management and state to involve 'real' chiefs in labour control, especially in critical situations such as strike actions, is frequently referred to in the literature. They were usually paramount or other prominent chiefs who wielded considerable power over the workers, but they tended to side with management and the state, and helped put down strikes (cf. Crisp 1984).

What these authors have in common is that they assume that the mediating role of chieftaincy between labour and capital has either come to an end or been seriously eroded in Africa. In my study of tea estates in Anglophone Cameroon (Konings 1995a), I found that the chief of Ndu in the Bamenda Grassfields continued to play an important intermediary role between capital and labour on the Ndu Tea Estate. This seems to be particularly because capitalism had not yet penetrated this area deeply and chieftaincy still occupied a powerful, even sacred, position in society (cf. Fisyi 1995; Warnier 2009). In these circumstances, estate management relied on the local chief for both the supply of land and labour, and control of workers at the workplace.

This explanation is supported by my previous research on the role of chieftaincy in capitalist development in Ghana and Cameroon. In northern Ghana, where circumstances are similar to those in the Bamenda Grassfields, I found that local chiefs also played a key intermediary role in the supply and control of labour on newly created public irrigation projects and capitalist rice farms (Konings 1986a). In coastal areas of Anglophone Cameroon, by contrast, where the plantation economy introduced during German colonial rule (1884-1916) extensively undermined local institutions and value systems and where chieftaincy was generally weak (Ardener 1962; Geschiere 1993), I found that local chiefs played a less significant intermediary role in the supply and control of labour than they did in the Bamenda Grassfields.

Like the tribal heads in the Ghanaian mines (Lentz & Erlmann 1989), chieftaincy in Ndu was never solely instrumental in labour control and functional to the demands of capital (Konings 1995a). While the chief was generally a reliable partner in development and often sided with the management, he also distinguished himself as the custodian of tradition and the champion of the interests of his (Ndu) subjects. As a consequence, he firmly resisted the management preference for female labour and was inclined to endorse his subjects' persistent loyalty to certain traditional norms and values that conflicted with the capitalist work ethic. He was also inclined to put pressure on management to advance the careers of Ndu men on the estate, a practice that led to frequent conflict between Ndu and other workers. This defence of traditional values and local interests in development projects in their local communities was also manifest in northern Ghana (Konings 1986a).

There is, nevertheless, sufficient evidence to support the view of Lentz & Erlmann that the intermediary role of the chieftaincy weakened over the course of time (Konings 1995a). First, the developing trade unionism on the Ndu Tea Estate attempted to transcend ethnic allegiances and defend the class interests of all workers against the state and management. The Ndu chief's keen opposition to the union, undoubtedly arising from the desire to preserve the traditional authority and values, eventually proved futile as he was accused of being a management stooge and the union leaders were hailed as the true representatives of workers' interests. Second, new power-holders emerged who could serve as ethnic brokers on the Ndu Tea Estate, as well as several ethnic associations that promoted ethnic solidarity and assistance. As a result, the chief's intermediary role has become marginalised and at present his assistance in labour control on the estate is needed by management, state and the union alike in critical situations, such as when workers engage in collective modes of resistance against control and exploitation. With the failure of the union and the Labour Department – as the modern brokers between capital and labour – to settle labour disputes, a final appeal is being made to the traditional broker to use his religious and moral authority over the workers to help reassert managerial control over the labour process.

Finally, my research appears to confirm the remarkable resilience of the chieftaincy and its capacity to adapt to changing conditions (van Rouveroy van Nieuwaal 1987). The present chief of Ndu is an excellent example of the tendency in the Bamenda Grassfields and elsewhere in Africa to enthrone well-educated youth capable of modernising traditional value systems. Soon after his installation in 1982, the current chief allowed women to work on a permanent basis on the estate, which can be seen as a significant contribution to women's emancipation in the Bamenda Grassfields. He has also established a cordial relationship with the union leadership and holds regular consultations. In fact, he has been able to integrate this potentially rival source of power into both the modern and traditional structures of authority in the local community. Some union leaders are members of the elite Development Committee and others have been co-opted as non-hereditary title-holders into the local community's traditional hierarchy of authority.

Chiefs also played an important role in a third prerequisite for agro-industrial development, namely the provision of land. Some chiefs, like the chief of Ndu, allocated vast amounts of land to agro-industrial enterprises for the construction of plantation estates (Konings 1995a). Others in Anglophone Cameroon either provided land for the CDC and Pamol smallholders or participated themselves, as land owners, in the CDC and Pamol smallholder schemes (Konings 1993a, 1998a).

Other chiefs in Anglophone Cameroon, in particular the Bakweri chiefs, refused to cooperate with the state and agro-industrial enterprises and firmly opposed the large-scale expropriation of their ancestral lands for plantation production during the German colonial period. Before and following the creation of the CDC on these lands in 1946/47, they were engaged in a relentless struggle to regain their lands and set up the Bakweri Land Committee (BLC) with the Bakweri modern elite (Molua 1985; Konings 2003a).

I will show in this book that the Bakweri chiefs and the modern Bakweri elite were engaged in various modes of resistance against the announced privatisation of the CDC on 15 July 1994. They claimed ownership of CDC lands, felt betrayed at not having been previously consulted about the CDC's privatisation and warned the government that the corporation could not be sold to non-natives without Bakweri consent and compensation. They often received solid support from other chiefs and the modern elite in the South West Province, notably the South West Chiefs' Conference (SWECC), which was formally constituted in 1990 (Eyoh 1998), and SWELA. However, it would appear that other Anglophone chiefs and organisations also supported their claims.

## Workers and trade unions

Agro-industrial enterprises in Anglophone Cameroon have always relied on wage labour for plantation production. Regional plantation agriculture was labour intensive and German planters needed about 18,000 workers by 1914. Pamol's labour force rose gradually from 1,200 to 3,500 and the CDC, the second largest employer in the country (being surpassed only by the government), initially employed between 20,000 and 25,000 labourers. Today, it employs approximately 14,000 workers (Konings 1993a, 1998a). Establishing a regular supply of labour was a major problem for plantation production for a long time. German planters experienced almost insurmountable problems procuring sufficient labour from local communities that were not only sparsely populated but also hated working for the expropriators of their land. This compelled the planters to import a considerable number of labourers from outside Cameroon, in particular from other West African countries (Rudin 1938; Rüger 1960). This imported labour, however, could not solve the acute labour shortage and also turned out to be expensive, which was a major reason why the scheme was quickly abandoned. The gradual opening up and pacification of the more densely populated areas of the interior revealed their enormous potential for solving the labour problem. Most of the people in the interior, however, were not ready to accept voluntary labour contracts. So various forms of coercion were employed during the entire German period to 'free' labour from the interior for the plantations. Initially large numbers of men from rebellious areas were simply seized and sent to the plantations for up to six years as a kind of penal labour force, sometimes receiving no pay at all. Later on, a labour-recruitment system was developed based on the continuous coercive pressure of private recruiters, local officials and suitably bribed African chiefs (Halldén 1968; Chilver 1971; Clarence-Smith 1989). Towards the end of German colonial rule, head taxes and hut taxes were imposed, which encouraged Africans to work on the plantations. Those unable to pay taxes in cash would be turned over to private employers who paid the tax and the fee of 10 Marks per head.

The most important inland recruitment areas were the Yaoundé region and the Grassfields area, both in the present Francophone West Province that was mainly occupied by the Bamileke, and the Anglophone North West Province that was occupied by various ethnic groups closely related to the Bamileke. During the British Mandate period there was a gradual transition from forced to voluntary labour migration that was facilitated by people's growing need for cash, improved conditions of service, the provision of land for food cultivation, the so-called 'chop farms', and active recruitment through ethnic, community and family networks. There were notable differences at first between the CDC and Pamol concerning labour-recruitment areas (Konings 1993a, 1998a).

When the CDC was established in 1946/47, it faced a serious problem with the supply of labour from Francophone Cameroon. Labour mobility from this area used to be encouraged by forms of forced labour imposed by the French (Kaptue 1986). By 1926 52% of the plantation labour force came from the French Mandate area (Table 1.1). This figure declined to only 1% in the 1980s. The determined efforts by the French Mandate Authority to prevent workers from leaving the area greatly contributed to this decline. Increased remunerative employment opportunities in Francophone Cameroon and the rising cost of living in Anglophone Cameroon in the aftermath of independence and reunification in 1961 led to a further reduction in labour migration from Francophone to Anglophone Cameroon (Ndongko 1975). Apart from a temporary influx of labour from neighbouring eastern Nigeria (Ardener *et al.* 1960) and a steady supply of labour from South West Province, this decline was largely compensated for by an increasing number of labour migrants from North West Province. It had a higher population density, developed cash-crop production much later and lacked job opportunities outside the traditional sector.

Table 1.1 *Regional composition of the CDC and Pamol labour forces (%)*

| | 1926 | 1941 | 1950 | 1960s | 1970s | 1980s | 1990s |
|---|---|---|---|---|---|---|---|
| *CDC* | | | | | | | |
| North West Province | 14.0 | 37.0 | 32.5 | 43.5 | 54.5 | 73.5 | 71.0 |
| South West Province | 33.0 | 27.5 | 33.0 | 25.0 | 38.0 | 24.5 | 27.0 |
| Francophone Cameroon | 52.0 | 25.0 | 13.0 | 4.5 | 5.0 | 1.0 | 1.0 |
| Eastern Nigeria | 1.0 | 10.5 | 21.5 | 27.0 | 2.5 | 1.0 | 1.0 |
| Total | 100 | 100 | 100 | 100 | 100 | 100 | 100 |
| *Pamol* | | | | | | | |
| North West Province | n.a | n.a. | n.a. | 5.0 | 27.0 | 41.8 | 54.0 |
| South West Province | n.a. | n.a. | n.a. | 13.0 | 47.0 | 44.4 | 33.5 |
| Francophone Cameroon | n.a. | n.a. | n.a. | 1.7 | 1.7 | 1.3 | 1.0 |
| Eastern Nigeria | n.a. | n.a. | n.a. | 80.3 | 24.3 | 12.5 | 11.5 |
| Total | n.a. | n.a. | n.a. | 100 | 100 | 100 | 100 |

*Source:* Konings (1993a and 1998a)

Pamol faced greater problems than the CDC in recruiting sufficient labour. Its main estates are in one of the most marginalised areas of Cameroon where the cost of living is extremely high because of regular food shortages. Cameroonian workers were thus more inclined to seek employment on CDC estates, and neighbouring eastern Nigeria became the main supplier of labour to the Pamol estates. In 1961, eastern Nigerians accounted for 80% of the total Pamol labour force (Table 1.1) but after reunification, the dominant position of Nigerian workers rapidly declined. However, managerial failure to recruit sufficient labour in Anglophone Cameroon formed an insurmountable obstacle to the complete realisation of the government's Cameroonisation policy and by 1970 Nigerian workers still accounted for 25% of Pamol's total labour force. From the 1970s onwards, a stabilisation in labour recruitment from Nigeria was seen at around 12%. Under constant pressure to 'Cameroonise', management staged a renewed recruiting drive in Anglophone Cameroon, first in the nearby Ndian and Manyu Divisions of South West Province and later in North West Province. As at the CDC, northwestern workers today form the majority on the Pamol estates (54 %).

It is striking that there have been few serious clashes between autochthonous and 'stranger' ethnic groups on the southwestern estates. Tensions between autochthons and allochthons are most likely to arise when stranger ethno-regional groups appear to occupy a dominant position.

The dominant position of eastern Nigerian workers at the CDC and particularly on the Pamol estates in the nationalist climate after the Second World War gave rise to serious friction between autochthonous Anglophone Cameroonian workers and eastern Nigerian strangers. Between 1947 and 1960, Anglophone Cameroonian workers on both companies' estates undertook a series of collective and informal actions aimed at removing Igbo and Ibibio supervisory and managerial staff (Konings 1993a: 69, 1998a: 80), repeatedly calling on management and the government to promote a rapid Cameroonisation of the labour force and management. After reunification, past animosities between Anglophone Cameroonian and Nigerian workers largely subsided, probably because the Nigerians became a relatively small, stranger minority group on the estates and were no longer perceived as a threat by Anglophone Cameroonians. Nigerian workers claimed that their best strategy was to assume a low profile so as not to generate envy and tensions (cf. Kleis 1975). Although conflicts did not totally disappear, the social distance between Nigerian and Cameroonian workers diminished (DeLancey 1973).

After this conflict between Anglophone Cameroonian and Nigerian workers, a new potential source of friction could have been expected in relations between the 'autochthonous' southwestern minority and the northwestern majority on the estates. Remarkably, extensive clashes between these two groups have not yet occurred. On the contrary, all researchers on estate labour agree that southwestern and northwestern workers usually manage to live and work peacefully together (Ardener *et al.* 1960; DeLancey 1973; Kofele-Kale 1981; Konings 1993a, 1998a). Both groups tend to organise not only on an ethnic but also on an inter-ethnic basis, as can be seen in the membership of churches and trade unions, and have engaged from time to time in common struggles against managerial control and exploitation in the workplace. One reason for this unexpected phenomenon is the consistent policy of the management, as well as church and union leaders, in mobilising and organising workers along multiethnic lines. This policy seems to have created a certain degree of understanding and tolerance among the workers for the other's socio-cultural background, thus fostering bonds of companionship and friendship across ethno-regional boundaries. Another reason is the widespread use of Pidgin English that has helped minimise communication problems between the various ethnic groups. A third reason is the marked preference of workers themselves for ethnically mixed living and working arrangements, which partly stems from their belief that witchcraft is most likely to occur among close relatives and tribesmen (Ardener *et al.* 1960; Konings 1993a). The most important reason, however, appears to be the shared living and working conditions on the estates, which are classic examples of occupational communities.[2]

Studies of such communities of miners, dockers and railwaymen in Africa confirm the solidarity and militancy of these workers (cf. Jeffries 1978; Sandbrook 1982; Parpart 1983; Waterman 1983; Crisp 1984).

Solidarity among plantation workers has, of course, never been total. There have always been cleavages within the CDC and Pamol labour forces. In addition to vertical divisions, such as those between local and migrant workers, manual and clerical workers, and plantation and factory workers, there have also been the horizontal cleavages of age, skill, experience and status. So although workers may have a common interest in resisting exploitation and subordination, the precise objectives of the different workers and their modes of resistance may well differ, or even collide.

Paige (1975) claimed that plantation workers tended to fight for incremental changes within the status quo and improvements in their living and working conditions. My previous studies of Anglophone Cameroonian plantation workers substantiate his claim to a large extent. CDC and Pamol workers have always remained highly sceptical of engaging in any overtly political action and their struggles have been primarily oriented at protecting their occupational interests within the status quo. What is peculiar to Anglophone Cameroonian plantation workers, however, is that they have constantly displayed a high degree of militancy in the defence of their occupational interests, as is shown by their numerous informal, collective and trade union actions (Konings 1993a, 1998a). Hardly any research has been carried out so far on the role of plantation workers during the agro-industrial crisis and reforms in Africa in general, and in Cameroon in particular. In this book I examine whether Anglophone Cameroonian plantation workers continued to resort to militantly oppositional actions during this period out of protest at managerial intensification of their exploitation and subordination in the labour process.

Plantation workers in Anglophone Cameroon have a long history of trade unionism. The CDC Workers' Union (CDCWU), for example, was founded in 1947 and soon became one of the largest and best organised trade unions in West Africa (Warmington 1960). It more or less dominated the industrial-relations scene in Anglophone Cameroon between 1947 and 1972, when it was dissolved during a state-initiated reorganisation of trade unions (Konings 1993a).

Paige (1975) is inclined to assume an identity of interests, ideological perceptions and actions between plantation unions and workers. He appeared to accept that unions usually shape, broaden and intensify their members' consciousness and actions, and represent and defend their interests. This is evident when he maintains that labour movements on the plantations tended to be '*reform* labour movements': they were inclined to refrain from mobilising their members for (radical) political action but instead championed the defence of their common occupational interests against their employers.

However there are indications that Paige (1975: 22) was not entirely unaware of the contradictory consequences of unions for workers' consciousness and actions. He sometimes seems to acknowledge that unions could also function as agencies of control over their members, offer assistance to the state and management efforts to integrate them into the capitalist mode of production, and stifle their initiatives and modes of resistance.

My own review of trade unionism in Anglophone Cameroonian agro-industrial enterprises tends to support Paige's claim that labour movements on the plantations are 'reform labour movements' (Konings 1993a, 1998a). However, it presents a more complex picture of the impact of plantation unions on workers' consciousness and actions than he does. It pays particular attention to the possible changes in the role of unions over the course of time and the contradictions that may arise between the union leadership and the rank and file, as a result of the constantly renewed efforts of state and management to transform trade unionism from a vehicle of labour resistance into an instrument of labour control.

The British Trusteeship Authority's introduction of a specific union model, which I described as 'free, but responsible trade unionism', resulted in the emergence of internal contradictions within Anglophone Cameroonian plantation unions. On the one hand, there were the skilled and clerical union leaders who realised early on the potential of an industry-wide class organisation for the protection of the interests of *all* plantation workers. Being moderate in their political views and economic demands, they clung to the ideals of union autonomy and responsibility that were impressed upon them by the Labour Department and the international 'free' labour organisations. On the other hand, there was also the large group of unskilled and semi-skilled workers who, in view of their management's recalcitrant attitudes, were less inclined than the union leaders to have faith in the efficacy of the institutionalised procedures of joint negotiation and collective bargaining, and were also more committed to militant action. Their support of the union leadership was highly conditional and instrumental: they expected their union leaders to deliver on their promises. When such expectations were not fulfilled, they tended to shift from the institutional mode of resistance to alternative modes of resistance, such as informal and collective actions. The attitude of Anglophone Cameroonian plantation workers towards their unions was clearly not exceptional in Africa: Crisp (1984), for example, found the same attitude among Ghanaian gold miners with basically similar characteristics.

It was after the reorganisation of trade unionism in Cameroon in 1972, which led to the establishment of state control over the unions, that the contradictions between the union leadership and the rank and file became increasingly obvious. Co-opted in the control structure over labour, the union leadership rapidly lost popular support. Even more significantly, it proved to be incapable of containing the rank and file's traditional militancy, as was reflected in the large-scale participation of Anglophone Cameroonian plantation workers in several illegal strike actions after 1972 (Konings 1993a, 1998a). I will show in this volume that these contractions became particularly visible during the agro-industrial crisis and reforms. The latter tended to weaken even further the bargaining position of the plantation unions despite the fact that Cameroonian trade unions were able to achieve a limited degree of autonomy in the political liberalisation process that started in 1990 (Konings 2009a).

## Smallholders and cooperatives

Contract farming is a growing phenomenon on the African continent. Generally speaking, it is a way of organising agricultural production whereby smallholders are forced to supply produce to agro-industrial enterprises in accordance with the conditions specified in written or oral contracts. These enterprises, in turn, have to provide access to critical productive resources such as credit, inputs and technical assistance, as well as to processing facilities and an assured market outlet.

Contract farming by large agro-industrial corporations has remained a controversial subject in the literature. It has been advanced by its advocates as a key strategy for rural transformation based on a dynamic partnership between smallholders and agro-industrial enterprises, and is said to offer opportunities for both parties. It provides agro-industrial enterprises with a regular supply of agricultural commodities at lower cost and risk than estate production does, and allows enterprises to present themselves as champions of regional development. At the same time, it enables participants to benefit from modern technology, marketing facilities and other services, and to boost their incomes. Significantly, it has found a prominent place in the IMF- and World Bank-inspired structural adjustment programmes (SAPs) for its potential to promote private-sector-oriented development and increase and diversify agricultural exports (Glover & Kusterer 1990; Little & Watts 1994; Grosh 1994).

Others are less convinced about the benefits of contract farming to smallholders. They reject the idea of equal partnership in these schemes, arguing that contract farming may subjugate the peasantry to increased control and exploitation by capital, leading to a peculiar form of proletarianisation (Feder 1977a, 1977b; Payer 1980). One of the most recent exponents of this theoretical tradition is Michael Watts. Drawing parallels between contract farming and the rise of flexible accumulation and subcontracting in advanced capitalist industrial organisation, Watts (1994: 64) concluded that contract farming transforms peasants into *de facto* piece workers, 'often labouring more intensively (i.e. longer hours) and extensively (i.e. using children and other nonpaid household labour) to increase output and quality'. In a similar vein, Clapp (1994: 81) refers to contract farming as 'a form of disguised proletarianisation: it secures the farmer's land and labour, while leaving him with formal title to both'.

What these opposing views have in common is that they ignore the great diversity in types of contract farming relations. Their arguments are based mainly on schemes with more or less homogeneous peasant participation, while contract farming schemes often show a considerable measure of social differentiation, with the various strata of participants differing widely in their relationship with management, their recruitment of labour, their access to the company's inputs and services, and their share in the incomes and benefits derived from these schemes. Moreover, contracts may vary from being exceedingly loose to very tight, resulting in different intensities of managerial control over participants' production and exchange. As a consequence, participants could more realistically be placed on a continuum ranging from autonomous producers to *de facto* proletarians (Gibbon 1997: 62-63).

Given this huge diversity, Little (1994: 217-18) suggested that it would be more useful to focus on the actual content of contracting relations and the motives and power relationships of the contracting parties rather than seeking blanket conclusions about contract farming as a generic institution. In addition to general market instability, he perceived the highly unequal power relationships in most of the existing schemes as a major threat to their long-term sustainability. He showed (*Ibid.*: 230) how autocratic managerial control gives rise to various forms of resistance by the contract farmers, including withdrawal from the scheme, a search for alternative markets, and even violent demonstrations and strikes, all of which jeopardise the scheme's viability. He therefore urged the introduction of intermediary organisations, such as farmers' cooperatives, which could represent the interests of producers. Such organisations have been generally weak or absent in contracting schemes in Africa and elsewhere and contract farmers have proved even more difficult to organise than plantation workers. Plantation workers work and live together and are thus more likely to discuss their common interests than contract farmers who work and live more in isolation (Paige 1975). Moreover, contract farmers are inclined to maintain good individual relationships with management and expect certain favours in return, rather than organising with other growers (Glover 1984). Little & Watts (1994) found that multinational agro-industrial enterprises, such as British American Tobacco (BAT), strongly opposed official grower representation and threatened to withdraw from local production if contract farmers attempted to organise into cooperatives. However, even when contract farmers are able to overcome obstacles to organisation, they usually lack the necessary power and autonomy to influence decision making (Clapp 1994: 82; Porter & Phillips-Howard 1997).

Several contract farming schemes have been created in Cameroon over time and the CDC and Pamol played a pioneering role in the establishment of contract farming schemes in Anglophone Cameroon. The 'old' CDC scheme and the Pamol scheme were both characterised by weak management control and supervision over the labour process and a large measure of social differentiation. Becoming increasingly dissatisfied with managerial lack of control over the processes of production and exchange, the CDC management introduced a 'new' scheme in 1977 that was devised and sponsored by the World Bank and other foreign financiers. This aimed at establishing a more homogeneous farming group, focusing on low-income rural groups rather than the richer, more progressive smallholders, with strict managerial control over participants' production and exchange.

The CDC and Pamol contract farmers demonstrated their ability to organise in defence of their interests against management and the state. Dissatisfied with the allegedly low producer price offered by the CDC, the participants in the 'old' CDC contract farming scheme were the first to organise into a cooperative. In 1986, during the serious crisis in the agro-industrial sector, they were followed by the Pamol contract farmers, with both cooperatives being created and dominated by larger farmers. While the latter claimed that the newly created cooperatives would defend the interests of all contract farmers, they were primarily concerned with guarding their own interests. Strikingly, the participants in the newer CDC contract farming scheme were precluded by management from forming a cooperative.

As in most other African countries, the performance of the Anglophone Cameroonian contract farmers' cooperatives has proved to be disappointing. The unprecedented crisis in the agro-industrial sector revealed the cooperatives' weaknesses and unequal bargaining position. Contract farmers were highly dependent on the large agro-industrial enterprises for the delivery of inputs and transport, as well as for the purchase and marketing of their produce. When management was no longer able to render these services during the crisis, the cooperative executive lacked the power to force them to stick to the terms of the contract. Even petitioning the state for intervention on the behalf of contract farmers proved futile in a situation where agro-industrial enterprises faced serious marketing and liquidity problems.

Disillusioned with the performance of their leadership, cooperative members have, like unorganised contract farmers, been inclined to resort to collective and informal modes of resistance. Some refused to adhere strictly to the scheme's regulations and to maintain their farms properly, while others even abandoned the scheme altogether. Most, however, tried to sell their produce on alternative markets where they were paid more promptly. Such informal actions by contract farmers were widespread in Africa and elsewhere (Konings 1993b; Little & Watts 1994). More conspicuous displays of displeasure included political strikes, demonstrations and other collective forms of resistance by contract farmers, such as the violent confrontations that took place in the Bakolori scheme in Nigeria (Beckman 1985).

# Organisation of the book and research methodology

Having set out the most important themes I will be exploring, I will now explain how the book is organised and how I arrived at the research findings it is based on.

The book consists of eight essays that examine the role of civil-society groups and organisations during the agro-industrial crisis and reforms in Anglophone Cameroon. Chapter 2 assesses the role of ethno-regional groups and associations, while Chapters 3 and 4 deal with the role of workers and trade unions during the agro-industrial crisis and the subsequent liquidation of Pamol. Chapters 5 and 6 study the protest actions of chiefs and workers against externally imposed attempts to privatise the CDC, and Chapters 7 and 8 focus on the role of the CDC and Pamol smallholders and their cooperatives during the crisis and the reform period.

The present study is based on several fieldwork periods undertaken in Anglophone Cameroon between 1985 and 2005. Various research methods were employed. First of all, I consulted primary and secondary sources in libraries, archives, departments and ministerial offices. The valuable material on regional agro-industrial enterprises and civil-society groups that is kept at the National Archives at Buea (BNA), the Provincial and Divisional Labour Offices in Buea, Limbe (Victoria) and Mundemba, and the CDC archives in Limbe-Bota was particularly useful. The CDC and Pamol managerial staff were usually cooperative and provided me with any statistical data and recent documents I requested. Secondly, I interviewed considerable numbers of workers, contract farmers, union leaders, cooperative leaders, managerial staff, government officials, chiefs, leaders of regional elite groups and associations, and other relevant informants. Most of these interviews were in English or Pidgin English, the *lingua franca* in Anglophone Cameroon. And thirdly, I observed the daily activities taking place on the CDC and Pamol estates over a period of some months.

During my fieldwork, I was assisted by various local research assistants who were familiar with the research areas and proved to be extremely helpful in gaining the confidence of relevant informants.

# Notes

1. For the numerous Anglophone complaints, see All Anglophone Conference (1993).

2. Unlike on the CDC and Pamol estates in Anglophone Cameroon, serious clashes between autochthonous and stranger workers reportedly occurred at agro-industrial enterprises in the southern part of Francophone Cameroon, especially on the SOSUCAM sugar estates in Mbandjock (Barbier *et al.* 1980; Ngend 1982). Two factors seem to be responsible for the violence between southern and northern workers on the latter enterprise in 1976. First of all, occupational and ethno-regional overlapping has always constituted a potentially explosive situation at SOSUCAM: the higher-paid positions are held by the better-educated and skilled workers from the south and the less well-paid jobs by the uneducated and unskilled workers from the north. And secondly, the unskilled sugar-cane cutters from the north tend to oppose any efforts at integration, preferring to live separately. These factors continue to create problems in ensuring a peaceful coexistence between the two ethno-regional groups and do not encourage solidarity.

# 2

# Ethno-regional groups and associations in the South West Province and the agro-industrial crisis

## Introduction

The agro-industrial crisis, which started in the early 1980s, has had serious consequences for the CDC and Pamol and brought them both to the verge of collapse. Pamol was put into voluntary liquidation by its mother company, Unilever, in October 1987 and has been up for sale ever since. The CDC was first denied public grants and subsidies, and has been preparing for privatisation since 1994. Both have been influential in regional development and control of the companies is an emotive issue that raises regional sentiments and has highlighted divisions between the Anglophone community and the Francophone-dominated state, as well as those between the South West and the North West elites. It was during political liberalisation that the Anglophone elite in general, and the South West elite in particular, started organising to defend regional interests surrounding the sale of the two companies.

## The liquidation and sale of Pamol

The Plantations Pamol du Cameroun Ltd (Pamol) was previously a subsidiary of the Unilever giant (cf. Wilson 1954, 1968; Fieldhouse 1978, 1994; Dinham & Hines 1983). Founded in the 1920s, it is one of the oldest agro-industrial enterprises in Cameroon. Its main estates produce palm oil and are in the Ndian Division of the South West Province that borders eastern Nigeria (Courade 1978).

Economically, the Ndian Division is one of the most important areas in the country: it has large oil deposits at Idabato around Rio del Rey, as well as timber and oil palms. Paradoxically, it continues to be one of the most isolated and marginalised regions in the country despite its natural riches. For a long time it was deprived of basic infrastructural provisions: it had no road connections with other parts of Cameroon and transport was only possible via a network of waterways (rivers, creeks, and the sea). When a road was finally constructed between Ndian and Kumba in the 1970s, it was badly maintained during the dry season and barely passable in the rainy season. The area appears to have closer links with Nigeria than with Cameroon itself, with many Nigerian fishermen, traders and peasants living in the area. The Nigerian currency is widely accepted and Efik is the *lingua franca* in the maritime areas of the division. Legal and illegal trade with Nigeria provides lucrative income opportunities for some of the local population (Konings 2005).

The main reason for the area's marginalisation seems to be political. During the inter-war period it was a no-man's land, in which the British authorities showed little interest. From 1945 onwards, it was an integral part of Kumba Division but being far from Kumba, it continued to be neglected by the district authorities. It was not until 1967 that it was separated from Kumba Division and declared an autonomous division by presidential decree. Even then hardly any development funds were allocated to the new division, as if it were still being penalised for the fact that during the 1961 plebiscite about 95% of the local population voted for integration into Nigeria rather than reunification with Francophone Cameroon. A few months before the plebiscite, one of the region's principal leaders, Mr N.N. Mbile, declared that his people were 'irrevocably [decided] never to accept union with the Cameroon Republic. .... If on this we shall have to be killed to the last man, it should be better that history records how a race of men died to the man fighting for their freedom' (cited in Johnson 1970: 166).[1] Following reunification, Ndian Division was never honoured with a ministerial seat in the federal government and its lack of national integration was also manifest in the low profile of the single ruling party in the area. A few months before the promulgation of the unitary state in 1972, the District Officer for the Ekondo Titi Subdivision reported:

The response to the call for buying and owning the party card is still slow. Meetings of cells and branches around the headquarters have not been held and I have no reason to believe that the organs in the remote villages are more effective. I called up some of the people and asked whether they owned the party cards and the answer they gave was amazing. They said since they do not travel they see no need to own the cards. Only people who are mobile need the cards because their kits are being inspected by the forces of law and order.[2]

For the local population, Pamol has always been the area's lifeline. They feel that the company has realised what political rulers and regional barons have persistently failed to do, namely to promote regional development. Pamol is the only private enterprise in the area that employs a sizeable labour force, with 3,000-3,500 workers in its heyday (see Table 1.1). It is responsible for 90% of Ndian Division's tax revenues. It has constructed labour camps with adequate water and electricity supplies, hospitals, schools and roads, and provides transport services for its workers and the local population. Local people still remember how a company launch, the M.V. Rio with a capacity of 45 passengers, used to ply the Ndian-Lobe route three times a week. And last, but not least, the company has always promoted smallholder schemes around its oil-palm estates since the 1960s.

Given its significant role in regional development over many decades, the Anglophone population and Ndian Division's population in particular were alarmed when the news spread that Pamol was in a deep crisis. For those familiar with the multitude of problems that were besetting the agro-industrial palm-oil sector, the crisis did not come as a complete surprise as agro-industrial enterprises engaged in local palm-oil production have always been plagued by chronically low productivity and high production costs (Konings 1989). Rising costs forced them to petition the state regularly to demand increased domestic palm-oil prices. A series of decrees between 1980 and 1985 ordering substantial wage increases throughout the country was a particular source of conflict between the state and agro-industry, as increases in wages were not (immediately) followed by increases in domestic palm-oil prices. Agro-industrial enterprises were often obliged simply to sell their produce at prices that did not even cover production costs. The severe drought in 1983, which slashed Pamol's output by over 30%, exacerbated the company's grave financial situation and forced management to put its development and rehabilitation plans on hold, borrow heavily from banks and resort to mass layoffs. For the first time, Unilever began to contemplate ceasing operations in Cameroon.

The crisis in the domestic agro-industrial sector was aggravated by two additional factors. First, government expansion of the sector had led to a staggering increase in output. In particular the massive expansion of the two parastatals that dominated the sector, the CDC and the *Société Camerounaise de Palmeraies* (SOCAPALM), had given rise to the unprecedented situation whereby locally produced palm oil exceeded domestic demand by about 40%. Second, the government's inability or unwillingness to control imports of cheap oil, notably of refined oil from Malaysia, led to a further drop in domestic demand for locally produced palm oil.

These two factors inevitably sparked keen competition that culminated in a price war between Cameroonian agro-industrial enterprises and forced prices down far below production costs and the government-recommended price. In the end, most companies could no longer avoid selling their palm oil on the world market. However, such exports were being made at a time when a 40% increase in the value of the CFA franc against the US dollar made locally produced oil even less competitive globally, while world market prices were sinking to their lowest level in forty years. In a desperate attempt to rid themselves of growing stocks of perishable palm oil, Cameroonian agro-industrial enterprises had to dump their produce onto the world market and suffered major financial losses in the process.

For private companies like Pamol, survival was even more difficult than for public and para-public enterprises. Public enterprises enjoyed substantial annual subsidies from the state, irrespective of their performance. They were exempt from paying certain taxes, were entitled to low-interest loans from the Central Bank and their plants were usually accessible by tarred road (Tedga 1990; Konings 1993a). This enabled them to proceed with expanding and modernising their estates, undercut prices on the domestic market and attract new customers. Thus, while sales of the two major palm-oil-producing parastatals doubled between 1984 and 1986, Pamol's sales plummeted.

In late 1985, Pamol's management decided to tackle its financial problems by cutting production costs as far as possible and seeking government assistance along with other agro-industrial producers. It also drew up a restructuring plan that proposed a series of cost-cutting measures including cultivating exclusively the best and flattest lands; promoting labour-saving cultivation methods such as a more extensive use of machinery and draft animals; closing one of its two mills to save major refurbishment costs and concentrate all its processing activities in one single mill; ceasing all its rubber operations in the country as they had proved uneconomic due to their limited scale and the dramatic fall in world rubber prices; and reducing its labour force. The plan also recommended the construction of a refinery. Producing refined oil had increased Unilever's market share in Ivory Coast and Pamol's management expected a similar effect in Cameroon (Sellers 1984). Unfortunately, the restructuring plan ended in failure. And some of the proposals, such as the closure of one of the mills, even resulted in higher costs, since the hiring of extra lorries to transport company produce to the surviving mill proved exceedingly expensive along Ndian Division's bad roads.

In December 1986, Unilever briefed the Biya government on the company's deteriorating financial position and urged it to immediately implement a series of protective measures for the ailing agro-industrial palm-oil sector, in particular an increase in domestic palm-oil prices, a special tax on all imports of edible oils and a ban on imports of heavy oil by the Cameroonian soap industry, and the granting of export subsidies. It repeated its complaint that Pamol was unable to compete with state-subsidised parastatals even though it was more productive and supplied higher-quality oil. It asked the government to end the situation of unequal competition by granting Pamol similar low-interest loan facilities to those the parastatals enjoyed, improving the roads to its estates and mill, and rendering all possible assistance in the construction of a refinery.

Pamol had previously been able to extract major concessions from the Cameroonian state by capitalising on its crucial role in the regional and national economy. But by 1987 the economic and political environment had changed to such an extent that the then Minister of Industrial Development and Commerce Nomo Ongolo rejected Unilever's request out of hand. He bluntly told the Unilever delegation that the severe economic crisis no longer justified the government allocating extra funds to the agro-industrial sector. Moreover, he felt that a multinational like Unilever should not call on government for assistance but instead make its own contribution to Pamol's recovery by reinvesting some of the substantial profits it had made in the country. Interestingly, Anglophones were quick to interpret the government's denial of support to one of their region's leading enterprises as a renewed attempt by the Francophone-dominated state to destroy their regional economic heritage. Some Anglophones even alleged that one of the hidden motives for denying support was that Ngomo Ongolo and other senior members of the corrupt Biya regime were personally keen to acquire a stake in Pamol. They knew very well that Unilever would decline to subsidise a company that had incurred a loss of FCFA 1.3 billion between 1984 and 1987, and would choose instead to wind up its activities in Cameroon.[3]

In July 1987, Unilever informed the government of its plan to sell Pamol. The government, in turn, told Unilever in no uncertain terms that the state would not be taking over the company. Already burdened with the massive losses incurred by the agro-industrial parastatals, it could not afford to buy out Pamol as well, especially since the company's debts amounted to some FCFA 4.2 billion and its neglected estates and mills were in need of costly modernisation. In view of the economic crisis, the government no longer wished to expand the state's investment in the agro-industrial sector. Instead, it adopted a policy to encourage the existing agro-industrial parastatals to become self-sufficient and profitable and, in the event of failure, either to go into liquidation or be privatised (Tedga 1990; Konings 1996b). It ended by strongly advising Unilever to sell the company to any Cameroonian businessmen interested in purchasing it. Such a transaction would be a major contribution to the realisation of one of the principal objectives of the government's 'New Deal' policies: encouraging sections of the Cameroonian elite to set up medium- and large-scale plantations (Konings 1993b; Takougang 1993).

Unilever accepted the advice and promptly began secret negotiations with a small group of well-known North West businessmen, including Mr Nangah, Mr Ngufor, Mr Buyo, Mr Kilo,

Mr Nuiouat and Mr Acha. This consortium was given legal advice by Mr Sendze, a prominent lawyer in Bamenda. Unilever had come into contact with this group through the mediation process of Pamol's management staff, which was mainly made up of North Westerners. Having personal interests in an eventual North West takeover of the company, some of these senior managers continued to act as brokers between Unilever and the North West business consortium and to provide the latter with vital information about the company's situation.

The North West group was well aware that any substantial investment in the domestic agro-industrial palm-oil sector was a risky undertaking. It justified its resolve to take over Pamol as follows:

- It was motivated in the first place by regional sentiments rather than (short-term) financial considerations. The group was keen to safeguard the employment of the company's labour force, the majority of whom originated from the North West Province (see Table 1.1).
- The group was convinced that the company's precarious financial position could be redressed in the long term provided the company was thoroughly reorganised and the government implemented forthwith all the protective measures for the agro-industrial sector previously proposed by Unilever.

Unilever eventually decided to sell the company to the North West group after the latter agreed to take over Pamol's liabilities in the form of long-term loans and to guarantee payment of the workers' wages and terminal benefits. A contract was then signed by the two parties but it was this contract that kindled regionalist sentiments among the South West elite.

As soon as the secret deal between Unilever and the North West group became known, the South West elite began agitating against the North West takeover of Pamol, appealing to the state to intervene on its behalf. In a strongly worded petition presented to the head of state by the highest-ranking southwestern army officer, General James Tataw, the South West elite declared categorically that it would never allow its ancestral lands, which had been occupied by Unilever for decades, to be colonised and exploited by North

Westerners. It claimed that a North West takeover of Pamol would inevitably strengthen North West domination over the South West. It therefore urgently appealed to the state to cancel the contract between Unilever and the North West group and support a South West takeover of Pamol.

This regional conflict painfully exposed the fragility of the post-colonial state's hegemonic project of national integration (Bayart 1979). In addition, the South West elite's request forced the Biya government to take a stand on this politically delicate issue, and thus risk accusations of serving regional rather than national interests.

Initially there appeared to be ample reason for government support of a North West takeover of Pamol. The North West group had taken considerable risks in deciding to buy Pamol given the enterprise's precarious financial position and the generally unhealthy situation of the domestic agro-industrial palm-oil sector. Despite the deep national economic crisis, the group had succeeded in raising the huge capital resources required for the takeover of the company and its liabilities. It undoubtedly possessed the entrepreneurial and managerial qualities needed to run the company. The takeover was also in line with the state policy of encouraging the various elite groups – whatever their ethnic or regional origin – to invest in medium-sized and large-scale agricultural plantations in any part of the country.

There initially seemed to be no convincing reason for the government to agree to the South West's appeal to call off the deal, especially since the opposition was based largely on regional sentiments. Nor had the South West elite provided any proof that it would be capable of raising the funds necessary to take over Pamol.

The South West elite however launched a political offensive to strengthen its bargaining position. It attempted to impress upon the government that Unilever's decision to sell the company to the North West group was unfair. Since Pamol was operating on South West ancestral lands, Unilever should have invited the South West group to make the first bid for Pamol. The group also stressed the close link between the company's plantation activities and regional development and the fact that this link was more likely to be preserved by a South West takeover. Finally, the group warned that a North West takeover would spark widespread regional and political discontent in the South West.

The effective mobilisation of the regional elite was clearly a decisive factor in the ultimate success of the South West's political offensive. In the face of such a demonstration of unity and determination, the government did not dare to disappoint the South West, a province of vital importance to the national economy in terms of its rich oil, timber and agricultural resources (Ndzana 1987). When the government finally announced its decision to cancel the contract between Unilever and the North West group, Unilever decided to put the company into voluntary liquidation on 13 October 1987. Exasperated by government policies, it flatly refused to renegotiate the sale of the company.

Immediately after this, a liquidator and a committee of inspection were nominated to represent the principal creditors, in particular the state and several banks. The liquidator appointed was Mr C.G. Mure, a Frenchman who owned a firm of accountants in Douala connected with Coopers and Lybrand. He seemed well qualified for the job as he had already been involved in the bankruptcy proceedings of several private and public enterprises in Cameroon.

At his first meeting with the creditors on 3 November 1987, he presented a situation report on the company's liquidation in which he argued that a public auction of the company's assets would be a disaster socially and economically for Ndian Division. He therefore proposed running the company as an ongoing business and looking for a solution to its long-standing problems before selling it to a reliable buyer. He claimed that his unorthodox proposal was both feasible and in line with the 1961 Companies Act of Anglophone Cameroon, as the situation at Pamol had not yet deteriorated beyond possible recovery. His proposal was approved by the creditors, which was significant as it was the first time in Cameroonian history that a company had chosen to remain in business while in the process of liquidation.

The liquidator assumed the function of chief executive of the company, being accountable for his actions only to the committee of inspection that was headed by the general manager of Meridien Bank International. He devised and implemented a series of measures to restore the company's finances, refusing to pay accruing company and income tax owed to the Treasury, interest on bank overdrafts and other liabilities on the grounds that the company was in liquidation. Together with other agro-industrial companies, he entered into negotiations with the government about revitalising the ailing agro-industrial palm-oil sector. Eventually he succeeded in persuading the government to raise domestic prices and impose a surcharge on imported palm oil to protect domestic production, measures that considerably enhanced Pamol's chances of survival. The liquidator then started modernising the estates, redoubled efforts to replant them, refurbished the mill, improved roads and bought new lorries to transport produce. He also began to diversify the company's production with a view to the risks involved in monoculture cropping, which had become evident in the continuing crisis in the palm-oil sector. In addition to replanting rubber trees, he had new crops introduced at Bai Estate, such as maize and a medicinal plant called *voacanga*. All these investments would be financed largely by the sale of palm oil, the company's main source of income and investment.

Sales of palm oil, however, remained problematic. In 1988, the liquidator signed an agreement with the management of the two leading parastatals, CDC and SOCAPALM, to stop the domestic price war but this covenant lasted less than two years. Renewed undercutting of prices by the parastatals forced the average selling price of palm oil down to FCFA 210/kg by March 1990, as against the government price of FCFA 323/kg. The Minister of Agriculture at the time, Mr J.N. Ngu, was well acquainted with the problems besetting the agro-industrial palm-oil sector since he had been the CDC's general manager for many years. In April 1991, he intervened to save the palm-oil sector from total collapse and in an attempt to stabilise the price, ordered that the two principal producers, CDC and SOCAPALM, be placed in charge of domestic sales of palm oil. Henceforth, Pamol's produce was to be sold to the CDC, which in turn would pay the company every two weeks for the palm oil it had delivered. This arrangement failed to prevent SOCAPALM from further undercutting prices and a renewed price war resulted in the CDC being unable to pay Pamol. Pamol was therefore confronted with an unprecedented liquidity crisis in the early 1990s and could not even pay its workers on time. To solve these problems once and for all, the liquidator was appointed president of a study committee which was to recommend a new set-up for palm-oil sales.

After a thorough investigation, the committee recommended creating a palm-oil producers' syndicate that would purchase all produce and reimburse producers for their production every fortnight. The syndicate became operational on 1 April 1993 and has been functioning satisfactorily ever since. Its first director was Mr Nyenku, a former Pamol manager.

From the very start, the liquidator carried out negotiations surrounding the sale of Pamol. His three main objectives were to sell the company for the highest possible price, to safeguard the jobs of the existing labour force as far as possible, and to ensure Cameroonian participation in the share capital of the new company. He announced that every section of the Cameroonian business community, irrespective of ethnic or regional origin, as well as company workers and contract farmers could be shareholders.

Several business groups and companies showed interest in buying Pamol. The most important were various southwestern groups, companies and associations, the Commonwealth Development Corporation (COMDEV), and the liquidator's own group.

The South West group was the first consortium to inform the liquidator of its continued interest in buying the company. This group, which was set up with the explicit aim of taking over Pamol, had formed a company, the so-called Cameroon Agro-Industrial Company Ltd (CAMAGRIC), under Chief Mosah Allen Misembe, a businessman hailing from Ndian Division. Closely connected with CAMAGRIC were long-established southwestern businessmen like Michael Atabong and Monango Williams, and some politicians and bureaucrats who had recently moved into business including Nerius Namaso Mbile and Sylvestor Dioh. Its legal adviser was Dr Henry Enonchong. The company began issuing shares at FCFA 25,000 each but, according to well-informed sources, CAMAGRIC was initially unable to raise more than FCFA 50 million, which included FCFA 10 million from the chairman himself. Obviously it was easier to mobilise the South West elite for a protest action against a North West takeover of Pamol than for a risky capital investment in the liquidated company.

CAMAGRIC's purchase bid of FCFA 500 million was categorically rejected by the liquidator as not reflecting the true value of Pamol's assets, which had been estimated by Hunting Technical Service of London at FCFA 5 billion. The liquidator in fact had misgivings about CAMAGRIC's ability to raise the vast capital resources needed to purchase the company, take on its liabilities and refurbish its estates and mill. The group tried all sorts of campaigns including aggressive letters and interviews, requests for political intervention and the spreading of tendentious and erroneous information to persuade the government to order the closure of Pamol. This would then enable the group to buy the company at the price it was offering. Such pressures yielded no results and the government no longer seemed inclined to intervene on behalf of the South West group. Represented on the committee of inspection of the liquidation, the government appeared to fully agree with the strategy of the liquidator, namely to restore the company to some degree of economic health before selling it to a reliable and financially stronger buyer.

There is evidence that some high-ranking government officials of southwestern origin were also connected with the South West group and CAMAGRIC, albeit mostly behind the scenes. In 1988 a delegation from this group led by Ogork Ebot Ntui, the then Minister with Special Duties at the Presidency, met with the liquidator, informing him that they wanted to buy Pamol using a loan from the Bank of Credit and Commerce International (BCCI), a bank regularly accused of maintaining close ties with the drugs mafia. Ogork Ebot Ntui was apparently interested in turning Pamol into an Indian hemp company and asked the liquidator to accept the post of personnel manager. When the liquidator refused, Ntui used his ministerial powers to frustrate Pamol's activities. Company lorries were held up for long periods at customs posts and, with the complicity of a bailiff in Kumba, a number were seized by the minister who later offered them for sale at public auction.[4]

Since 1991 the newly created South West Elites Association (SWELA) has made the purchase of Pamol one of its priorities in development plans for the South West Province.[5] It has continued to pressurise the regional and national administration to hand the company over to South Westerners and has also attempted to raise the capital required. For example, it organised a series of meetings in 1993 to exhort its members to subscribe to shares costing FCFA 50,000 each in any eventual takeover of Pamol.[6] This campaign has not yet borne fruit.

The Commonwealth Development Corporation (COMDEV) was another serious candidate, offering FCFA 3.2 billion for Pamol. The purchase was to be made through a proposed new company called *Société d'Exploitation de l'Entreprise Pamol* (S.E.E. Pamol). COMDEV was prepared to provide a loan of FCFA 1.2 billion at 9% interest repayable over ten years. The minimum capital of the new company would be FCFA 1 billion but COMDEV would subscribe to only 20% of the share capital. It committed itself to promoting contract farming schemes that would place 60% of palm-oil production in the hands of contract farmers by the year 2000. It also promised to construct a refinery with a daily minimum capacity of 20 tons.

At one stage in the negotiations, the Meredien Bank International, whose general manager was president of the inspection committee for the liquidation, proposed a joint venture with participating interests as follows: COMDEV 20%, Meredien Bank International 40%, and Palma Limited Company 40%, the last being a holding company with shares held by Pamol staff, contract farmers interested in the future of Pamol and Cameroonian businessmen from a variety of sectors. This offer initially appeared attractive but political pressure on the negotiations from the South West side eventually blocked the deal with COMDEV. Subsequently, Meredien Bank International also withdrew from the joint venture.[7]

In September 1993, Pamol workers and managerial staff announced that they had more confidence in COMDEV than in SWELA because of COMDEV's international reputation, proven financial background and experience in managing companies and plantations in Africa including Cameroon.[8] That Pamol workers and managers preferred COMDEV to SWELA is not altogether surprising since most of them hail from the North West Province. However, I found that southwestern workers also had more faith in COMDEV than in SWELA. Pamol workers and management staff felt overwhelmingly that the English-speaking origins of COMDEV were an additional reason to welcome its takeover of Pamol. Unlike the French, the British were thought not to be out to dominate Anglophone Cameroon. Moreover, the English-speaking business culture fitted well in Anglophone Cameroon.

Apparently the liquidator too became interested in purchasing the revitalised company under the same conditions as those spelt out by COMDEV. To this end, he formed a consortium of

Cameroonian investors with solid international backing. However in September 1993, Pamol workers and managerial staff vehemently rejected the presence of the liquidator in any group of prospective buyers 'in view of his gross mismanagement of the company in liquidation'.[9] This is a graphic example of their marked change of attitude towards the liquidator during his time in office. He was once hailed as the 'saviour of Pamol' and commanded enormous respect among the workers[10] but when the initial euphoria over the company's possible survival was over and Pamol started to face liquidity problems, workers and managers alike became increasingly disgruntled with him.

The liquidator turned out to be extremely arrogant and authoritarian. Contrary to the Unilever style of management, he was in the habit of treating even the most senior managers with disdain bordering on contempt. For example after renewed deterioration in the company's situation, he refused to consult any of them. His French nationality, too, came to be increasingly problematic after the Biya regime fuelled existing animosity between Francophones and Anglophones (Gaillard 1992). His appointment was perceived retroactively as yet another example of Francophone domination of the Anglophone region. Pamol workers and managers deeply resented his poor command of English and were infuriated when he created the impression that he preferred Francophone to Anglophone workers and managers. He recruited a dozen Francophone graduates to understudy the Anglophone managers with an eye to eventually taking over their duties. This led to considerable confusion in the existing chain of command and fierce conflicts between the Anglophone managers, the liquidator and his Francophone graduates.

There was general consensus within the company that the salary being paid to the liquidator was too high as it was far in excess of the incomes of even the most senior managers. Without consulting anyone, Christian Mure appears to have rewarded himself with fees and allowances amounting to FCFA 430 million during his five-and-a-half years in office (October 1987-May 1993) even though he spent most of his time in Douala where he lived and ran his firm of accountants. He commuted between Douala and the Pamol Headquarters in Lobe once or twice a week by chartered plane, which cost the company more than FCFA 1 million per trip. Little wonder then that many people both within and outside the company believed he was not keen to sell the company because of his vested interest in continuing the liquidation process.

There is no doubt that Christian Mure's close contact with the corrupt and authoritarian Biya regime (van de Walle 1993; Jua 1991) was widely resented within the company. Several informants told me that the liquidator was given to boasting about his connections with high-ranking officials right up to the presidency. They also alleged that he dipped into company coffers to aid Biya's re-election in the 1992 presidential elections, providing South West Minister John Ebong Ngolle, a close friend, with a new Pajero and a substantial sum of money to campaign for Biya in the South West Province. Understandably, his contacts with the Biya regime did not endear him to the workers and managerial staff, the vast majority of whom supported the candidature of John Fru Ndi, the chairman of the SDF, in the presidential elections. It is reported that after Biya's victory in the fraudulent elections, the liquidator led a group of Biya loyalists to the house of Dr I.N. Timti, a northwestern manager, on what he described as a mission of 'condolence'. He is reported to have remarked, 'Please accept my sympathy that your leader has lost the elections, as you will not replace me as the company's general manager'.[11]

These factors, together with the liquidator's inability to pay staff during the company's severe cash-flow crisis in 1992/93, led the workers to embark on a two-month strike starting on 10 March 1993. On that fateful day, the liquidator barely escaped a lynching by workers and was rescued just in time from his hiding place on the estate by the military.

On 26 April 1993, the committee of inspection resolved that it would take over responsibility for the liquidation and justified its action as follows:

- all attempts to obtain reliable information from the liquidator had failed;
- the liquidator had persistently frustrated the committee's requests for regular auditing of the company;
- the company's financial situation had deteriorated dramatically without any plausible explanation although it was discovered

afterwards that its liabilities had increased from FCFA 4.5 billion to FCFA 7.5 billion during the liquidator's time in office; and

- the liquidator was no longer in a position to proceed with the company's liquidation since the workers had warned him not to return to the estate.[12]

The Mundemba High Court suspended the liquidator from duty on 4 May 1993 and later officially dismissed him on 15 November 1993. He was ordered to refund FCFA 361 million of the princely FCFA 430 million he had received in fees and allowances during his time in office. Reliable sources claim he appropriated over 3,000 tons of palm oil and about FCFA 50 million after his suspension.[13]

The committee of inspection created a local management committee led by Dr I.N. Timti to run the company on 8 May 1993. It hoped that the company's future would be rosy after Christian Mure's dismissal and that after being placed on a sound footing by the local management committee, the company would then be sold quickly. This would prove to be wishful thinking. The company's future appeared even bleaker after the newly appointed coordinator of the local management committee, Dr Timti, started embezzling the company's meagre resources.

The company's liquidation lasted until October 1996 when its creditors agreed to buy the company through a debt equity swap as settlement of its outstanding debts. A new company called Pamol Plantations Public Limited Company took over the assets of the company under liquidation, and the creditors became shareholders. The Cameroonian state then acquired majority shares in the new company. Its new general manager was Moses Obenofunde, a former general manager of the Meridien Bank in Douala, who had previously served as the chairman of the committee of inspection and one of Pamol's liquidators after Christian Mure's dismissal.

The Cameroonian government, the major shareholder, immediately made it clear that it was observing a hands-off policy towards the new company and that it was committed to its eventual privatisation. The new company continued to face huge problems, as noted by its general manager in 1998:

Palm oil is currently coming into Cameroon from the big Malaysian and Indonesian suppliers at low prices. We have had to drop our prices by over 30 per cent and this has damaged our turnover. We have a social duty to employ people but at the moment I have to ask them to take a 20 per cent cut in salary, to become third-party contractors working in our fields, or dismiss them.[14]

Mr Obenofunde and his successor in 2005, Obi-Okpun Wanobi Osang, have tried to execute a carefully restructured programme aimed at improving production and reducing costs.

## State withdrawal and privatisation of the CDC

The CDC is the largest agro-industrial enterprise in Cameroon and is the country's second-largest employer, surpassed only by the government. It used to employ 25,000 workers and at present has about 15,000 permanent and casual workers (see Table 1.1). It is one of the few agro-industrial enterprises in the world that specialises in a variety of crops: rubber, palm oil, tea and bananas are its four major crops.

Founded in 1946, the CDC is one of the oldest agro-industrial enterprises in Cameroon but its roots can be traced back to the German colonial period (1884-1916) (Ardener *et al.* 1960; Epale 1985; Konings 1993a). At its foundation, the CDC was charged by the British administration with developing and managing estate lands that had been expropriated from the local population, notably the Bakweri during the German colonial period (see Chapter 5), for the benefit of the people of the Trusteeship territory. It was also to provide for the spiritual, educational and social welfare of its employees. Any profit realised after the corporation had met its statutory obligations, discharged its normal functions and placed in reserve such sums as might be required for the effective running of the enterprise was to be paid to the public authorities to develop the Trusteeship territory (Konings 1993a).

Students of plantation agriculture, such as Beckford (1972), have blamed the persistent poverty and underdevelopment of Third World economies on this mode of production. In the case of the CDC however, this thesis finds little support as the corporation has been a major instrument of modernisation and is largely credited with whatever socioeconomic development has occurred in Anglophone Cameroon. It has created employment for many men and women, constructed numerous roads, ensured water and electricity supplies, built and staffed schools and awarded a substantial number of scholarships, provided medical care for a relatively large proportion of the local population and stimulated the supply of goods and services to itself and its workers. In addition, it played an important role in the commercialisation and modernisation of peasant production as an intermediary in marketing the Bakweri peasantry's banana production during the 1950s (Ardener 1958; Geschiere 1995) and in the establishment of regional smallholder oil-palm and rubber schemes since the early 1960s (Konings 1993b). As a result, the CDC has often been seen as the economic lifeline of Anglophone Cameroon.

In 1960, a year before Cameroonian reunification, an important change took place in the corporation when COMDEV took over the management and invested £1 million. It managed the corporation until 1974 when a North Westerner, J.N. Ngu, was appointed general manager. Following reunification, one can see increasing intervention by the Francophone-dominated federal state in this Anglophone corporation and the corporation's increasing dependence on foreign financial institutions for its modernisation and expansion. Between 1967 and 1987, it expanded its area under cultivation from about 20,000 to 40,000 ha using loans supplied by several external financiers, including the World Bank, the International Development Association (IDA), the European Investment Fund (FED), COMDEV and the (French) Central Fund for Economic Cooperation (CCCE). In compliance with the terms of its external loans, the federal state in 1966 began contributing to the corporation's equity share capital, which had previously been divided between the Federal State of West Cameroon and the West Cameroon Marketing Board. The Federal Minister of Planning and Territorial Development became the corporation's supervisory minister.

In the wake of the promulgation of the unitary state, Decree No. 73/597 of 28 September 1973 charged the corporation with a mission to contribute to national development and announced a new Moratorium and Articles of Association under which the CDC had to operate. One article made the United Republic of Cameroon and the National Produce Marketing Board (ONCPB) the exclusive shareholders in the corporation. In 1977 the government ordered the CDC management to expand outside the South West Province in another attempt to transform the CDC from a regional to a national corporation. As a result, the CDC now owns estates in the North West, West and Littoral Provinces. Since 1982 the chairman and the general manager are no longer appointed by the CDC's Board of Directors but by decree. Strikingly and despite these integrative efforts, the people of Anglophone Cameroon have continued to regard the CDC as 'their' corporation.

The CDC has been one of the few agro-industrial enterprises in Cameroon that has had generally positive operating results, though these have fluctuated over the years. As a public enterprise, it continued to receive large annual government subsidies and grants, irrespective of performance. For example, between 1981 and 1987, the CDC received approximately FCFA 93 million from the government. Like other agro-industrial enterprises in Cameroon, it has been suffering from the severe economic crisis since 1986 although in the three years prior to the crisis (1983/84-1985/86), the corporation was still making substantial profits totalling FCFA 3.2 billion. The crisis, however, had a dramatic impact on the corporation's financial situation: during the period from 1986/87 to 1990/91 it suffered a loss of about FCFA 19 billion (Konings 1995b). There is no doubt that the sharp fall in commodity prices on the world market was principally responsible for the corporation's virtual bankruptcy. Nevertheless, there were other factors that also contributed to the emergence and continuation of the crisis. In addition to the political elite's apparent refusal to control imports of cheap tea and palm oil, there have been frequent reports of the managerial elite's involvement in massive embezzlement, reckless expenditure, waste, and power struggles based on ethnic and regional considerations.

The South West-North West divide has, in fact, often paralysed the corporation's administration. Since reunification, the chairman of the CDC's Board of Directors has usually been a South Westerner. Prominent SWELA members like Nfon Victor Mukete, Chief Samuel

Endeley, John Ebong Ngolle and Nerius Namaso Mbile have also held this position. The daily management of the corporation, however, has been dominated by North Westerners. The appointment of North Westerner John Niba Ngu as general manager was 'advised' by the corporation's external financiers but was strongly resented by the southwestern managerial elite. First, there were also suitable southwestern candidates for this post, particularly Mr I.N. Malafa who used to be senior to Mr Ngu in the corporation's hierarchy, having served as the deputy general manager during the final years of the COMDEV management. Second, the southwestern managerial elite feared that Ngu's appointment would reinforce North West domination of the CDC management. Ngu's thirteen years in office were marked by strong anti-North West feelings and he was regularly accused by the South Western managerial elite of favouring his own countrymen. Ngu's serious conflicts with two of the southwestern chairmen of the CDC, Nfon Victor Mukete and Chief Samuel Endeley, have become almost legendary.

When Biya started to appoint some South Westerners to key positions in the South West to reduce North West domination and achieve regional balance, his friend Ngu was replaced in 1988 by Peter Mafany Musonge, a Bakweri. Ngu was then appointed Minister of Agriculture, a post which, incidentally, had meanwhile become supervisory minister of the CDC. In this capacity, Ngu continued to interfere in the CDC, denying his successor the freedom to discharge his duties. The southwestern managerial elite alleged that Ngu was using his brothers on the management staff to pressurise or even to get rid of Musonge. Together with other sections of the southwestern elite, they put constant pressure on Musonge to reduce North West influence in the corporation. Particularly after the foundation of the SDF, SWELA and the Bakweri elite urged Musonge to sack those northwestern managers suspected of being SDF supporters. In a strongly worded petition, the Bakweri Elite Youth Wing declared in July 1991:

> This is a reminder of an earlier letter to you this year in which we requested you to support our fight against SDF and their 'Graffi' domination that has caused the Bakweri people to be deprived of what belongs to them. Mola, you have to redundant the following

'grasslanders' who are strong supporters of the SDF. They are Mr Ngeh F., Chie W., Tatani, Ndenesho, and Fomuso. Do this now. We are behind you. You are also supported by Chief Justice S.M.L. Endeley and all Vikumas.[15]

Without doubt, these internal conflicts within the CDC management impeded its capacity to combat the economic crisis. Managerial problems were aggravated by the fact that the government was no longer prepared to offer any financial assistance to the ailing parastatal. To save the country from total collapse, the management and the unions on the CDC estates agreed to adopt a series of adjustment measures aimed at reducing costs and increasing productivity (see Chapter 3). This managerial strategy, which was aimed at economic recovery, was reinforced in 1989/90 when the IMF and World-Bank-inspired SAP demanded a restructuring of the parastatal sector. The CDC management then had to sign a four-year performance contract (1989/90-1993/94) with the government (Tedga 1990), under which the corporation was expected to achieve a set of objectives related to plantation development, production costs, quantity and quality of output, and staff productivity. In return, the government wrote off some of the corporation's debts amounting to FCFA 9 billion and exempted it from paying certain taxes.

The various adjustment measures brought some relief to the company's liquidity problems but owing to the continuing decline in commodity prices, the company's position remained precarious. In June 1992, the Biya government, which was highly dependent on French support and aid, managed to obtain a FCFA 7 billion low-interest loan for the ailing company from the French CCCE. Although this loan provided much-needed capital for investment purposes, the increased control of France over the corporation was strongly resented by CDC workers and managers, as well as by the general public in Anglophone Cameroon. It was rumoured that the CCCE was interested in taking over the management of the CDC oil-palm estates and this again resulted in widespread protests in Anglophone Cameroon.

This regional outcry against supposedly increasing French control of the corporation was in sharp contrast to regional sentiments about attempts to transfer the management of two major CDC crops to

English-speaking companies. Few protests were voiced in Anglophone Cameroon when the corporation entrusted management of the banana sector to the American multinational Del Monte in 1987. Regional newspapers even praised the negotiations between the CDC and COMDEV in late 1992 for a potential transfer of the management of the corporation's three tea estates to COMDEV for a period of ten years.

From 1992 onwards, persistent rumours circulated in Anglophone Cameroon that the Biya government was about to either sell, shut down or privatise the CDC. While World Bank sources confirmed that the external financiers were putting pressure on the government to do so, the government continued to deny these rumours. On 15 July 1994 however, the government issued a decree announcing the privatisation or liquidation of a first batch of 15 public enterprises, notably in the transport and agro-industrial sectors. The CDC was one of the most conspicuous victims of this decree and the announcement caused commotion in Anglophone Cameroon. All the existing parties, organisations and associations, among them the SDF, SWELA, chiefs and Anglophone pressure groups, such as the Cameroon Anglophone Movement (CAM) and the All Anglophone Conference (AAC) (Konings & Nyamnjoh 2003), seemed to forget their differences as they rallied in protest against what they perceived as 'the attempt of the Biya government to sell this sizable corporation, which has been for long the pride of Anglophone Cameroon, to France'. Some also alleged that privatisation was a 'plan by Biya to compensate his "tribesmen" and allies with a slice of the parastatal cake'. One local paper claimed that the government was offering the CDC 'at low cost to cronies' (Konings 1996b: 212).

Protest marches were held in Anglophone towns. Protesters carried banners with slogans such as 'France: hands off Anglophones' and 'Hands off or we will burn the plantations'. CDC workers went on strike as they thought privatisation would mean retrenchment. A memorandum to Biya, co-signed by Anglophone pressure groups including the newly created Southern Cameroons National Council (SCNC), chiefs and prominent local landowners contended that the CDC was not for sale as local landowners, in particular the Bakweri, had neither relinquished ownership of CDC land nor received any royalties for its use since the corporation's foundation in 1946, and CDC workers had injected over FCFA 5.5 billion into the corporation as compulsory savings during the crisis. In August 1994, the Biya government sent a delegation of Anglophone ministers to the capitals of the two Anglophone provinces to appease the population. They were jeered, however, and accused of wanting to benefit from the spoils. In Buea, the capital of the South West Province, they met an assembly of the powerful association of southwestern chiefs that expressed to the delegation the region's bewilderment at being sacrificed on the altar of uncontrolled liberalisation. In Chapter 5, I will show that the traditional and modern elite of the Bakweri has continued to be the most prominent group in Anglophone resistance against any government attempt to privatise the CDC.

The privatisation protest movement was one of the recent developments in Anglophone Cameroon that made the Biya regime painfully aware of the growing unity and determination among Anglophones in their struggle for redress of the marginalisation and subordination of their region within the Francophone-dominated state.

## Conclusion

This chapter has provided evidence of the argument put forward in the previous chapter that the regional agro-industrial crisis and reforms in Anglophone Cameroon have reinforced existing regional sentiments among the South West elite. However these regional sentiments appear ambivalent. This is manifest in the struggle for control of the two major agro-industrial enterprises in the South West Province. At times, they have tended to adopt an Anglophone identity and resisted any attempt by the Francophone-dominated state to dismantle the common Anglophone colonial legacy. Consequently, when rumours started to spread that the Biya regime intended to sell the few remaining Anglophone Cameroonian companies to Francophone or French business interests, they rallied behind the northwestern elite in defence of Anglophone patrimony. But as soon as they suspect the northwestern elite of being interested in establishing control over economic resources in the South West, they are inclined to adopt a South West identity for fear of renewed

North West domination over their province. Believing themselves to have suffered greater disadvantage than North Westerners in the Francophone-dominated post-colonial state, the South West elites appear to be more inclined to adopt a South West identity than an Anglophone identity.

Significantly, this study also provides evidence that, in the wake of the introduction of multipartyism in late 1990, Anglophone interests in general and South West interests in particular have been represented first and foremost by the emerging non-political associations and pressure groups of the South West and Anglophone elite rather than by the newly created political parties in the Anglophone region. As Nyamnjoh & Rowlands (1998) acutely observe, ethno-regional associations appear to have increasingly become the prime movers in the regional political economy. While personal animosities among southwestern political leaders prevented them from founding a strong political party, even the popular North West- based SDF gradually started losing its initial appeal in Anglophone Cameroon. It still participated in Anglophone protest marches against the privatisation of the CDC, mainly because the majority of CDC workers and managers are from the North West and are strong SDF supporters. However, it was becoming increasingly evident that the SDF was presenting itself as a national rather than a regional party and was adopting an ambivalent, half-hearted stand towards the Anglophone problem and Anglophone demands for a return to the federal state (Krieger 1994; Konings & Nyamnjoh 2003).

## Notes

1. For Mbile's political career, see Mbile (2000).

2. Political Report on Ekondo Titi Subdivision for March 1972, by Michael Nkamsi D.O., in Buea National Archives (BNA), File Cd (1972)2, Political Reports on Ekondo Titi Subdivision. See also Monthly Political and Economic Report for the Month of April 1970, in BNA, File 1969/1, Divisional Economic and Political Reports.

3. *The Messenger*, 14 October 1993, pp. 8-9.

4. Minutes of a meeting with labour officials, Pamol management, staff representatives, trade unionists and the administration to discuss the non-payment of Pamol workers' salaries, held in the Conference Hall of Korup National Park on 8 March 1993, in File MTPS/SWP/MND.49/Vol.2, General Correspondence – Plantations Pamol du Cameroun Ltd.

5. For SWELA, see Nyamnjoh & Rowlands (1998); Konings & Nyamnjoh (2003) and Nkwi (2006).

6. See Report of the National Security Bureau at Ekondo Titi, dated 22 September 1993, in File G 4002/49, Vol. 3, Pamol Cameroon Ltd – General Correspondence.

7. Plantations Pamol du Cameroun Ltd (Company in Liquidation) Annual Report, 1989-1990; and Report on Pamol Situation as at 16 May 1989. These documents can be found in the Pamol Headquarters Archives.

8. See Memorandum to the Chairman, Inspection Committee of Pamol, presented by the workers of Pamol deliberating at Lobe on 16 September 1993, in Pamol Headquarters Archives at Lobe Estate. For COMDEV's role in plantation production in Cameroon, see Konings (1993a).

9. *Ibid.*

10. See, for instance, *Cameroon Tribune*, 8 February 1989, p. 5.

11. *The Messenger,* 17 June 1993, p. 14.

12. Minutes of Meeting of Creditors' Committee of Pamol held at Douala on 26 April 1993, Pamol Headquarters Archives at Lobe Estate.

13. *The Herald,* 3-10 November 1993, p. 10. The liquidator, Mr C.G. Mure, then appealed to the South West Court of Appeal in Buea. Remarkably, this court reversed the decision of the Mundemba High Court and ruled that Mr Mure was not to pay back any money to the company and that the company's shareholders and creditors could either continue to employ him or appoint a new liquidator. The latter decided to drop him. They then appointed Evariste Njaba and Moses Obenofunde as joint liquidators.

14. Pamol Summit Reports (1998).

15. *The New Standard,* 30 July 1991, p. 6.

# 3

# CDC workers and the agro-industrial crisis

## Introduction

Surprisingly, while it is now widely accepted that wage workers have been among the most seriously affected by the economic crisis and structural adjustment programmes (SAPs) in Africa, their responses have hardly been studied. The existing literature tends to focus on the actions of central labour organisations and their defence of members' interests. There seems to have been a large variation in the role played by these organisations in African states: it is said to have been 'spectacular' in Zambia (Simutanyi 1992), 'considerable' in Nigeria (Olukoshi & Aremu 1988), 'unexpected[ly] low' in Ghana (Herbst 1991) and 'absent' in Cameroon (Mehler 1993; Konings 2007b). Although there are references to the responses of workers themselves, these are seldom based on research at the local level. This may give rise to easy generalisations and even to incomplete or false interpretations of workers' responses as numerous studies of organised labour have highlighted the remarkable difference in workers' consciousness and actions between and within African states, and the contradictions between the rank and file and the union leadership (Jeffries 1978; Sandbrook & Cohen 1975).

Nigeria is one of the few countries in Africa for which empirical studies on local workers' responses to the economic crisis and SAPs exist. These studies draw different conclusions. Oloyede (1992), for example, claims that shop-floor workers in a local subsidiary of a Dutch electronics multinational were more likely, on the basis of a rational calculation of benefits and costs, to adopt an individual survival orientation than a collective oppositional posture to managerial adjustment measures, with the benefit in this case being individual security or tenure, and the cost being the likely further weakening of collectivism, which individual pursuit can bring about. Some other case studies, however, do not support Oloyede's claim:

Bangura (1991) and Bangura & Beckman (1993), for example, argue that Nigerian industrial workers have continued to oppose managerial adjustment measures.

This chapter examines the response of plantation workers in Nigeria's neighbour, Cameroon. It focuses on CDC tea pluckers who have had to cope with the severe crisis affecting the corporation since 1986/87 and the subsequent structural adjustment measures aimed at cost reduction and increases in productivity (see Chapter 2). Soon after the signing of a four-year performance contract (1989/90-1993/94) with the government, the CDC's general manager announced a managerial crusade against undisciplined and unproductive workers:

> In the Contract Plan drawn up and signed by the Government of Cameroon and the Corporation, the corporation is required to meet certain standards of efficiency and to be self-supporting and profitable….. That is why we have to be generally very strict on discipline and sanction any manifestation of laxity….. Maximum efforts shall be required of employees so as to continuing producing more at lower and lower cost; laxity and *laissez faire* which are characterised by an alarming rate of absenteeism and uncompleted tasks shall not be tolerated.[1]

A study of tea pluckers' responses to the crisis is all the more interesting as the labour force on one of the two selected estates was female-dominated. This enables an exploration of the possibility of gender-related differences in pluckers' responses, taking into account the frequent assumption in managerial circles that female workers are more docile and disciplined because of their persistent subordination to patriarchal domination in society (cf. Elson & Pearson 1984; Mies 1986; Ezumah & Fonsah 2004).

This chapter is divided into two parts. The first discusses the role of CDC trade unions during the agro-industrial crisis and the second part assesses the role of workers on CDC tea estates during the agro-industrial crisis, showing their various modes of resistance to the intensified control and exploitation in the labour process.

70

# Trade unionism in the CDC and the agro-industrial crisis

Trade unionism in the CDC has a long history. Immediately after the corporation was established in 1946/47, a trade union was organised on its estates and duly registered. This union, the Cameroon Development Corporation Workers' Union (CDCWU), was soon to become one of the largest and most powerful in West Central Africa (Warmington 1960; Konings 1993a).

In contrast to the CDC management, the British Trusteeship Authority was not opposed to the formation of this union, if only as it offered a more sophisticated means of labour control. As in other British colonies, the Labour Department was quite successful in propagating a specific trade union model within the newly established union, one that may be best described as 'free, but responsible' trade unionism (Sandbrook 1975). This model actively advised trade unionists to stay out of politics and solve conflicts with their employers in a cordial manner through negotiations and collective bargaining rather than through strikes. The strike weapon was only to be used as a last resort if all other means of settling disputes, including conciliation and arbitration, had failed.

I have demonstrated elsewhere that the introduction of this type of trade union model resulted in the emergence of internal contradictions between the moderate CDCWU union leaders, who were mainly recruited from among the supervisory staff and clerical workers, and the rank and file that comprised the vast majority of unskilled and semi-skilled workers. The latter were less inclined than union leaders to have faith in the efficacy of the institutionalised procedures of joint negotiation and collective bargaining, and were more committed to militant action (Konings 1993a; see also Chapter 1).

These contradictions in the relationship between the rank and file and the union leadership were never fully worked out during the CDCWU's existence (1947-1972). This was mainly due to the fact that the generally moderate union leadership was pressurised by the rank and file into adopting an aggressive bargaining policy with regard to the management and the government, employing the strike option as a 'tactical weapon' (Paige 1975). Not only was strike action frequently threatened, it was also regularly employed, with workers called out on strike if all peaceful means of settling a conflict had been exhausted. As a result, union leaders tended to enjoy massive support among the rank and file.

By the end of the 1960s however, the post-colonial state was increasingly beginning to intervene in the system of industrial relations and to curtail union autonomy with a view to curbing labour militancy and establishing 'total' control over civil society (Bayart 1979). The 1967 Federal Labour Code virtually outlawed strike action in the country, seriously weakening the bargaining position of unions. Despite strong resistance on the part of the CDCWU leadership, trade unionism in the CDC came under state control in 1972. In a subsequent reorganisation, a single central labour organisation was formed, first called the National Union of Cameroon Workers (NUCW) but rechristened the Cameroon Trade Union Congress (CTUC) in 1985. Existing unions, like the CDCWU, were dissolved and new unions were created to organise workers engaged in the same or related fields of activities within each administrative division in the country.

This reorganisation had a number of disastrous consequences for trade unionism at the CDC. First, it became subordinated to the single party. Its primary responsibility was to turn workers into party militants and educate them about the need for increased production and constant dialogue with the employers. There were high expectations among the party leadership that the new union model was going to accomplish what the Trusteeship model of autonomous trade unionism had failed to achieve, namely the transformation of trade unionism into an instrument of labour control and a responsible partner in national development.

The second major consequence was the fragmentation of the union, which created serious obstacles to united trade union actions. Since the reorganisation of trade unionism on a divisional basis, CDC workers have belonged to five different agricultural workers' unions, with membership depending on the administrative division in which they are employed. As most CDC estates are in the Fako Division of the South West Province, the majority of CDC workers belong to the Fako Agricultural Workers' Union (FAWU).

Thirdly, the union became paralysed by a lack of funds. Through the introduction of a new distribution system for contributions, the divisional unions received no more than 50% of members' contributions. Moreover, a state-controlled National Committee for Trade Union Contributions in Yaoundé was made responsible for collecting and allocating the check-off contributions across the whole country, resulting – unsurprisingly – in frequent and often prolonged delays in the remittance of monies to the divisional unions and in the large-scale misappropriation of funds. This financial crisis has prevented the divisional unions from employing more than a few full-time officers and from organising any activities such as educational courses.

Finally, the union was stripped of any popular participation in the decision-making process. Trade unionism became virtually a one-man affair in the person of the president of the divisional union. He owed his position more to the party's selection than to workers' support and was unlikely to be removed from office as long as he enjoyed the party's support. He ran the union without regularly consulting the rank and file on policy matters or the allocation of funds and Executive Committee, congress and mass meetings became rare events. The union president also tried to control the shop stewards who had been introduced in 1968. Rather like party elections, union members were presented with a list of screened candidates and all the workers could do was approve the union's nominees, leaving them with virtually no say in who would represent them. In protest, workers sometimes refused to vote. Any shop steward who caused the management trouble or opposed the one-man rule of the union ran the risk of being victimised by the president.

It was after the reorganisation of trade unionism in 1972 that contradictions between the union leadership and the rank and file became increasingly obvious. Co-opted in the control structure over labour, the union's leadership rapidly lost popular support. And even more significantly, it proved to be incapable of containing the rank and file's traditional militancy, as reflected in the large-scale participation of CDC workers in several illegal strike actions after 1972 (Konings 1993a).

Interestingly, following the introduction of a multi-party system in the country in December 1990, CDC workers began to pressurise the union leadership to fight for a return to union autonomy. Most of the CDC workers hail from the North West Province and are strong supporters of the Social Democratic Front (SDF), the major opposition party based in Bamenda in the North West Province, which started the fight against the one-party state (Mehler 1993). Cornelius Vewessee, once chairman of the CDCWU and, since 1974, president of the FAWU, also joined the opposition and soon became one of the most outspoken advocates of trade union autonomy. In February 1991, he declared:

> The workers expect an independent and strong trade union organisation that would be autonomous in relation to all political parties and state bodies and institutions…. This will relieve the trade union of the rubber stamp element in the country's political life. If the trade union does not become more militant and resolute in its demands, it will not be of much help to the workers.[2]

Vewessee also dared to condemn the corrupt leadership of the Confederal Bureau of the Cameroon Trade Union Congress (CTUC) for its continuing alliance with the ruling party, the Cameroon People's Democratic Movement (CPDM), and its complete neglect of the defence of workers' interests during the economic crisis and structural adjustment programme, a criticism that would have been impossible before the introduction of multipartyism in 1991. His relentless efforts yielded some success: on 2 April 1991, the CTUC leadership publicly announced that union members were henceforth free to join any party they chose. However during the executive elections at the CTUC Congress in May 1992, which were clearly manipulated by the ruling CPDM party, Vewessee failed to dissuade most delegates from voting an alternative member of the CPDM's Central Committee, Etame Ndidi, into the office of president of the central labour organisation (Konings 2000, 2006, 2007b, 2009a).

Unfortunately, before the union leadership became involved in the struggle for a return to trade union autonomy, it was already being confronted with the unprecedented economic crisis in the corporation (see Chapter 2). This further weakened the bargaining position of the state-controlled unions *vis-à-vis* management. Their principal strategy became to protect workers against retrenchment, even if this demanded curtailment of past gains.

In 1987, trade union presidents on the corporation's estates were approached by CDC management to assist in the planning and implementation of adjustment measures. Management had apparently assumed that union assistance would be important in controlling any anticipated resistance by workers to a painful adjustment programme. This assumption was questionable as such assistance on the part of the union leaders was just as likely to enhance worker dissatisfaction with the union leadership and result in their refusal to cooperate. However, the union presidents eventually agreed to assist the management in its struggle for economic recovery.[3] There were a number of factors behind this decision including the fact that, since the reorganisation of trade unionism in 1972, the union had become used to solving problems with the management and the state through peaceful negotiation rather than confrontation. In this particular case, union presidents agreed with the management that, given the corporation's inability to secure any loans or public subsidies during the crisis, cost reductions and productivity increases were necessary prerequisites for economic recovery. Furthermore, they were assured by management that nobody in the corporation would be exempt from making sacrifices for the sake of economic recovery. Finally, they hoped that the implementation of an adjustment programme would safeguard the jobs of the sizeable CDC labour force.

On 23 August 1987 the union presidents agreed to a substantial increase in productivity by estate workers. For example, the daily quota of green leaves expected of tea pluckers was raised from 26 kg to 32 kg. Union leaders assured management that they would elicit workers' support in this.[4] As the corporation's financial position continued to deteriorate, management proposed further austerity measures to the union presidents. After some negotiation, a new agreement was signed on 6 January 1990 that entailed drastic cuts of about 30-40% in the salaries and fringe benefits of workers and managerial staff. The corporation used to supply workers with free housing, water, electricity and medical facilities but now they were obliged to make substantial contributions towards the supply of these services themselves. The most draconian measure, however, was the introduction of a compulsory savings scheme that forced workers to save at least 15% of their wages to assist in the corporation's recovery.[5] It has been estimated that these compulsory savings by workers and cuts in fringe benefits between February 1990 and February 1992 totalled about FCFA 2.9 billion.[6]

Following the achievement of a degree of trade union autonomy in 1991, union presidents became somewhat more responsive to the hardships their workers were facing and began to criticise the adjustment programme they had previously supported. At their urgent request, the CDC general manager organised a meeting to reassess the January 1990 agreement and on 14 March 1992, the FAWU president, Cornelius Vewessee, insisted on the termination or modification of workers' financial contributions to the corporation's recovery programme. He justified this remarkable change in the unions' position as follows:[7]

- The unions had expected that workers' increased output and financial sacrifices would have forestalled or at least minimised any retrenchments. This had proved wishful thinking, and the management had embarked on mass lay-offs. For example, between 1986/87 and 1990/91, the labour force at the Tole and Ndu Tea Estates was cut from 1546 to 974 and from 1750 to 1333 respectively.

- The unions had expected the government to take appropriate measures to stabilise the prices of essential commodities and standardise the wages of the agro-industrial parastatals but this had not happened. Nor had the National Social Insurance Fund continued to pay family allowances to workers. In fact, prices had skyrocketed after the opposition's 'Ghost Town' campaign,[8] wages had been frozen since July 1985 and taxes increased by 100%. As a result, CDC workers 'would now seem to be carrying out forced labour as a majority of the labour force has no take-home wages at the end of the month'.

- The unions had supported the 6 January 1990 agreement because the CDC was unable to obtain financial assistance at that time. This situation, however, had recently changed with a CCCE grant to the corporation of FCFA 7 bn. As a result, workers were no longer willing to make further sacrifices.

- The unions would no longer tolerate the fact that workers were making sacrifices for economic recovery while the political and managerial elite 'continued to loot the parastatals'.[9]

Management refused to cancel the 6 January 1990 agreement. The only concession it was willing to make was a 3% reduction in the compulsory savings rate to partially compensate workers for tax increases. This was unacceptable to the unions. As management refused to reconsider its offer, FAWU president Cornelius Vewessee declared a collective trade dispute on 13 May 1992, and when management tried to employ delaying tactics, CDC workers in the Fako Division went on strike (21 to 26 May 1992). Management then agreed to various amendments of the 6 January 1990 agreement including reintroducing free accommodation and water for the workers and a 24% reduction in medical costs.[10]

Although there was a slight improvement in the relationship between the union leadership and the management after these amendments, tensions and conflicts have never completely disappeared. The union presidents regularly complain about the management's lack of consultation with them, while the management, in turn, constantly stresses that the unions should concentrate more on an increase in labour productivity in times of crisis than on the representation of workers' interests.

## Tea pluckers and the agro-industrial crisis

In 1991-92 in an attempt to understand CDC workers' responses to the adjustment measures, I carried out intensive research on two regional CDC tea estates that had been set up during the 1950s when the British Trusteeship Authority started to actively promote local tea production (Konings 1995a, 1996c, 1998c, 2009b). The first, the Tole Tea Estate, was created in the Fako Division of the South West Province in 1954. It is the only CDC estate to employ predominantly female pluckers, the majority of whom come from the North West Province, which is the traditional labour reserve for the coastal plantations (DeLancey 1974). The second estate, the Ndu Tea Estate, was started in 1957 and is in the Donga-Mantung Division of the North West Province. It was owned by a British-Indian multinational, the Estates and Agency Company Ltd (EAC) that had substantial tea interests in India and Sri Lanka, and was taken over by the CDC in 1977. At present, it is the only CDC estate in the North West Province and one of the few CDC estates without labour camps. It employs almost exclusively local male labour.

The gender difference in the labour forces employed on these estates is by no means accidental (Konings 1995a). It is the outcome of two potentially conflicting factors: the capitalist preference for female pluckers and patriarchal control over female labour in the local communities (Stichter & Parpart 1988). Tea estates, in fact, were among the few capitalist enterprises during colonial rule that gave preference to female labour and there has long been a demand for female labour on tea estates throughout the world. The rationale for this was the managerial belief that women tended to be more productive than men in certain tasks (they had 'nimble fingers' and were, therefore, naturally suited to plucking), as well as being more docile and cheaper. This formed a direct threat to the customary patriarchal control over female labour.

In 1952, just a few years before the two estates were set up, Kaberry published her classic study of women in the present North West Province in which she emphasises the contradictory position of women in society. On the one hand, there is a general recognition that women play an indispensable role in society as child bearers and food producers but on the other, they are subordinated to patriarchal controls in society. These contradictions may not, however, be as puzzling as they first appear. Control over women's vital productive and reproductive labour used to constitute the basis of men's prestige, power and wealth in society. In a more recent study of women in the North West Province, Goheen (1993: 250) observed:

> Women grew the food crops and were expected to provide the necessities of daily life from their farms. Women's productive labour forced men to participate in (lucrative) trading networks; their reproductive labour increased the size of the household and thus the status and the labour force of the male head. Any surplus value women produced over and above that required for household needs and petty barter was in the hands of men, who retained all the profits.

Managerial demands for female pluckers proved to be more successful on the Tole Tea Estate than on the Ndu Tea Estate because capitalism had had a more disruptive effect on social formations in the South West Province than in the North West Province. Consequently, patriarchal opposition to female employment on the newly established tea estates was less pronounced in the former than the latter province. The introduction of plantation agriculture in the South West Province during German colonial rule resulted in the large-scale expropriation of land and a regular flow of migrant labour, especially from the North West Province, to coastal estates. The CDC, which took over most of the former German plantation lands, was not dependent on the goodwill of the local chiefs for the supply of land and labour when the Tole Tea Estate was created in 1954. Furthermore, chieftaincy was a relatively weak institution in the segmentary societies of the South West Province and was often a colonial creation (cf. Geschiere 1993). Despite the pervasive ideology of patriarchal dominance in their communities, these chiefs were in no position to contest managerial decisions about employing female labour as they had no authority on CDC estates. Moreover, when the Tole Tea Estate was established, female employment on CDC estates was not a new phenomenon and CDC management used to encourage workers' wives to seek employment there (Konings 1993a).

In comparison with the South West Province, there was little capitalist penetration in the North West Province. Determined to create a tea estate at Ndu in 1956/57, the EAC management was heavily dependent on the goodwill of the local chief and elders for land and labour since chieftaincy continued to be a powerful institution in the centralised states of the North West Province (Nkwi & Warnier 1982; Warnier 2009) and was still capable of resisting any serious capitalist onslaught on local value systems and patterns of authority. During negotiations, the chief of Ndu strongly opposed the managers' proposals to employ female pluckers on the estate, insisting instead on the employment of local male labour as a prerequisite to the setting up of the estate in his area of jurisdiction. This was a condition that would not only halt the migration of local male labour to coastal areas but also forestall the construction of labour camps, common to the coastal estates. In this way, he hoped to safeguard not only traditional male control over women's productive and reproductive labour but also the continuous integration of male workers into the local community and their loyalty to the traditional code of ethics and authority patterns.

In the end, he agreed that women could be employed on the estate for specific activities, notably weeding, on a casual or temporary basis and provided their employment did not affect their productive and reproductive responsibilities in the local community. The EAC negotiating team had no other choice but to comply with the conditions set out by the local chief.

From the start, the labour force on these estates shared some common characteristics (see Table 3.1). First, they tended to be either illiterate or poorly educated, which is not surprising. For this category of workers, plantation labour forms a rare employment opportunity in the capitalist sector. Second, workers are mainly men and women who have tried to escape from the control of (male) elders in their local communities and build an autonomous existence. Table 3.1 shows that most of the women employed on the Tole Tea Estate tended to be 'husbandless' (cf. Bryceson 1980). Some were young, single women who had no access to land but were expected to work as unpaid labour on family farms. Most, however, were older women who had lost relatively secure usufruct rights to land as a result of the death of a husband or divorce. Rather than becoming dependent on family elders for their survival, they preferred to migrate to the tea estate where they could be sure of a regular monthly wage income. Ndu workers, in contrast, tended to be local men who had failed to become family heads and were thus eager to escape from the control of those who had succeeded. They saw plantation labour as a route to a relatively autonomous existence and, above all, to social mobility in the local community. There was often a specific sequence in the attainment of such social mobility objectives: first to build a house and to marry one (or more) wives who would be responsible for the cultivation of food; then to set up a coffee farm and raise cattle; and eventually to invest in the acquisition of honorific titles that give access to the same power and wealth in the local community that is available to hereditary office and title holders. These were not easy objectives for poorly paid estate workers, and very few managed to accomplish them all.

Table 3.1 *Demographic characteristics of tea estate workers in Cameroon (%)*

|  | Tole women | Ndu men |
|---|---|---|
| **Age** | | |
| 15-24 years | 7.5 | 3.5 |
| 25-34 years | 32.5 | 25.0 |
| 35-44 years | 41.0 | 38.5 |
| 45-54 years | 17.0 | 28.0 |
| 55 years and over | 2.0 | 5.0 |
|  | 100 | 100 |
| **Marital Status** | | |
| single | 9.0 | 8.0 |
| married | 32.0 | 90.5 |
| widowed | 27.0 | 1.0 |
| divorced/separated | 25.0 | 0.5 |
| free union |  | 7.0 |
|  | 100 | 100 |
| **Educational Level** | | |
| illiterate | 78.0 | 56.5 |
| primary education | 20.5 | 39.5 |
| post-primary education | 1.5 | 4.0 |
|  | 100 | 100 |
| **Religion** | | |
| Christian | 94.0 | 92.0 |
| ancestral belief | 6.0 | 7.0 |
| Muslim |  | 1.0 |
|  | 100 | 100 |
| **Years of Service** | | |
| 0-5 years | 17.0 | 12.5 |
| 5-10 years | 19.5 | 24.5 |
| 10-15 years | 39.0 | 17.5 |
| 15-25 years | 19.5 | 31.5 |
| 25 years or more | 5.0 | 14.0 |
|  | 100 | 100 |

*Source:* Data supplied by estate offices.

Thirdly, the labour force on these estates tended to be highly committed and became increasingly stable. Over 60% of the Tole and Ndu workers were employed on the estate for more than ten years (see Table 3.1). In general, both groups had a high stake in plantation labour. Tole female workers tended to be not only husbandless but also household heads with children to support. They were often highly dependent on plantation labour for the reproduction of their families, lacking both the time and energy to engage in additional income-generating activities. Most had acquired a small food farm for subsistence and trading purposes but experienced difficulties in combining food production and trade with their daily workload on the estate and in the household. Ndu workers, too, worked for a long period on the estate, eager to realise their social mobility goals. Although they became involved in a variety of potentially lucrative economic activities, such as coffee production, cattle rearing and trade during their careers, they would retain their jobs on the estate. Plantation labour served as an insurance against future misfortune in their expanding economic activities and as a source of further investment.

Despite these common characteristics, there are also some differences between the Tole female workers and the Ndu male workers. One major difference is the degree of contact with their home towns. Unlike the Ndu male workers who remained firmly integrated in their local community, Tole female workers maintained very few close links with their region of origin. The single women in particular seem to have largely severed their ties with their home towns and villages and their escape from patriarchal control tended to prevent them from maintaining contact with family members and gaining access to land at home. Their 'exit option' from wage employment is usually a switch to petty trade in urban centres rather than a return home. Even married female workers on the Tole Tea Estate seem to find it difficult to keep up intensive contact with family members at home. Geographical distance and a six-day working week present serious obstacles to regular communication. Many female workers only visit their home towns in the annual period of leave or for special occasions, such as funerals of close kin.

There are divisions within the labour force on the two estates that are based mainly on education, occupation, gender and marital status as well as ethnic and regional origin. There is a division, for instance, between the vast majority of illiterate and poorly educated field workers and the tiny group of better educated clerical workers. The latter tend to look down on the field workers and to treat them with little respect when they visit the estate offices. There is also a division between male and female workers. The root of this cleft is the pervasive ideology of male dominance. For example, male workers expect the (male) management to give them preference over female workers when there is an opportunity for further training or promotion, and to fire female workers first when retrenchment is required. They are reluctant to work under female supervision and regularly harass their female colleagues. There is a persistent fear among married men that wage employment will make their wives too headstrong or independent. There is also a division between married and unmarried female workers. Unmarried women tend to be relatively free from patriarchal controls but are accorded very little respect, being labelled as loose women or prostitutes. Married female workers, on the other hand, are highly respected but are still subordinated to male dominance. Some husbands insist that, according to African tradition, women are responsible for the upkeep of the family and they tend to make very little financial contribution to their family's upkeep, spending their wages as they choose. Others, especially men from the North West Province, even claim that they are traditionally entitled to their wives' wage income.

Finally, there are divisions along ethnic and regional lines. There is a greater ethnic and regional heterogeneity among the Tole female workers than among the Ndu male workers. On the Tole Tea Estate, there is a clear North West-South West divide: 67% of Tole female workers originate from ethnic groups in the North West Province and 29% from ethnic groups in the South West Province. On the Ndu Estate, almost all workers hail from two ethnic groups in the North West Province: 73% belong to the local ethnic group, the Wimbum (Jeffries 1962; Probst & Bühler 1990), and 23% come from the neighbouring ethnic group, the Nso (Goheen 1996), most of whom live in villages near the estates. Although ethnic and regional heterogeneity is a potential source of conflict, with rivalry being sparked by suspicions of favouritism in hiring or promotion or due to disagreements with supervisors or co-workers, there have been few incidences of serious, protracted ethnic clashes on either estate. Interestingly, although the labour force at the Ndu Tea Estate is ethnically less heterogeneous than at the Tole Tea Estate, it was nevertheless the scene of more overt ethnic tensions and conflicts in the 1960s. This was partly due to Ndu chauvinism: since the estate was located on Ndu land, the chief and local people used to claim that Ndu workers be given priority when vacancies occurred for leading positions.

Generally speaking however, estate workers of different ethnic groups and regions live and work peacefully together. It has been the consistent policy of the management and church and union leaders to mobilise and organise workers on a multi-ethnic basis, and this seems to have created a certain degree of understanding and tolerance among workers for each other's sociocultural background and to have fostered bonds of companionship and friendship across ethnic boundaries. The general use of Pidgin English has helped to overcome barriers of communication between the various ethnic groups. The most important reason for this relative harmony, however, appears to be the sharing of similar living and working conditions on the estates, which are classic examples of occupational communities. The internal divisions that do exist have never prevented tea pluckers from regularly engaging in common actions to protect their interests. Estate workers display a rather ambivalent attitude towards plantation labour: they appreciate it as it provides them with a regular source of income but they have an acute sense of being exploited and of subordination in the labour process.

As in other parts of the world (cf. Loewenson 1992), estate workers in Cameroon receive relatively low remuneration for their arduous work but, unlike in many places (cf. Kurian 1982), there is no difference in the remuneration of male and female workers on Cameroonian estates. Before the economic recession, tea pluckers on CDC estates used to earn an average net monthly wage of FCFA 20,000-25,000. However quite a number of pluckers were unable to earn this much due to the link between the remuneration of workers and the system of task work. Achieving the daily targets set by management entitled a worker to a daily basic wage; while non-completion of the allotted task was punished by a pro-rata payment according to the work completed. While workers' incomes have seriously decreased during the economic crisis, managerial controls over the labour process have intensified to improve labour discipline and productivity.

Since the first days of estate tea production, the union leadership and the Labour Department have consistently instructed pluckers that their union was the normal intermediary channel between workers and management. As a result, workers have usually turned to the union in the first instance for representation and defence of their interests. Their support for their union has never been unconditional however. They expected union leaders to act promptly and actively during individual and collective disputes and to produce results. When such expectations were not realised, workers began to bypass the union and use alternative methods, such as informal actions, pursued on an individual or small-scale basis, or collective actions (Cohen 1980; Crisp 1984). This was particularly true of the period of state-controlled unionism. Loss of confidence in the union seems to have been more evident at the Tole Tea Estate than at the Ndu Tea Estate. The degree of participation in union affairs has always been conspicuously lower among female pluckers than among their male counterparts because of the patriarchal union structure and women's multiple productive and reproductive responsibilities outside the labour process (cf. Parpart 1988; Pittin 1984).

Confronted with the (initially) close cooperation between the union leadership and the management in the planning and implementation of austere adjustment measures, the response of the tea pluckers was complex and varied. Some workers opted for a single strategy, others for several strategies, simultaneously or consecutively. A growing number of pluckers have become survival-oriented in the climate of insecurity. In the interest of keeping their jobs they are inclined to acquiesce in whatever stringent economic recovery measures management may introduce. They try to impress the management with above-average output and avoid conflicts with their supervisors. This seems to be more marked among Tole female pluckers than Ndu male pluckers, which is no doubt attributable to the fact that the Ndu male pluckers are still strongly integrated in the local community and enjoy an easier exit option than the Tole female workers.

Some workers continue to rely on the unions to handle their individual and collective grievances but a growing number are bypassing the unions and lodging their complaints directly with the Labour Department. It is overburdened with work, which results in long delays in settling disputes. What is even more striking is the fact that the majority of workers have clung to their informal and collective resistance during the crisis. Since the corporation's foundation in 1946/47, such actions have usually been oriented at combating managerial efforts such as attempts to increase labour productivity, notably through an increase in task work; to strengthen control over the labour process; and to minimise wages and other conditions of service. Such managerial efforts, which are obviously crucial to capital accumulation, were intensified during the economic crisis and became central to the corporation's adjustment measures. The workers' persistent resistance to these efforts is principally manifest in their informal actions, which is quite understandable: collective actions are extremely risky in a situation where strikes are virtually outlawed and are likely to elicit severe managerial reprisals in the form of summary dismissals. Collective action is a last resort when other means of settling long-standing disputes have failed. Significantly, however, the number and intensity of informal actions, which are difficult to control by the management, have increased during the crisis in response to the various adjustment measures introduced by the management.

## Tea pluckers and managerial efforts to maximise labour productivity

On 23 August 1987, union presidents informed pluckers on both estates that they had agreed with the management to an increase in the amount of green leaves to be picked daily from 26 kg to 32 kg. Most pluckers strongly resented this and told their union presidents that the new norm was too high as many had already had difficulties in reaching the old quota.

The Tole female pluckers continued to resist the implementation of the new norm on the estate. Eventually, the CDC's general manager had to call upon FAWU president Cornelius Vewessee to make renewed attempts to persuade the women to accept the agreement. At a mass meeting organised by the union on 23 October 1987, the women reluctantly agreed to accept the new norm on condition that every worker in the corporation was obliged to contribute to its economic recovery. The Ndu male pluckers could not forestall the implementation of the new norm on the estate but soon started to express their dissatisfaction. During the executive elections of the Donga-Mantung Agricultural Workers' Union (DUAW) in September 1987, they refused to re-elect their president, Johnson Tanto Massa, and instead voted a non-estate worker, G.N. Majam, into office. Then they started a go-slow in November 1987, which resulted in all of them being paid pro-rata. It was only after they had been given the opportunity to check upon the implementation of the new norm on the other CDC tea estates that they were willing to call off their actions.

A year later, on 3 October 1988, Tole female pluckers went on strike alleging that they were unable to fulfil the new requirements in spite of working from 6.30 a.m. to 6 p.m. each day. They no longer felt obliged to adhere to the agreement as their condition for accepting the new norm – the contribution of *all* workers to the economic recovery programme – had not yet been met by the management. The union president, Cornelius Vewessee, strongly condemned the pluckers' strike actions, pointing out that they were illegal as they had not followed the prescribed procedures for settling conflicts. He was booed and jeered by the angry pluckers. The CDC general manager then threatened the strikers with dismissal if they did not report for work the next day, with the result that most pluckers decided to resume work. Seventy-nine remained on strike but they were summarily dismissed by management. Many of them stayed in the area surviving on farming and trading.

No further collective actions on this issue have been reported. There is, however, evidence that pluckers are increasingly resorting to informal actions to protest against managerial efforts to raise labour productivity. Unexpectedly, the corporation's statistical data seem to suggest that there has been an increase rather than a decrease in various forms of informal resistance during the crisis, such as arriving late at work, absenteeism, malingering and poor work performance. The proportion of the total days lost due to uncompleted work rose from 7.22% in 1987/88 to 8.24% in 1989/90, while those lost as a result of unauthorised absence rose from 5.27% in 1987/88 to 5.71% in 1989/90.[11] Although this increase might appear small, it is nevertheless significant if one takes into account the intensification of managerial efforts to increase labour discipline during the economic crisis. The rate of absenteeism at the Tole Tea Estate has certainly caused concern: the estate manager reported to the union that absenteeism was responsible for the loss of over 1700 person-days during July and August 1992. He estimated the corporation's financial loss at about FCFA 11 million and warned the union president that he would not hesitate to dismiss more than a hundred workers if the union and shop stewards failed to address the situation.[12] The managerial crusade against undisciplined and unproductive workers appears not to have been successful.

## Tea pluckers and managerial efforts to strengthen control over the labour process

Supervisory staff constitute an essential link between the estate management and the workers in the labour process. They are expected to communicate the orders of estate managers to the workers and maintain discipline in the labour process.

Like other CDC workers, pluckers have always drawn a clear line between 'bad' and 'nice' supervisors. Bad supervisors treat workers as objects of production and are largely insensitive to their plight. They may be differentiated into two types (see Adesina 1989): supervisors who are notoriously authoritarian and bossy and who command their subordinates without taking into account their opinions and advice; and those who are over-zealous in their duties, interested only in increasing output and who supervise their subordinates closely and without compassion. Nice supervisors, by contrast, are those who treat their subordinates as human beings in the labour process and take their personal and domestic problems into consideration when exercising their supervisory powers. They are usually less strict and allow workers a certain measure of autonomy in the execution of their allotted tasks.

Since the start of the economic crisis, the management has put enormous pressure on the supervisory staff to exercise tight control over their subordinates, to use their authority to the full and, if necessary, to discipline workers without compassion. Increasingly authoritarian supervision seems not to have had the desired effect of strengthening managerial control over the labour process but rather to have provoked workers, making them feel like slaves who are constantly being pushed to increase production for no reward.

Although there used to be numerous collective actions aimed at the transfer or dismissal of strict supervisors, such actions have abated during the economic crisis. Workers seem to have realised that not only are these actions risky but they will almost certainly be ineffective, with the management actively backing exacting supervisors and being unlikely to give in to collective demands for their removal.

However, there still seems to be widespread informal resistance to intensified managerial control over the labour process, which manifests itself in the following forms.

- *Insubordination.* It is not uncommon for workers to simply refuse to carry out orders, even if refusal might result in a considerable loss of output. For instance, some Ndu pluckers refuse to work during heavy downpours in the cold, rainy season. Others refuse to do overtime on Saturdays during the peak plucking season as they see Saturday afternoons as a time for resting, visiting friends and relatives or working on their own coffee farms. Estate records suggest that insubordination is increasingly being accompanied by insults and abuse and even physical attacks on supervisory staff.
- *Attempts to discredit supervisory staff.* At times, pluckers play tricks on supervisors and discredit them with their superiors. This may include falsely accusing them of bribery or corruption in the hope that management will take action against them.
- *The threat of using mystical powers.* Pluckers sometimes threaten to harm or kill a supervisor through sorcery and witchcraft. It is difficult to know whether this is mere bluff or seen as a real threat.

## Tea pluckers and managerial efforts to minimise wages and conditions of service

Workers have always fought for improved living standards and steadfastly resisted managerial efforts to curtail their wages and fringe benefits. It is small wonder that they were furious about the 6 January 1990 agreement between the management and unions that introduced a compulsory savings scheme and drastic cuts in their fringe benefits. Their bitterness was reflected in various collective actions.

Directly after signing the agreement, the newly elected DUAW president, Mr G.N. Majam, was accused by the shop stewards of betraying workers' interests. The shop stewards subsequently refused to communicate the terms of the agreement to the workers and when Mr Majam himself tried to explain the agreement, he barely escaped a severe beating by angry workers. Following Mr Majam's dismal failure to persuade workers to accept the agreement, the CDC's general manager decided to go to Ndu personally. At a mass meeting, he threatened workers by claiming that non-acceptance of the agreement would inevitably lead to the closure of the estate because of the corporation's precarious financial position. This left them with no other option but to comply.

A year later on 4 January 1991, Ndu workers went on strike without informing the shop stewards or the union leadership. Faced with serious financial problems after the drastic cuts in their incomes, they were angry that their family allowances had not been paid for eighteen months and that they, unlike other CDC workers, had not received any Christmas advance. Attempts by the Labour Department and the union to settle the strike failed and it was only after the payment of family allowances on 9 January 1991 that work resumed.

In early 1992, all CDC workers in the Fako Division, including the Tole female pluckers, started to agitate for the abrogation of the 6 January 1990 agreement and the immediate payment of nearly two years of family-allowance arrears. Their demands were supported by the FAWU president, Cornelius Vewessee. The workers went on strike on 21 May 1992 and refused to negotiate with management until Vewessee returned from the CTUC conference he was attending in Yaoundé. On his return on 26 May, they called off the strike and authorised him to negotiate with the management, which eventually resulted in an amendment of the 6 January 1990 agreement.

Besides sporadic collective actions, workers have engaged in a variety of informal actions in protest at reductions in income, including output restrictions, sabotage and involvement in illegal income-generating activities. Some pluckers do not abide by plucking standards and mix bad leaves with good ones, a practice that enables them to complete their task more quickly and achieve more weight and income. Others cut down tea bushes and use them for firewood, while others steal tea from the factory and sell it to middlemen. The management has frequently complained that the theft of tea has reached unprecedented levels and has caused the company serious losses. Increased theft is closely connected with the workers' interpretation of this criminal offence: it would appear that they regard this and other illegal activities as an opportunity to take what is due to them in return for their hard labour, and for reducing the degree of their exploitation in the labour process (Gordon 1977).

## Conclusion

This study of CDC plantation workers presents a more complex picture of labour responses to the economic crisis and SAPs than the case studies available of Nigerian industrial workers. CDC tea pluckers have employed a variety of strategies to cope with managerial adjustment measures. A growing number are adopting an individual survival orientation rather than an oppositional posture and doing their utmost to make a good impression on management through hard work and disciplined behaviour in the hope that this will help them escape the regular retrenchments. Some workers are relying on the bargaining strength of the state-controlled unions to protect their interests but many workers are bypassing the unions and lodging their individual and collective complaints with the Labour Department, which is still perceived by most workers as a neutral intermediary between management and labour. Unexpectedly, the majority of workers have continued to resort to sporadic collective actions and frequent informal actions to protest at their intensified exploitation and subordination.

A number of factors account for the continuing resistance of many CDC workers. One is their remarkable degree of solidarity. The various internal divisions among workers have never impeded them from regularly resorting to joint actions against their employer although their solidarity has been weakened somewhat by the present economic crisis. This solidarity has been promoted by their shared living and working conditions and a *linga franca* (Pidgin English), which allows for easy communication (cf. Ardener *et al.* 1960; DeLancey 1973). A second factor is the workers' persistent belief in the efficacy of militant action. The illiterate and poorly educated estate workers have always put less faith in institutionalised bargaining procedures than the relatively moderate union leadership that is mainly composed of clerks and supervisory staff. The regular failure of these procedures to achieve workers' aims and the establishment of state control over the unions have strengthened this belief that militant action is the only way of bringing management to its knees and redressing long-standing grievances.

A growing lack of motivation among workers during the crisis has also played a role. Increased productivity has not resulted in increased wages and workers' real incomes have been seriously eroded. Most workers, and women in particular, are still reluctant to resign and lose their regular monthly wage income, however meagre it may be, but a growing number, mostly men, are no longer interested in keeping their job at any cost, especially as they have lost confidence in the corporation eventually recovering economically. Some workers have already resigned, having collected their long-service awards and gratuities as well as their voluntary and compulsory savings. They are using this capital to invest in farming, trading and other potentially lucrative activities. Others are contemplating resignation. No longer committed to their jobs and having worked out alternatives, workers are becoming more militant and less reluctant to show resistance.

Another factor influencing workers' attitudes is their daily exposure to glaring socio-economic inequalities on the estates. Although the corporation's adjustment measures have effected a substantial reduction in the high salaries and fringe benefits of the managerial staff, there is still a wide gap in incomes and living standards between them and the workers. Workers' acute feelings of exploitation and subordination are undoubtedly reinforced by the sharp contrast between their own misery and managerial opulence. Finally, CDC workers' continuing resistance has also been influenced by their perceptions of the state. In his comparative work, Burawoy (1985) used the concepts of 'productive politics' and 'global politics' to tackle the complex relationship between the labour process and the state. Like most Cameroonians, CDC workers attribute the economic crisis primarily to the corruption and mismanagement of the ruling regime rather than to the sharp fall in commodity prices. The majority belong to one of the opposition parties, mostly the popular Social Democratic Front (SDF). They are unwilling to make voluntary sacrifices in the name of economic recovery as long as the regime in power lacks legitimacy and is only interested in the 'politics of the belly' (Bayart 1989).

Management has failed dismally to control workers' resistance during the crisis and there is no reason to believe that it will succeed in the near future. On the contrary, there are indications that labour resistance may increase. The unions have largely regained their former autonomy and their leadership has become more critical of the adjustment measures that it had previously agreed upon with management. CDC workers have always admired militant union leadership and are inclined to support any union action in defence of their interests.

I did not find any evidence to support the widespread assumption that female workers in developing countries are more amenable to control than male workers. There was a slight difference in the degree and modes of resistance between Ndu male pluckers and Tole female pluckers: Ndu male pluckers were somewhat more militant because they enjoy an easier exit option due to their close links with their local community. On the other hand, Tole female pluckers have shown themselves to be more inclined to circumventing the state-controlled unions and engaging in alternative modes of resistance because of the union's patriarchal structure and their own multiple productive and reproductive responsibilities outside the labour process.

## Notes

1. Circular in File MEPS/SWP/BU.134/vol. IV, General Correspondence CDC. These documents are to be found in the archives of the Provincial Delegation of Labour and Social Welfare in Buea.

2. *Cameroon Post*, 20-27 February 1991, p. 11.

3. See letter from Mr C.P.N. Vewessee, President FAWU, to Provincial Delegate of Labour and Social Insurance, Buea, dated 13 May 1992, in File MTPS/IDTPS/SWP/LB.2/Vol. XXVII, Complaints from CDC.

4. See Report of the Divisional Inspector of Labour, Limbe, on Mass Meetings with the workers of the CDC Estates/Services in connection with the economic crisis, in File MEPS/SWP/BU.134, Vol. IV, CDC General Correspondence.

5. See Agreement between the CDC General Manager and the Presidents of the Divisional Agricultural Workers' Union from Fako, Meme, Moungo, Ndian, Menoua and Donga-Mantung, dated 6 January 1990.

6. See *Cameroon Post,* 19-26 February 1992, p. 6.

7. See Minutes of the Second Appraisal Meeting of the 6 January 1990 Agreement between the CDC Management and the Workers' Unions that was held in the general manager's office on 14 March 1992, in File MTPS/IDTPS/SWP/LB.2/Vol. XXVII, Complaints from CDC.

8. This was a campaign of civil disobedience organised by the opposition parties to force the Biya regime to call a sovereign national conference. It involved the stoppage of all work, trade and traffic in the towns except on Friday evenings and Saturdays, which resulted in huge personal and public financial losses and aggravated the economic situation still further. See Konings (1996a).

9. See also the Labour Day speech by Mr C.P.N. Vewessee on 1 May 1991, in *Messager(e)*, 13 May 1991, p. 4.

10. See Addendum to the Agreement of 6 January 1990 between the CDC and its workers represented by the Presidents of Fako, Meme, Moungo, Ndian, Menoua and Donga-Mantung Agricultural Workers' Unions, in File MTPS/IDTPS/SWP/LB.2/Vol. XXVII, Complaints from CDC.

11. See *CDC Annual Reports and Accounts,* 1987-90, Yaoundé: SOPECAM.

12. See letter from Mr R.M. Achiri, Estate Manager Tole Tea, to President, Agricultural Workers' Union, dated 16 September 1992, in File MTPS/IDTPS/SWP/LB.2/Vol. XXVII, Complaints from CDC.

# 4

# Trade unions and Pamol's crisis and liquidation

## Introduction

Trade union formation was more difficult on the Pamol estates than at the CDC and it was not until independence and reunification in 1961 that a permanent trade union, the Pamol Cameroon Workers' Union (PCWU), was set up at Pamol. The PCWU proved to be weaker than the CDCWU. Although it was able to preserve a large degree of autonomy *vis-à-vis* the state between 1961 and 1972, its leadership, both the moderate and the militant elements, found it hard to represent and defend workers' interests. Since the leadership often failed to deliver on promises, workers were inclined to circumvent the union and defend their own interests by engaging in collective action. Like the CDCWU, the PCWU was dissolved in 1972 and integrated into state-controlled trade unionism until political liberalisation in the early 1990s when trade unions regained a certain measure of autonomy.

In the first part of this chapter, the role of Pamol trade unionism is examined from its start until the company's crisis in 1980. The second part discusses its role during Pamol's crisis and subsequent liquidation (1980-1994).

## The birth and development of trade unionism on the Pamol estates

Trade unionism has a long history on the Pamol estates (Konings 1998a). The first initiatives by senior workers to form a union were taken in the early 1940s, soon after the British administration passed legislation permitting trade unionism in West Africa. Confronted with growing labour militancy and emergent nationalism in their colonies, the British came to consider the formation of free but responsible trade unions as a more sophisticated strategy for labour control than outright repression of workers' organisational efforts (see Chapters 1 and 3).

Setting up trade unions on the Pamol estates, however, proved difficult. Like most other employers in West Africa, Pamol's management was initially opposed to them, fearing that the rank and file would be mobilised to militant action. Unilever appears to have never been in favour of trade unions, preferring instead to deal directly with workers' representatives (Berlan *et al.* 1978). Moreover, the vast majority of Pamol's estate workers were illiterate and employed on temporary contracts, and a large proportion were Nigerian. Such groups of workers obviously showed little interest in joining a local union. There was also the problem of leadership. Just as at the CDC, most initiatives regarding union formation then were taken by clerks and senior technical workers who had the education, skills and status required to handle the bureaucratic procedures involved in unionism and play the complex games involved in collective bargaining. At the same time, they were often mistrusted by the illiterate workers who were suspicious of white-collar workers representing their interests and who had more faith in militant action than in collective bargaining. In its 1948 report to the United Nations, the British Trusteeship Authority perceptively observed:

> The development of trade unions is still in the most elementary stage and the majority of the workers have no conception of the proper functioning of a trade union. The labourers are very distrustful of the clerks, and the high percentage of illiteracy among them constitutes a serious handicap to the understanding of sound trade union principles. They have little faith in collective bargaining and, in times of unrest, they have often repudiated their union's leadership which is composed mainly of clerks and resorted to strikes and acts of violence which seems to them to be the only means of enforcing their demands.[1]

One final difficulty was communication between workers on the various Pamol estates. One of Pamol's rubber estates, the Bwinga Estate, was located in Fako Division, which is relatively far away from the Pamol headquarters in the Ndian Division. The other estates are located in isolated areas and difficult to reach. This constituted a serious obstacle to setting up a company union.

All the initiatives to establish unions on the Pamol estates either failed or were short-lived during the British Trusteeship era.[2] On the advice of the Labour Department however, management introduced consultative committees at the divisional and central level that allowed joint consultation even though they were clearly dominated by the management. They often served merely as a means of disseminating management information to workers. A 1956 inspection report on the Ndian Estate gives an idea of their functioning:

> There is no trade union membership. The estate is divided into four divisions and in each there are divisional consultative committees which meet monthly. There is also a Central Joint Consultative Committee which meets every two months or more often if necessary. Examination of the minutes shows that the meetings have been called on most occasions by the management. Items by the workers' side are usually produced as 'other matters'. A paternal attitude seems to prevail, with the workers' side offering a vote of thanks to the management at the end of the meetings.[3]

In the absence of any permanent trade union organisation and adequate consultative machinery, Pamol workers nevertheless showed a significant capacity to defend their interests by engaging in sporadic, and usually short-term, collective actions. These were localised strikes that were restricted to one estate, or even to one division on an estate, and were motivated by local workers' specific, sometimes long-standing, grievances about managerial control and exploitation, such as white managerial staff members' racist attitudes towards workers, an extreme authoritarian exercise of duties, ethnic discrimination and favouritism by supervisory staff, low remuneration or increases in task work (Konings 1998a).

Independence and reunification on 1 October 1961 put an end to any previous attempts to organise Pamol workers in Nigeria and Cameroon into one union. Senior workers on the Lobe Estate, who had failed to set up a union during the uncertain, hectic period preceding independence, now decided to form a union that would embrace all Pamol's estates in Cameroon. Following consultations with senior workers on other Pamol estates, they announced the establishment of the Pamol Cameroon Workers' Union (PCWU) on 28 October 1961.

The founders initially saw the union as an organisation that would defend the interests of Cameroonian workers not only against management but also against Nigerian workers.[4] This attitude is understandable if one takes into account the strong resentment of Cameroonian workers to the dominant position of Nigerian workers on the Pamol estates at the time. The Registrar of Trade Unions, however, refused to register a union that was keen to exclude Nigerian workers from membership, as this would fuel existing tensions between Cameroonian and Nigerian workers. The founders then agreed to open up membership to the whole Pamol labour force, and the union was registered on 4 August 1962.

The Labour Department advised the union leadership on organisational and administrative matters and helped them to draw up a constitution that clearly reflected the model of 'free but responsible trade unionism' it had been successfully propagating in the British Trusteeship era.[5] Like other employers in West Cameroon, Pamol's management had meanwhile changed its attitude towards unionism. Trade unions could no longer be opposed as they enjoyed continued state support and the existing trade unions were generally behaving responsibly.[6]

The PCWU gradually increased its membership from 1, 850 in 1963 to over 2,400 in 1970, a figure that included about 75% to 80% of the total labour force.[7] The union's strategy was to approach the supervisory staff first and if they decided to join, they invariably became leaders of the different branches and members of the National Executive Committee (NEC). They would subsequently try to convince their subordinates of the benefits of unionism and, when necessary, bring pressure to bear on them to join the union.

Unlike trade unions in most African states (Ananaba 1979; Freund 1988), the PCWU and other trade unions in Anglophone Cameroon were able to preserve a large measure of autonomy *vis-à-vis* the state for a considerable period of time. This was due to two factors. First, the political elite in Anglophone Cameroon still felt a strong attachment to British values and institutions and simply took over the model of free but responsible trade unionism that had been introduced during the British Trusteeship period. Second, trade union leadership in Anglophone Cameroon continually assured the government that it was determined to play a responsible role in national development and to steer clear of partisan politics. This assurance meant that the West Cameroon government did not interfere in trade union matters and, more importantly, did not try to establish control over the unions.

It was not until the creation of a one-party state in 1966 (Johnson 1970; Bayart 1979) that growing intervention by the federal state in the system of industrial relations could be observed, starting with the promulgation of the 1967 Federal Labour Code. This had two important consequences for trade union action in the Federal Republic. First, in the matter of collective disputes, it required all channels available for a peaceful settlement – principally conciliation and arbitration – be exhausted before a strike was called. Illegal strike action could be punished with the termination of strikers' contracts. Second, it introduced shop stewards, the so-called staff representatives, into the larger enterprises across the country. This did not, in fact, involve a complete break with the past but the local union representatives were given a legal status and their position was regulated and became protected by law. The Labour Code assigned a double role to staff representatives: on the one hand, the representation and defence of workers' interests at the local level and, on the other hand, the promotion of the enterprise's output. This role was ambivalent and delicate since staff representatives were subjected to constant pressures from above and below. Workers expected them to defend their interests at all costs, even to the extent of violating the law on strike action while employers viewed them as the lowest chain in the labour control structure and continually exhorted them to present any workers' grievances during joint consultations and help increase labour productivity.[8]

Significantly, after the creation of the PCWU in 1961, there was a fierce, largely ethnically based struggle for power within the union's National Executive Committee (NEC) that was dominated by southwestern workers. This was particularly manifest in the selection of a suitable candidate for the pivotal function of general secretary. Well-qualified candidates could not stand for office or lost elections simply because they were not acceptable to leaders belonging to the local ethnic majority groups, especially the Balondo. It is even doubtful whether the first two general secretaries could be called 'workers' and their appointment was obviously the outcome of an ethnic compromise.

The first general secretary was Prince E.A. Anjeh (1961-1964). At the time of his appointment, he was a trader based in Kumba and was well known to Pamol workers because he supplied the estates with goods. His successor was Mr P.L. Itoe (1964-1968), a barber on the Lobe Estate who enjoyed great popularity among workers especially among the Balondo, his own ethnic group. Both men could be characterised as moderate and responsible union leaders and came close to being the Labour Department's ideal type of union leader. Their 'productionist' and 'economistic' conception of trade unionism (Bates 1971) was clearly reflected in Prince Anjeh's welcome address at the first PCWU conference that was held on the Lobe Estate on 4 August 1962:

> I must make it very clear that every worker within your plantation industry, particularly in Pamol Cameroons Ltd, should learn to work harder so as to receive the co-operation of the management, in order to improve the industry and to improve his lot.[9]

Neither adopted the aggressive bargaining style of trade union leaders on the neighbouring CDC estates who were inclined to back up their demands with strike threats (see Chapter 3). Although leaders were able to extract concessions from the management, their moderate style of leadership promptly created the impression among the rank and file that they were being weak in their defence of workers' interests and thus unequal partners in the bargaining process. This impression was reinforced by the management's strategy of presenting and rejecting union claims as a direct onslaught on the company's important role in regional and national development, supported by the government. Both union leaders rapidly lost the support of the overwhelming majority of workers who favoured a more militant style of leadership. They were regularly accused of being 'under the dictatorship of the management' or 'management stooges'.[10] Workers' growing discontent became manifest when they engaged in collective actions undertaken without the knowledge of the union leadership, and even in attempts to topple the union leadership.

Remarkably, the union's national executive committee, which was still dominated by southwestern workers, unanimously appointed a North Westerner as general secretary following the October 1968 general strike (Konings 1998a: 93-94). The new general secretary, Mr J.Y. Tumenta was a senior clerical worker and had won massive support among the workers during the 1968 strike because of his increasingly militant attitude towards management.

Immediately after his appointment, he began attacking the company for dismissing five union leaders after the 1968 strike and its merciless exploitation and oppression of workers:

> The dismissal of five NEC members of PCWU further indicates that this management is opposed to trade unionism in a Democratic Republic such as Cameroon. Every union member or leader and all Staff Representatives' future in the Pamol Service is dark because Pamol management is opposed to any democratic practice that is going to stop the Pamol management from 'dictating' as they are continuing to do.

> The Federal Labour Code of 1967 means nothing to Pamol management. It would appear as if Pamol said to themselves – because of our investments in this country, we should ignore all national laws in areas controlled by us and suppress and exploit as speedily as we can. Its policy is tantamount to slavery and/or apartheid because a white man can flog you and call you 'black monkey' and if you show any sign of annoyance, he can charge you with rudeness and insubordination and summarily dismiss you.[11]

Management evidently became worried about the new leadership and soon adopted an obstructive strategy towards the union. Despite warnings, Mr Tumenta continued to criticise the company in the press and in January 1969 the management decided to sever all relations with him and boycott the union.[12] The boycott lasted until

1 September 1969 when Mr Tumenta informed the company that the Prime Minister of West Cameroon had advised him to restore normal management-union relations. Management then made known its willingness to resume contact with the union.

Not surprisingly, management continued to mistrust Mr Tumenta and seldom invited him for consultations or negotiations about workers' problems. He too seemed less inclined to expend much time and energy on representing workers' grievances to a permanently hostile management. He was increasingly interested in creating a union of agricultural workers across the whole of West Cameroon.

Tumenta's pursuit of his own personal ambitions and his growing neglect of workers' interests disappointed Pamol workers. They had expected his militant style of leadership to extract more concessions from management than the moderate styles of his predecessors. Workers rapidly lost confidence in their once immensely popular leader and no one protested when he was dismissed by the union's national executive on 28 February 1970.[13] His successor was Mr I.A. Fomukong (1970-1972). Like Tumenta, he hailed from the North West Province and had previously been a carpenter in the company before becoming one of the union's organising secretaries. He proved to be an energetic and competent leader and managed to improve relations between the union and management and negotiate a number of improvements in workers' living and working conditions.[14] Both management and the rank and file were satisfied with Fomukong's leadership during the difficult transition to state-controlled trade unionism. His term in office, however, came to an end in 1972 when the PCWU was dissolved and unionism became subordinated to the single party, a further step in Ahidjo's 'hegemonic project' (Bayart 1979).[15] Not surprisingly, the establishment of state control over trade unionism in the country had similar effects on the PCWU as on the CDCWU (see Chapter 3) and weakened the role of trade unionism on the Pamol estates even further.

First, state control was aimed at transforming unionism from a vehicle of labour resistance into an instrument of labour control. One should not, however, exaggerate the effects of state control: it tended to be more visible at the central level than at regional and local level. Indeed, the impact of the party on trade unionism in the isolated Ndian Division seems not to have been very noticeable. In public, union leaders were expected to glorify the party and propagate the party's new rhetoric about the need for hard work and constant dialogue with the employer but in practice they often pursued their own course of action, to the extent of even secretly organising strike actions. Trade union members were forced to buy party membership cards, yet there were no party meetings. Local and regional party leaders only occasionally turned up at the estates, usually when workers were on strike. They were then apt to strongly condemn illegal strike actions and advise workers to exercise patience. They also came for festive occasions and fund-raising purposes. Workers resented being extorted by the party elite.

Second, trade unionism on the Pamol estates became fragmented. After the dissolution of the PCWU, its membership was taken over by three different agricultural workers' unions in the South West Province: the Ndian Agricultural Workers' Union (NAWU) that was responsible for workers on the Ndian and Lobe Oil Palm Estates, and the Meme Agricultural Workers' Union (MAWU) and the Fako Agricultural Workers' Union (FAWU) that were responsible for organising the Bai and Bwinga Rubber Estates respectively. This chapter concentrates on the NAWU, which became by far the most important union on the Pamol estates as it dealt with workers employed in palm oil production, the company's main activity. NAWU's dominant position was further strengthened in 1986 when Pamol stopped its rubber activities in Cameroon, which led to the closure of the Bwinga Estate and experimentation with new crops on the Bai Estate.

Third, trade unionism on the Pamol estates became paralysed by a lack of funds due to the introduction of a new system for the distribution of check-off contributions (see Chapter 3). One of the gravest consequences of the financial crisis was that the divisional unions experienced difficulties paying the salaries of its full-time officers and organising union activities, such as seminars.

Fourth, trade unionism on the Pamol estates virtually became a one-man affair in the person of the president of the divisional union, who owed his position more to the party's selection than to workers' votes. The presidents of the divisional unions of agricultural workers in the South West Province tended to continue in office after their initial election. Mr M.I.C. Mokeo, for example, has been president of NAWU since its foundation to the present day.

# Case 4.1 *NAWU President, Mr M.I.C. Mokeo*

Mr Mokeo hails from the Ndian Division. He is a motor mechanic by profession. He was employed by the Ministry of Interior at Kumba before joining Pamol in 1969. Being active as a senior skilled worker in the Lobe Estate garage, he soon became a staff representative and, following the dissolution of the PCWU in 1972, he was elected president of NAWU.

He has a long-standing conflict with the company about his work performance and occupational category. He has received several written warnings for poor work performance. Moreover, the management postponed the implementation of a recommendation to upgrade him made by the South West Joint Classification Board in the early 1970s. It was not until 1986 that he was promoted to Category 7G at a monthly salary of FCFA 110,000 and immediately declared redundant. In 1989 he claimed FCFA 60,570,000 in damages from the company for late promotion and wrongful sacking during his tenure of office as a Staff Representative.

Compared to some of his predecessors, like Mr J.Y. Tumenta, he is poorly educated. As a result, his letters tend to be unintelligible. That is why the Pamol Personnel Manager, Mr M.Y. Nyenku, has often invited him to his office for clarifications, but he never responded to such invitations.[16]

He is said to be unpredictable, unreasonable and aggressive. He is therefore a constant thorn in the flesh of Pamol managers and labour officials. They have used several strategies to deal with him. Their usual strategy is simply to ignore him. Sometimes they call him to account for 'unfounded' allegations or 'irresponsible' actions. And, above all, they seize any opportunity to get rid of him.[17]

He runs the union as a one-man affair. He has failed to account for the use of union dues and has often neglected the representation of workers' interests. He is therefore unpopular among the workers and staff representatives. To regain workers' confidence, he has on occasion threatened the management with strike actions and has even secretly organised some strike actions.

He has always been a loyal party member. He has been well rewarded for his loyalty. The party has maintained him in office and has even facilitated his trade union career, notwithstanding his unpredictable and sometimes 'irresponsible' trade union leadership. Besides being president of the Divisional Union of Agricultural Workers in the Ndian Division, he also became president of the Divisional Union of Trade Unions in the Ndian Division. This was not yet the end of his ascendancy in the union hierarchy. In the executive elections of the CTUC in May 1992, in which the CPDM bribed the delegates to elect leaders to be sympathetic to the party, he was voted into office of first vice-president of the central labour organisation. He used his newly gained power position in 1993 to topple his arch-enemy, Mr C.G. Mure, the company's liquidator.

Given their formidable financial and organisational problems, it is understandable that the new divisional unions were virtually absent on the Pamol estates during their first years. The union leadership made no attempt to represent or defend workers' interests and Pamol's management took advantage of the situation and took decisions on labour issues without consulting the union leadership. The apparent atrophy of the union and the intensification of managerial control over the labour process drove the workers to resort to collective actions (Konings 1998a: 104-106). In an effort to regain workers' confidence, NAWU president Mokeo became more active and militant in the late 1970s, not only threatening management with strike actions but even calling workers out on strike.

Pamol started to face an unprecedented financial crisis in 1980. It weakened even further the bargaining position of the state-controlled unions *vis-à-vis* the management.

## The role of trade unionism during Pamol's crisis and liquidation

To combat the crisis and save the company from total collapse, the management felt compelled to implement a series of austerity measures that severely affected their workers. These involved labour retrenchment, the non-payment of overtime and drastic cuts in fringe benefits, including the abolition of the company's building and motorbike loan scheme and its scholarship scheme.

These measures caused great anxiety among the workers, who feared losing their jobs and a serious decline in their income. Industrial relations deteriorated when management initially refused to follow the rules for retrenchments. Many workers were laid off without the required consultation with the union and staff representatives, and some staff representatives were laid off without the prior authorisation of the Labour Inspectorate, as demanded by the Labour Code.[18] The workers accused the union president and staff representatives of patently neglecting to defend workers' interests.

Persistent pressure from the workers on the union leadership had some effect. During the deepening crisis in 1983 the union president and staff representatives insisted that the management follow the correct procedures regarding retrenchments.[19] Although they conceded that further redundancies were inevitable in the company's struggle for survival, they gave the management to understand in no uncertain terms that austerity measures should affect workers and managerial staff alike. In August 1983, they subsequently proposed remedial measures aimed at reducing the number of managerial posts and curtailing the fringe benefits enjoyed by expatriate staff. These included abolishing the posts of plantation director and chief engineer, replacing the Ghanaian marketing manager with a Cameroonian national, discontinuing vacation flights twice a year for the families of expatriate managerial staff, withdrawing end-of-the-year bonuses for senior staff in the form of an extra month's pay and drastically cutting the high allowances given to managerial staff to boost their prestige.[20] The management rejected these proposals outright, claiming they would demoralise managerial staff.

In 1983 management engaged in another illegal practice when workers who had been declared redundant were forced to accept alternative jobs against their will. Anyone who refused to cooperate was deemed to have terminated their contract of employment of their own volition, which made them ineligible for termination benefits they would have been entitled to. After protests by staff representatives, the union declared a trade dispute on 10 October. It was eventually settled by the Provincial Inspector of Labour, who ordered the management to pay four months' wages to 22 workers for the time they were (forcibly) idle and to reinstate them.[21]

Other measures taken during the crisis provoked the workers as well and led to mounting labour unrest that was manifest in various strike threats and sabotage activities. The most important ones are considered below.

Although well aware that field workers strongly resented working on religious holidays, management ordered them to work on 21 May 1982 (Ascension Day). The union president, Mr Mokeo, personally prevented workers at the Kokundu Division of the Lobe Estate from going to the fields by turning back the lorry and announcing at muster that workers should return home. He even tried to elicit the assistance of the police. This was, of course, rejected. As a result of Mokeo's actions, the company lost a full day's production in Kokundu Division and the workers lost a day's wages. Afterwards, Mr Mokeo was once again severely reprimanded by management.[22]

There was an agreement between the union and management that the company could increase working hours during the peak season. In the 1983 peak season, factory workers were asked to do twelve-hour shifts but were vehemently opposed to this as overtime was no longer paid but compensated for with time off. Following several complaints, they stopped work on 11 April, threatening to revert to eight-hour shifts if overtime was not paid. Their representatives discussed the issue with management on 22 April. It was agreed that any time workers had to do a twelve-hour shift, two hours of overtime would be paid and the other two hours would be compensated for with time off. In addition, workers would be given more and better food during such a shift. The workers, however, rejected the agreement and maintained they would not work more than eight hours. They expressed their discontent in violent actions. Rather than reporting their actions to the security forces or terminating their employment, management elected to transfer them to the fields to avert a further escalation of the dispute. They were replaced by field workers to keep the mill running[23] but this did not produce the desired results. The factory workers became increasingly demoralised by the withdrawal of existing incentive schemes and the inhumane treatment they received from the technical director, Maurice Buermans. In early 1987 seven instances of sabotage were reported in the factory, resulting in a total loss of

FCFA 25 million.[24] There were also strikes in the fields, for example three instances of attempted strikes at the Lobe Estate in 1984 alone.[25]

On 16 November 1984 a meeting was held at which the most important item on the agenda was the end-of-the-year bonus, as stipulated in the collective agreement. Staff representatives demanded an extra month's pay instead of the company's traditional gift of beef for its workers, pointing out that managerial staff had always received an extra month's pay. The management rejected their demands on the grounds that it could not afford an extra month's pay for every worker because the company had not yet recovered from the 1983 financial crisis. Staff representatives then proposed that the management convert the value of the beef into cash and pay that amount to the workers instead. Management claimed it needed time to study the proposal. When staff representatives returned to their various estates, they wrongly gave the workers the impression that they would receive an extra month's pay in place of their beef. On 20 December, the company's managing director ordered the cash equivalent be paid to workers. When the Lobe Estate workers were informed of this by clerical workers in the Lobe Head Office, they decided to strike the next day to press their demands for the payment of a whole extra month's pay. On 26 December they were joined by Ndian Estate workers who sympathised with their cause and although the union president claimed that the strike was organised by the workers themselves, there were strong indications that he himself was behind it.

Attempts by the party, the administration, management and the union to persuade workers to call off the strike failed. The management then set a deadline of 28 December for the resumption of work and 182 strikers were summarily dismissed for not turning up for work on that day. After the strike, the management attempted to dismiss Mr Mokeo as well, alleging that he had masterminded it. However, the Divisional Inspector of Labour, Mr M.L. Moto, refused to authorise his dismissal on the grounds that management had insufficient evidence to support its allegations.[26]

Mounting labour unrest during the crisis compelled Pamol's management to operate more cautiously. In 1986 it consulted staff representatives about its restructuring plan and asked them to sensitise workers to the company's severe financial problems. It also informed them of its intention to lay off 240 workers. To ensure that the required procedures were strictly adhered to, it consulted Mr E.K. Lottin, a retired senior labour officer. Following recommendations by the staff representatives and a thorough examination of each individual case by Lottin, only 135 workers were eventually laid off.[27]

On 2 August 1987 the management told staff representatives that Unilever intended to sell the company because of the precarious financial situation. The staff representatives demanded that termination benefits be paid to workers prior to the sale.[28] Faced with an uncertain future, some workers preferred to be paid off and leave the company. Most planned to invest their newly acquired capital in farming, trading or other entrepreneurial activities. And following its failure to sell the company to the North West consortium (see Chapter 2), Unilever announced on 13 October 1987 that it had put the company into voluntary liquidation.

On the day of liquidation, the newly appointed liquidator, Mr C.G. Mure, served workers with letters of termination but at the same time instructed them to continue working until further notice. Workers had no choice but to comply. From the memorandum they sent to the President of Cameroon a few days after the liquidation however, it is clear that most had little faith in the company surviving after Unilever's dramatic withdrawal from plantation production in Cameroon. In the memorandum, they requested that:

- the government give every possible encouragement to Cameroonian business groups that might be interested in running the company as an ongoing concern; and
- in the event of bankruptcy, the company's industrial, residential and plantation assets be transferred to the employees to cover their severance pay.[29]

Following the liquidation, workers' employment prospects were extremely bleak and representation and defence of their interests by the union leadership and staff representatives was virtually non-existent. Owing to its financial problems, the company was no longer able to transfer the required contributions from wages to beneficiary bodies, thus accumulating huge debts to the National Social Insurance Fund, the credit union and the trade unions. Lacking income, NAWU was (again) not in a position to organise union activities. After some time, however, the liquidator agreed with the union president that the company would make some funds available to the union for special occasions. In 1990 he sold a tractor to the union at the cost of FCFA 3 million to enable the union to earn extra income from agricultural activities. Like his predecessors, he tried to ignore the union president as far as possible. Their relationship became strained due to personal animosities. The French liquidator, who had lived and worked in Cameroon for many years, once even claimed that he was 'more Cameroonian than Mr Mokeo'. The liquidator also rarely consulted staff representatives, arguing that the company's survival, recovery and eventual sale was more important for the time being than representing workers' interests. In November 1987, the company was exempted from conducting staff representative elections by the Divisional Inspector of Labour 'until such a time that the company's future was known'. It was not until 17 March 1990 that new elections were held on Pamol's estates. These elections were organised by the management and the union without the required assistance of the Divisional Inspector of Labour who, in reaction to this breach of procedure, nullified the elections. As a result, the staff representatives elected in 1982 continued to stay in office. It is no surprise that they faced legitimacy problems among the workers.[30]

Initially, the workers did not protest against the union's failure to represent their interests since they, like the liquidator, were also interested primarily in the company's survival. They regained hope when the liquidator continued to employ them, pay their wages, and even recruit new workers to replant the estates. He was soon hailed as the company's saviour. A speech delivered by a staff representative on 22 October 1988, on the first anniversary of the liquidation, illustrates the high esteem the liquidator enjoyed among the labour force at the time:

> But as God would make it, the saviour Mr C.G. Mure....mobilised us and urged us to work harder and effective in order to earn a living till such a time when a buyer would be got. In December

1987 we began to have hopes when for the first time in the history of Pamol, the liquidator presented to each of us a Christmas gift of 3,000 francs CFA and 5 litres of palm oil.[31]

Their faith in the liquidator meant that workers were prepared to fight for the corporation's survival and even to make further sacrifices. When the parastatals once again began undercutting the prices of palm oil on the domestic market in 1989 – and thus threatening the company's future – staff representatives sent another memorandum to the country's president requesting that 'the government should urgently intervene and bring order, discipline and price stability to the palm oil industry'.[32] As soon as it became clear that the government was unable to find an immediate solution to the problems in the agro-industrial palm-oil sector, the workers declared themselves ready for austere adjustment measures. On 21 March 1990, the management and the union presidents signed a survival agreement that included the introduction of a compulsory savings scheme and drastic cuts in workers' fringe benefits such as payments for housing, electricity and company health-care services.

From 1990 onwards, however, there was growing dissatisfaction among workers with the performance of both the liquidator and the union president, Mr Mokeo. The company was facing serious liquidity problems, resulting in the irregular payment of wages and salaries, and workers began blaming these problems on the liquidator's policies. While the company was having trouble selling its palm oil on the domestic market, he was continuing to invest in the rehabilitation of the estates and recruit new labour. Liquidity problems even forced him to close down the Ndian Estate for a few days in late November 1990.[33] Moreover, the liquidator appeared arrogant, barring managers and workers from participating in the decision-making process and bullying both in public. In addition, being French, he began hiring an increasing number of (better paid) Francophones to replace Anglophone supervisors and managers, thus fuelling Anglophone-Francophone tensions within the company.

Workers also blamed Mr Mokeo for a lack of concern for workers' problems following the company's liquidation. Their discontent with the union president's performance was expressed at a central staff representatives' meeting on the Lobe Estate on 7 September 1991. Staff representatives rebuked him for his persistent failure to handle workers' grievances regarding poor medical care, the liquidator's erroneous calculation of termination benefits in November 1987, the irregular payment of wages and salaries, and the non-payment of family allowances. Nor had he ever consulted with them or attended meetings they had officially invited him to. He had refused them access to the staff representatives' office and equipment at the Lobe Estate, using these facilities instead for his personal ends. And finally, he had collected union funds from management without accounting for the money spent. The workers resolved that the management should stop paying Mokeo any union dues until he had accounted for the funds he had already received and that he should hand over the staff representative office and equipment.[34] Two days after this meeting, Mr Mokeo dismissed the chairman of the meeting, Chief Fritz D. Nyassa, from office and suspended the other 16 staff representatives who had attended the meeting.[35] The staff representatives unanimously condemned his action on 4 March 1992, accused him of one-man rule and mismanagement and declared they would no longer recognise him as president.[36]

In the absence of any representation by the union president, workers resorted to strike actions. Two local strikes were prompted by the non-payment of wages. On 15 October 1991 workers in the Bulu section of the Ndian Estate went on strike due to the non-payment of September's wages although after negotiations between management and staff representatives, work was resumed the next day.[37] In the night of 15/16 March 1992, a group of newly recruited workers in the Mundemba Camp on the Ndian Estate moved from camp to camp armed with cutlasses to inform the workers that a violent strike would take place the following day in response to the non-payment of February's wages. Early in the morning, security forces moved on to the estate to guard strategic installations and later in the morning the senior divisional officer of the Ndian Division met workers in an attempt to calm tempers. He told them action was being taken to advance FCFA 2,000 to each newly recruited worker.[38]

Largely ignored by the management and strongly derided by staff representatives, the union president began asserting himself in 1992 when the company was experiencing formidable problems in paying its workers. This happened at a time when trade unionism in Cameroon had regained a large measure of autonomy. In the wake of the political liberalisation process, the Confederal Bureau of the CTUC announced on 2 April 1991 that union members were free to join the party of their choice. Nevertheless, the ruling party, the CPDM, was still trying to maintain a certain degree of control, particularly at the central level. In executive elections for the CTUC congress in May 1992, which were clearly manipulated by the CPDM, Etame Ndedi, an alternate member of the party's central committee, was voted in as president of the central labour organisation (Konings 1995b, 2000). On the same occasion, Mr Mokeo, who had remained loyal to the party, was elected first vice-president, which increased his power in both the union and the party and gave him access to the highest echelons of government. He intended to exploit this position in his struggles with his arch enemy, the liquidator. With increasing hostility towards the management and a militant style of leadership, he was able to regain a large measure of support from workers who were being subjected to severe hardship as a result of the long-term non-payment of wages.

Mokeo organised two general strikes in 1992 – one on 18 May and the other on 15 June – for the following reasons:

- The company's non-payment of March, April and May's wages.
- The company's violation of its 1990 survival agreement. While management had imposed austere adjustment measures on workers, it had not kept its promise to pay them regularly. The union president demanded that management immediately cease deducting certain amounts of money from workers' wages, including compulsory savings and rents.
- The company's refusal to transfer workers' contributions to the National Social Insurance Fund, the credit union and trade unions.

The union president threatened anyone who intended to break these strikes with a severe beating. The 15 June strike was particularly violent. Infuriated by the managerial elite's apparent lack of concern for workers' sufferings, strikers directed their actions at the liquidator personally and at the top management at Lobe Head Office. They stormed the building, smashing windows and doors, breaking the windscreen of the administrative manager's car and deflating the tyres of other cars parked in front of Head Office. Barricades were erected. The forces of law and order had trouble controlling the angry workers who were out to mishandle the liquidator and the deputy general manager. Etame Ndedi, the president of the central labour organisation, who happened to be on tour in the area, was asked to intervene and eventually succeeded in persuading the workers to halt their violent actions.

It was extremely difficult to get the strike called off so that negotiations could start. The workers were intransigent, insisting that they would not resume work until their three months' of back wages had been paid. They argued that negotiations would have absolutely no effect because they had been misled several times in previous negotiations. It was only after urgent appeals by Mokeo and Etame Ndedi that they reluctantly called off the strike.

Conciliation was reached the same day. The union agreed on a renewal of the survival agreement for a further two-year term. Management, in turn, promised to observe the terms of the agreement as far as possible, in particular the regular payment of wages. It also promised that workers' severance pay, estimated by the liquidator at FCFA 800 million, would be paid out prior to any sale of the company. After a statement of account, a decision would be taken on how the trade union and credit union dues would be paid.

During negotiations, the divisional officer of the Ekondo Titi Subdivision warned the management at Pamol not to dismiss any of the strikers. However, 28 workers were in fact dismissed, accused of assaulting fellow workers and damaging company assets on the day of the strike.[39]

In the aftermath of these two strikes in August 1992, the liquidator reintroduced Joint Consultative Committees (JCCs) that had been abolished with the introduction of shop stewards in the 1967 Federal Labour Code. These committees were set up to improve communication between workers and management with the aim of assisting management to find solutions to the problems facing the company. They were not meant to replace staff representatives, who already had well-defined functions, but the liquidator would henceforth only consult the JCCs. Thus, instead of improving industrial relations in the company, the JCCs became a new source of conflict, as the staff representatives accused the liquidator and the JCCs of undermining their legal position in the company. Relations deteriorated even further when political motives began to play an increasingly important role in the company. With the approach of national presidential elections, which were scheduled to take place on 11 October 1992, the atmosphere in the company became tense. Most workers and managers supported the candidature of the SDF's chairman, John Fru Ndi. When he visited the company during his election campaign, he assured the northwestern managers, like Dr I.N. Timti, that the company's administration would be handed over to them should he win the elections. Strongly opposed to the liquidator's policies, they encouraged the union to topple the liquidator, arguing that he was arrogant and dictatorial, unconcerned about workers' problems and, above all, a staunch supporter of the party in power and its candidate, Paul Biya.[40] During the election period, the liquidator felt physically threatened by the workers who had tried to ambush him. Soon afterwards, he proved, once again, incapable of paying wages on time. The workers alleged that this was because he was making large contributions to President Biya's election campaign from company coffers.

Lack of payment led to a rebellion among Nigerian workers in February 1993 in the wake of the government's announcement on 8 January that aliens living in Cameroon without a valid residence permit would be expelled from the country with effect from 28 February 1993. Most Nigerian workers had no passports or residence permits and obtaining these documents posed insurmountable problems for them: they were expensive – FCFA 18,000 for a passport and FCFA 60,000 for a residential permit – and, more importantly, they had received no wages since November 1992. Realising that they could not meet the deadline of 28 February, they decided to resign and return to Nigeria. Management accepted their resignations but was unable to pay their wage arrears, compulsory savings and end-of-contract benefits estimated at about FCFA 20 million.

On 14 February, the Nigerian workers' representatives discussed the payment of their entitlements with management. The liquidator behaved arrogantly during these discussions and the Nigerian representatives lost their tempers and began physically attacking him and other senior managerial staff. They were later advised to return for a final decision on 23 February.

However on 23 February, over 200 Nigerian workers invaded the Head Office. They attempted to set the building on fire but were prevented from doing so by the timely intervention of heavily armed soldiers and gendarmes. A meeting then took place that was also attended by the Nigerian assistant consul general. The liquidator was conspicuous by his absence. After deliberations, it was agreed that the Nigerian workers would be allowed to stay until 4 March when the liquidator would be present to pay out their final entitlements. The consul was asked to address his angry countrymen in the Ibibio language and they dispersed grudgingly while 'alerting the forces of law and order to get their guns ready because they may have to be killed if their money was not paid on the 4th of March'.[41] When they reported back on 4 March, a client had just purchased oil and the proceeds from this sale were used to discharge nearly 30 workers. Others were paid off a few days later. The payment of other workers' wages was then suspended as a result of a two-month strike that started on 9 March.

While the conflict between management and the Nigerian workers was developing, the union president, Mr Mokeo, declared a trade dispute on 20 February on the grounds that management had failed, firstly, to pay wages and salaries for a period of three months, trade union dues, family allowances and end-of-contract benefits to the over 200 Nigerians who had resigned, and, secondly, to respect the union leaders. At a mass meeting at Lobe football field on 22 February, Mr Mokeo stressed that the non-payment of wages was a serious breach of the survival agreement that had been renewed in 1992. He then threatened to call a strike on 1 March should wages not be paid by 27 February, an ultimatum that was well received by his audience. Workers were particularly embittered about the liquidator recruiting expensive managerial staff while they themselves were starving due to the non-payment of wages.

Meetings were organised by the management and the local administration to avert the impending strike. In a final meeting on 8 March presided over by the senior divisional officer of the Ndian Division, the liquidator explained at length why Pamol could not pay its workers, but he failed to convince workers' representatives. The atmosphere soon degenerated as tempers were lost. The liquidator finally agreed to pay workers on 19 April when the newly created oil syndicate would be coming into operation.[42] However his pledge did not keep workers from embarking on a general strike the next day that was to last two months. It would prove to be the longest in Pamol's history and threatened the company's survival, occurring as it did at the beginning of the peak production period (April-June).

On the first day of the strike, Ndian Estate workers blocked all the estate roads and the main entrance to the oil mill. Armed with sticks to ward off any attempt to disrupt their strike action, they then paraded around the area carrying placards. The actions by Lobe Estate workers were even more violent: they cut off electricity and the water supplies, locked the gate, stopped the mill's operations, brought traffic to a standstill and ransacked the liquidator's house. They wanted to kill the liquidator, who had taken refuge to the doctor's house, but he was rescued just in time by the security forces. Workers threatened to resume their violent actions should the military, who were posted on the estate at the company's cost throughout the strike, dare to provoke them in any way.

From the very start, it was clear that Mr Mokeo actively supported the strike. Workers were highly dependent on their union president to represent their interests to the powers that be. Fully exploiting his ascendancy in the union and party hierarchy, Mr Mokeo soon led a union delegation to Yaoundé to inform the Prime Minister and the Minister of Labour and Social Insurance of the current situation at Pamol. A government delegation subsequently visited Pamol and reported back negatively to the government on the company's management.

Since the government took no further action, workers gradually tired of the strike and appealed to the union president to negotiate a settlement. At a meeting with him at Lobe Estate on 5 April, staff representatives pointed to the negative consequences of the strike, including workers' financial problems, the high rate of crop looting, expected crop losses during the peak production period, the deteriorating condition of estates and estate roads, the depreciation of the mill and its high maintenance costs, the wide gap between the workers and the liquidator created by the strike, and the lack of intervention by government. They demanded that the union president seek immediate government intervention regarding the resumption of work.[43] The union president, however, asked them to be patient and not to become discouraged.

The strike continued until 8 May when the committee of inspection set up a local management team headed by Dr I.N. Timti to run the company. Dr Timti's appointment was probably a result of his popularity among workers due to his active role in the strike when he was the only manager who could move around freely. Mr Mokeo joined the follow-up committee that was supposed to play an intermediary role between the committee of inspection and the local management team. To demonstrate his new power position in the company, he demanded one of the company cars.[44] After the strike, the newly appointed Dr Timti managed to obtain an advance of FCFA 60 million from the Palm Oil Producers' Syndicate for essential services and the payment of wage arrears.

The company's financial position remained precarious and workers had little faith in its survival unless it was taken over by a reliable enterprise, preferably COMDEV.[45] On 16 September 1993, staff representatives presented a memorandum to the chairman of the committee of inspection about any future sale of the company, asking him to take into account the following demands in any negotiations:

- A prospective buyer should give priority to paying workers' end-of-contract benefits and compulsory savings in full.
- Convincing proof should be demonstrated of sound financial backing and adequate investment plans to guarantee the company's future.
- The Cameroonian government should be a partner in the new company and hold nominal shares.
- Workers should be allowed to buy shares in the new company.
- The previous liquidator, Mr C.G. Mure, should be excluded from any group of prospective buyers in view of his gross mismanagement of the company during his term in office.

Workers warned the chairman that they would resist any buyer who did not live up to their expectations.[46] Although a number of prospective buyers have come forward, the company has yet to be sold.

## Conclusion

This chapter has documented the emergence and development of trade union formation on the Pamol estates. After the setting up of a permanent union in 1961, the union leadership used different strategies in the era of trade union autonomy (1961-1972) to promote workers' interests. However both moderate and militant strategies failed to bring about any substantial improvement in workers' living and working conditions. Dissatisfied with their leadership's performance, workers were inclined to bypass the union and resort to collective action in defence of their interests.

The evidence presented in this chapter seems to run counter to the widespread assumption in government and party circles that state-controlled trade unionism is more effective in controlling workers than autonomous trade unionism. State-controlled trade unionism actually helped sharpen the existing contradictions between the union leadership and workers, as was manifested in workers' lack of recognition of the union leadership and their persistent collective actions.

The union leadership however appears to have never fully complied with a primary trade union role of labour control. In fact, it was regularly inclined to identify with workers, even calling strikes to regain their confidence. The most important union leader, Mr M.I.C. Mokeo, was not only a long-time skilled worker and staff representative at the company but also had personal conflicts with management concerning his own performance and his ranking and retirement conditions, which were aggravated by his aggressive, unpredictable behaviour. Largely ignored by management and the Labour Inspectorate but gradually rising in the union hierarchy, he capitalised on workers' growing discontent with their deteriorating position during the company's crisis and liquidation. He seized on the issue of the non-payment of wages to organise Pamol's discontented workers against his personal enemy, the liquidator, and incite them to illegal strike action. The historic 1993 strike allowed him to topple the liquidator and set himself up as an intermediary between the committee of inspection of the liquidation and the local management team.

## Notes

1. *Report on the Cameroons under United Kingdom Administration for the Year 1948,* London: HMSO, 1949, p. 110.

2. For a detailed account of these initiatives, see Konings (1998a).

3. Inspection Report: Ndian Oil Palm Estate, 4 February 1956, in File BU.Ea/2, Tour of Inspection Reports – Ndian Estate Pamol Ltd, dated 28 May 1958.

4. Interview with Mr I.A. Fomukong, former General Secretary of PCWU, at Lobe Estate on 25 November 1993.

5. *The Constitution of the Pamol Cameroons Workers' Union,* Calabar: Competent Press, 1963.

6. See letter from Mr R.G. Dawson, General Manager of Pamol, to Senior Labour Officer of West Cameroon, Buea, dated 5 March 1962, in BNA, File Qd/a (1959)3, Pamol Ltd: General Correspondence.

7. See figures presented in File BU.102, Vol. 2, Pamol Cameroon Workers' Union, Lobe-Kumba.

8. For a detailed discussion of the staff representatives' position and role, see Konings (1993a and 1998a).

9. Welcome Address by E.A. Anjeh, General Secretary of PCWU, to the First Conference held at the Lobe Oil Palm Estate, West Cameroon, dated 4 August 1962, in File BU.Ib/59 BU. 102, Pamol Cameroon Workers' Union, Lobe-Kumba.

10. See, for example, letter from Mr Geoff Ek'ka T. Anje, Area President of Bai Branch and Member of Central Executive of PCWU, to Registrar of Trade Unions, Buea, dated 28 March 1968, in File MTLS/WCD/BU.102, Vol. 2, Pamol Cameroon Workers' Union, Lobe-Kumba.

11. Mr J.Y. Tumenta, General Secretary of PCWU, 'Our Case with the Management', in File MTLS/WCD/BU. 102, Vol. 2, Pamol Cameroon Workers' Union, Lobe-Kumba.

12. Letter from Mr D.J. Lucking, Personnel Manager of Pamol, to Mr E.K. Lottin, Labour Delegate and Senior Labour Officer, Buea, dated 4 February 1969, in File BU.95/S.2, Vol. 1, Plantations Pamol du Cameroun Ltd.

13. See letter from Mr S.E. Ayuk, General President of PCWU, to Mr J.Y. Tumenta, General Secretary of PCWU, Mbonge, dated 28 February 1970, in File MTPS/WCD/BU.102, Pamol Workers' Union, Lobe-Kumba.

14. See *Pamol News* no. 8, January 1971.

15. For a detailed report of these developments, see Konings (1993a: 135-138).

16. Letter from Mr M.Y. Nyenku, Personnel Manager of Pamol to Mr M.I.C. Mokeo, President of NAWU, dated 22 October 1977, in File MTPS/SWP/BU.95/S.2, Vol. 2, Complaints from Pamol du Cameroun Ltd.

17. See, for instance, letter from Mr M.L. Moto, Divisional Inspector of Labour and Social Insurance, to the President of the Divisional Union of Trade Unions, Ndian Division, dated 26 September 1987, in File MTPS/IPTPS/SWP/BU. 189/S.2, Vol. 3, Election of Staff Representatives – Plantations Pamol du Cameroun Ltd.

18. See letter from Mr J.N. Fomunjong, Divisional Inspector of Labour and Social Insurance, Mundemba, to Honourable Minister of Labour and Social Insurance, Yaoundé, dated 4 June 1981, in File MTPS/SWP/MND/49, Vol. 1, General Correspondence – Plantations Pamol du Cameroun Ltd.

19. See Report of the National Security Post Ekondo Titi, 10 August 1983, in File G 4002/C.30, Plantations Pamol du Cameroun Ltd – General Correspondence.

20. See letter from Union Officials and Pamol Staff Representatives to the Managing Director of Pamol, dated 24 August 1983, in File MTPS/SWP/BU.95/S.2, Vol. 2, Complaints from Plantations Pamol du Cameroun Ltd; and letter from Mr E.K. Lottin, Provincial Inspector of Labour and Social Insurance, to the Governor of the South West Province, Buea, dated 30 January 1984, in File MTPS/SWP/BU.95, Vol. 2, Complaints from Plantations Pamol du Cameroun Ltd.

21. See letter from Mr E.K. Lottin, Provincial Inspector of Labour and Social Insurance, to the Governor of the South West Province, Buea, dated 30 January 1984, in *ibid.*

22. See letter from Mr W.N. Kimbeng, Estate Manager, Lobe, to Mr M.I.C. Mokeo, President of NAWU, dated 25 May 1982, in File MTPS/SWP/MND.49, Vol. 1, General Correspondence – Plantations Pamol du Cameroun Ltd.

23. See Minutes of Extraordinary Meeting between Staff Representatives and Management held at D.L. Martin Memorial Club on 27 April 1983.

24. See Minutes of Meeting of Lobe Technical Service Employees and Some Members of Management held at the Lobe Management Club on 7 April 1987, in File MTPS/SWP/MND.5, Vol. 2, Complaints from Pamol Lobe Estate.

25. Minutes of the Divisional Union of Agricultural Workers of Ndian Division held at Lobe on 20 February 1984, in *ibid.*

26. See various reports in File MTPS/SWP/BU.95/S.2, Vol. 2, Complaints from Plantations Pamol du Cameroun Ltd; and *Cameroon Tribune,* 30 January 1985, p. 5.

27. See Circumstantial Report on Redundancy in Plantations Pamol du Cameroun Estates by the Provincial Delegate of Labour and Social Insurance, Buea, to the Minister of Labour and Social Insurance, Yaoundé, dated 17 February 1987, in File MTLS/WCD/BU.135, Vol. 1, Pamol Cameroon Ltd – General Correspondence.

28. Minutes of Extraordinary Central Staff Representative Meeting held at Lobe on 2 August 1987, in File MTPS/SWP/Bu.95/S.2, Vol. 2, Complaints from Plantations Pamol du Cameroun Ltd.

29. Memorandum from Pamol Employees to the President of the Republic of Cameroon, dated 17 October 1987, in File MTPS/SWP/BU.95/S.2, Vol. 3, Complaints from Plantations Pamol du Cameroun Ltd.

30. See Circumstantial Report on the Panorama and Current State of Affairs in the Plantations Pamol du Cameroun Ltd, Ndian, by Mr Ilang Ahmed Ibrahim, Provincial Inspector of Labour, Buea, dated 11 November 1990, in File MTPS/IPTPS/SWP/BU.95/66/S.3, Vol. 1, Follow-Up Complaints from Ndian Division.

31. Address presented by the workers of Plantations Pamol du Cameroun Ltd on the occasion of the first anniversary of their survival in liquidation at Lobe on 22 October 1988, in File G 4002/49, Vol. 3, Pamol Cameroon Ltd – General Correspondence.

32. Memorandum from Pamol Employees to the President of the Republic of Cameroon, dated 7 November 1989, in File MTPS/DPTPS/SWP/BU.103, Vol. 1, Plantations Pamol du Cameroun – General Correspondence.

33. See letter from Divisional Inspector of Labour and Social Insurance, Mundemba, to Provincial Inspector of Labour and Social Insurance, Buea, dated 6 December 1990, in File MTPS/IPTPS/SWP/BU.169/S.2, Vol. 2, Inward Float File, Labour Office, Mundemba.

34. Letter from the Secretary, Central Staff Representatives, to the Divisional Chief of Service for Labour and Social Insurance, Mundemba, dated 11 September 1991, in File MTPS/SWP/MND.15, Vol. 2, Complaints from Pamol Labe Estate.

35. See letter from President of the Divisional Union of Trade Unions, Ndian Division, to Central Staff Representatives, dated 9 September 1991, in File MTPS/SWP/MND.1/S.2, Vol. 1, Staff Representative Elections – Pamol, Lobe.

36. Minutes of the Meeting held between the Divisional Chief of Service for Labour and Social Insurance, Mundemba, to the President of NAWU, and the Staff Representatives of Plantations Pamol du Cameroun Ltd in the Labour Office at Mundemba, dated 4 March 1992, in File MTPS/SWP/MND.48, Cameroon Trade Union Congress – General Correspondence.

37. Letter from Provincial Delegate of Labour, Buea, to Divisional Inspector of Labour and Social Insurance, Mundemba, dated 1 November 1991, in File MTPS/DPTPS/SWP/BU.103, Vol. 1, Pamol – General Correspondence.

38. Letter from Divisional Chief of Service for Labour and Social Insurance, Mundemba, to Mr J.N. Ndi, Estate Manager, Ndian Estate, dated 18 March 1992, in File MTPS/SWP/MND.20, Vol. 3, Complaints from Pamol Ndian Oil Palm Estate.

39. See several reports on these 1992 general strikes in Pamol in File MTPS/DPTPS/SWP/BU.103, Vol. 1, Pamol – General Correspondence; File G 4002/49, Vol. 3, Pamol Cameroon Ltd – General

Correspondence; File G 4002/C.30, Plantations Pamol du Cameroun Ltd – General Correspondence; and File MTPS/SWP/MND/21/ S.1, Vol. 1, Ndian Agricultural Workers' Union.

40. See Report of the National Security Post, Ekondo Titi, dated 11 October 1992, in File G 4002/C.30, Plantations Pamol du Cameroun Ltd – General Correspondence.

41. *Weekly Post*, 3-10 March 1993, p. 1; see also Circumstantial Report on the gloomy social climate prevailing on Plantations Pamol du Cameroun Ltd by the Divisional Inspector of Labour and Social Insurance, Mundemba, dated 27 April 1993, in File MTPS/IPTPS/ SWP/MND.24, Vol. 3, Complaints from Plantations Pamol du Cameroun Ltd.

42. Minutes of a Meeting with Labour Officials, Pamol Management, Staff Representatives, Trade Unionists and the Administration to discuss the problem of non-payment of salaries to Pamol workers, held in the Conference Hall of Korup National Park on 8 March 1993.

43. Minutes of the Meeting of Pamol Workers' Representatives with the President of the Ndian Agricultural Workers' Union held at the Lawn Tennis Club, Lobe, on 5 April 1993.

44. For the various reports on the 1993 general strike, see *Cameroon Post*, 1 April 1993, p. 15; File MTPS/DPTPS/SWP/BU.103, Vol. 1, Pamol – General Correspondence; and File G 4002/49, Vol. 3, Pamol Cameroon Ltd – General Correspondence.

45. Memorandum to the Chairman, Inspection Committee of Pamol, Presented by the Workers of Plantations Pamol du Cameroun Ltd Deliberating at Lobe on 16 September 1993.

46. *Ibid.*

# 5

# Chieftaincy and the privatisation of the CDC

## Introduction

Privatisation has been a key instrument in the stabilisation and Structural Adjustment Programmes (SAPs) imposed on Africa by the Bretton Woods institutions. It is an essential part of the overall strategy to open up African economies to market forces and promote private-sector development. Since public enterprises are considered to have performed dismally, African governments have been under considerable pressure from international donors to sell them to domestic and foreign private capital. Given their troubled economic condition and acute dependence on foreign financial flows, governments have officially accepted privatisation so as not to forfeit the international support that is so crucial for their political survival.

The actual number of privatisations has remained modest in Africa (cf. Grosh & Makandala 1994; Mkandawire 1994; Tangri 1999) due to technical and financial constraints as well as socio-political factors. Interestingly, some of these reflect the same political concerns that led to the creation of so many public enterprises in the years after independence: an inability to attract foreign investment to politically and economically unstable African nations, the absence of a well-developed domestic entrepreneurial class, and the pursuit of patron-client relationships by neo-patrimonial African states (Sandbrook 1985; Tangri 1999). Resistance to privatisation by civil society, in particular by professional bodies, student organisations and trade unions, has also been highlighted because privatisation often involves the sale of public property to well-placed nationals or foreign enterprises and generally results in massive lay-offs (Olukoshi 1998; Konings 2002).

While there is abundant literature on the role of chieftaincy in African post-colonial states (van Rouveroy van Nieuwaal & Ray 1996; van Rouveroy van Nieuwaal & van Dijk 1999), none examines the role of chieftaincy in current privatisation projects. There seems to be more inerest is the role of chieftaincy in political liberalisation than in economic liberalisation.

This chapter focuses on the virulent opposition by Bakweri chiefs in Anglophone Cameroon to the government announcement on 15 July 1994 of the privatisation of the CDC. The chiefs claimed Bakweri ownership of CDC lands and felt betrayed at not having previously been consulted about the CDC's privatisation, warning the government that the corporation could not be sold to non-natives without Bakweri consent and compensation. The Bakweri chiefs' resistance to the CDC's privatisation is part of a long-standing struggle for the return of their vast lands, which were expropriated during German colonial rule for plantation agriculture and, in 1946, leased by the British Trust Authority to the newly created CDC. In this resistance, they were always assisted by the modern Bakweri elite who, like their chiefs, felt aggrieved by the loss of their ancestral lands. Following the announcement of the privatisation of the CDC, Bakweri chiefs received support from other sectors of Anglophone Cameroon's traditional and modern elite, who have seen the privatisation of the CDC as a renewed onslaught by the Francophone-dominated post-colonial state on Anglophone identity and colonial heritage. This alliance of traditional and modern elites forms a powerful force to ensure that justice will prevail on the issue of Bakweri land ownership. It has forced the government to repeatedly postpone the privatisation of the CDC and enter into negotiations with the landowners.

This chapter first describes the protracted struggle by Bakweri chiefs for a return of the expropriated ancestral lands, which provides the necessary historical background to the subsequent discussion on their current resistance to CDC privatisation.

# Bakweri chiefs and the retrieval of CDC lands

The Bakweri are a small ethnic group that live on the slopes of Mount Cameroon in the Fako Division of the South West Province of Anglophone Cameroon (Ardener 1956, 1996; Matute 1990). Compared to the highly centralised states in the North West Province of Anglophone Cameroon that are ruled by powerful, even sacred, chiefs (cf. Fisyi 1992, 1995; Konings 1999), the social organisation of the Bakweri, like that of most other ethnic groups in the South West Province, is segmentary. Chieftaincy tended to be a weak institution in the various autonomous Bakweri villages, and often a colonial creation. It was only during British indirect rule that chieftaincy became rooted in local communities and two paramount chiefs were installed to act as the district heads of Buea and Victoria (Mbake 1975; Geschiere 1993; Takougang 1994).

When Cameroon became a German protectorate in 1884, the Germans saw the Bakweri as an aggressive and savage people who might create problems for the opening up of the hinterland. In 1891, the Bakweri of Buea, under the leadership of the legendary Chief Kuva Likenye who was the only Bakweri chief who had established a measure of military control over surrounding villages (Ardener 1996: 76-78; Geschiere 2009), defeated a German expedition. However, it was not until 1895 that their area was truly pacified.

The fertile, volcanic soils around Mount Cameroon proved suitable for large-scale plantation agriculture and more than 100,000 hectares of Bakweri land were expropriated by the German colonial state. The original occupants were expelled and sent to restrictive native reserves (Konings 1993a: 37; Clarence-Smith 1993: 197) as German companies rushed to the area in a frenzied bid to get the best tracts of land (Epale 1985: 23-34). In protest, the Bakweri showed little enthusiasm about working on the plantations, certainly not for in menial jobs. They were, as a result, no longer branded as aggressive and savage by the Germans but as apathetic or downright lazy, a stereotype that has remained to this day (Courade 1981/82). To solve the area's serious labour problems, German planters were compelled to recruit labour from other areas in Cameroon and while most migrant workers initially returned to their region of origin after a short spell of work on the estates, an increasing number decided to settle near the plantations when they retired, thus aggravating the land problem even further (Konings 1993a, 2001). This resulted in extensive squatting by Bakweri and migrants alike on plantation lands that were only partly cultivated. Due to the extreme overcrowding on the reserves, intruders frequently ignored or resisted eviction notices although planters were sometimes obliged to surrender some of their land, and the government purchased areas for the benefit of native communities (Epale 1985: 94-95).

Following British occupation of the area during the First World War, the property of German planters was confiscated and turned over to the Custodian of Enemy Property. Shortly afterwards when the British took over the administration of the area, the plantations were merged and a government department was set up to manage them. By 1922, however, the British Mandate Authority had decided to dispose of them as the administrative costs of maintenance were excessive. It seriously considered returning plantation lands to the original owners but eventually abandoned the idea and instead concluded that it would be in the best interests of the territory and its inhabitants to return the plantations to the foreign private enterprises (Fonsah 1993; Fonsah & Chidebelu 1995). According to Eyongetah & Brain (1974: 103), one of the principal reasons for the British Mandate Authority handing over the plantations to foreign planters was:

> that it would have been impracticable to split the plantations into small plots for Cameroonian owners – since without capital backing, the buildings and machinery would fall into ruins. Moreover, it feared that the natives' lack of experience would mean that disease would be spreading among the crops and the cocoa plots would be destroyed.

The estates were put up for auction in 1922 but with restrictions on bidding by German nationals. However there was little interest shown in the plantations and very few were sold for various reasons including the considerable capital resources needed to put the plantations, which had been neglected since British occupation, back into operation; the problems of recruiting and controlling labour; low commodity prices on the world market; and uncertainty about the future of the mandated territories (Epale 1985: 79-80). Another auction was held in London in November 1924 but without restrictions on German bids this time, and almost all the estates were bought by their former German owners (Fonsah 1993; Fonsah & Chidebelu 1995).

At the start of the Second World War, German estates were expropriated again by the Custodian of Enemy Property but after the war, a decision had to be reached once again on how to dispose of the properties. In the meanwhile, the young educated Bakweri elite had founded nationalist and ethnic associations such as the Cameroon Youth League (CYL) led by P.M. Kale and Dr E.M.L. Endeley and the Bakweri Improvement Union under the leadership of J.A. Kale and D.M.L. Endeley (Ebune 1992: 101-138). This contributed considerably to a growing awareness of colonial injustices towards the Anglophone population in general and the Bakweri in particular, notably the large-scale expropriation of Bakweri lands by the Germans that had resulted in the subsequent shortage of land among the Bakweri people. As soon as they got wind of ongoing British deliberations about the future of the former German plantations, they approached their chiefs demanding action in defence of Bakweri interests. This eventually led to the formation of the Bakweri Land Committee (BCL) (cf. Molua 1985). The BLC's original membership totalled 48, including 25 chiefs, with members of the Buea chiefly family playing a prominent role in the organisation. Paramount Chief G.M. Endeley was its president, his cousin, D.M.L. Endeley, was its secretary and the latter's brother, E.M.L. Endeley, was another of the driving forces behind it (Matute 1990: 125-28). On 8 June 1946, Chief Endeley informed the Resident in Buea of the BCL's formation and stated that its major objective was 'to take charge of all the land in Victoria Division which virtually belongs to the natives'. It was his fervent wish that the committee continue to exist 'as long as the Bakweri people live'.[1]

The BLC sent several petitions to the British administration and the United Nations.[2] In a petition addressed to the Secretary of State for the Colonies on 24 August 1946, the BLC demanded that:

- the former German plantations be handed back to the people of the British Trusteeship Territory of the Southern Cameroons;

- the part of the plantations originally belonging to the Bakweri people be handed over to the Bakweri administration; and
- any profits made on the plantations by the Custodian during the last five years be paid to the Native Administration concerned as compensation for the loss of land expropriated from the Bakweri by the German government.[3]

After considerable deliberations, the British Trusteeship Authority declined to surrender the former German plantation lands to their original owners as they had little faith in the Bakweri peasantry's ability to increase agricultural output. They therefore advocated a continuation of plantation production in the Trust Territory because substantial investments had already been made, and considerable profits had been derived from this form of production by the German planters. Nevertheless, the administration was more reluctant this time to hand over the plantations to foreign private enterprises, being aware that such a transfer would badly hurt the rising expectations of the Bakweri and would certainly lead to vehement opposition by the BLC. Instead, it announced in November 1946 that the former German plantation lands would be leased to a newly established statutory corporation, the Cameroon Development Corporation (CDC). It hoped that the foundation of a public corporation, which would run the former German plantations for the benefit of the people of the territory, would reduce Bakweri opposition.

The proposed public corporation, the CDC, eventually came about with the passage of two ordinances during a special session of the Nigerian Legislative Council from 9-12 December 1946. The first, the Ex-Enemy Lands (Cameroons) Ordinance No. 38 (1946), provided for the acquisition of the former German plantation lands that had been vested in the Custodian of Enemy Property for the duration of the Second World War. Under the terms of this ordinance, the Governor of Nigeria was to declare them 'native lands' and hold them in trust for the common benefit of all inhabitants of the territory. This final acknowledgement by the British administration that the former German plantation lands were Bakweri property was subsequently endorsed in a special resolution on Bakweri lands adopted at the Sixth Meeting of the United

Nations Trusteeship Council in March 1950. The second ordinance, the Cameroons Development Corporation Ordinance No. 39 (1946), provided for the foundation of the proposed corporation, the CDC. All the lands acquired by the Governor under the first ordinance would be leased to the corporation, whose main objective was to develop and manage the lands in the interests of the people of the trust territory.

Following the passing of these two ordinances, the Governor of Nigeria immediately bought the plantation lands from the Custodian of Enemy Property for a sum of £850,000 and leased them to the newly established corporation for a period of 60 years that was renewable for an equivalent term at the corporation's discretion (Konings 1993a: 39). The CDC, in turn, was supposed to pay a monthly rent to the treasury but this was never passed on to the Bakweri.

Although the first ordinance recognised Bakweri title to the CDC lands, the Bakweri Land Committee was not satisfied. It complained bitterly that it was not treated with the courtesy of being informed about government intentions regarding these lands. It had lodged several petitions in 1946 and continued to demand the return of these lands to the Bakweri people.

Unwilling to give up the struggle, the BLC decided to send a representative to the United Nations, which had granted it a hearing after receiving its petition. E.M.L. Endeley was chosen to present its case. However this move was hampered by the British administration. While it had given the impression that it would finance Endeley's trip to New York, it had actually only paid his passage as far as Lagos, thus forcing Endeley to return to Cameroon (Epale 1985: 153).

In reaction to ongoing Bakweri protests, the British administration asked W.M. Bridges, a senior district officer in the Southern Cameroons who was well acquainted with Bakweri society,[4] to investigate Bakweri land complaints and recommend appropriate solutions. Bridges began his investigation in 1948 with the assumption that 15 acres (6 hectares) of land would be more than adequate for each Bakweri household and eventually concluded that a surrender of 25,000 acres of CDC land would satisfy Bakweri land requirements. He proposed using the land to cultivate food crops on a controlled tenancy basis and that the CDC provide technical advice, social welfare services and market facilities for approved crops (Konings 1993b: 159). His report was presented to a visiting UN mission by the British administration with a view to countering the arguments advanced by the BLC, which stressed that the Bakweri were not asking for an increase in land ownership but for a return of all their lands.

In 1961 the British left the Trust Territory but neither the Bakweri land problem nor the settlement scheme proposed by the government had been resolved. The 31 December 1959 agreements that legalised the secession of the Southern Cameroons from the newly independent Republic of Nigeria demanded that the CDC surrender all its rights, titles and interests under the previous leases and certificates of occupancy to the government of the Southern Cameroons. It, in turn, agreed to lease all those lands to the CDC for a period of 99 years as of 1 January 1960. At the end of that period CDC lands would be transferred to the legitimate owners, namely the Bakweri.

After the reunification of the British and French Cameroons in 1961, the Bakweri land problem disappeared from the national agenda as the new political leaders increasingly turned their backs on regional and parochial issues in their pursuit of national unity (Konings & Nyamnjoh 1997: 210). Moreover, the post-colonial state became more interested in the expansion of the agro-industrial sector for the necessary modernisation and increase of agricultural production than in a return of plantation lands to their legitimate owners (Konings 1993a: 17-34). In addition, post-colonial governments adopted and even extended the policy of the British Trusteeship Authority of co-opting leading members of the traditional and modern Bakweri elites onto the Board of Directors and management of the CDC.

On 6 July 1974, the government promulgated law No. 74-1 that laid down the rules governing land tenure in Cameroon (Fisiy 1992: 34-38). Making a distinction between private and national lands, this would later serve as the basis for rejecting prior Bakweri claims to CDC lands on the grounds that they were national lands. This was a clear violation of the UN-sanctioned 1946 ordinances that created the CDC and the 1959 agreements between the CDC and the government of the Southern Cameroons.[5] This bold rebuff of previous ordinances and agreements remained largely unchallenged because the autocratic rule of President Ahmadou Ahidjo had, by this time, silenced all the organisations that were not under government control. The BLC died a natural death, although occasional memoranda were presented to the government by its most dedicated members.

For the Bakweri, however, the land issue continued to be a matter of priority, especially as the government was making full use of the powers it had been granted by the 1974 land law to confiscate increasing amounts of native land in the name of 'the imperative interest and defence of the economic policies of the nation'.[6] Exactly 20 years later when it announced the privatisation of the CDC, the government would learn that the BLC, like the legendary phoenix, was merely lying dormant before rising once again at an appropriate moment.

## Bakweri chiefs and the privatisation of the CDC

Privatisation has been put forward by international donors as a magic formula capable of curing the ailing Cameroonian economy. At the start of the economic crisis in the mid 1980s,[7] there were some 175 public enterprises in the country that employed around 80,000 people (Tedga 1990: 125-44; van de Walle 1994b: 152). These enterprises served both economic and political ends. Besides being avenues to economic modernisation and growth, they also allowed the government to engage in prebendal politics and cement a hegemonic alliance that incorporated the country's emerging elite into the state apparatus (Bayart 1979). A patrimonial logic existed in many African post-colonial states (Chabal & Daloz 1999) but was particularly strong in Cameroon, a country with stark ethnic and regional cleavages (van de Walle 1994a; Nyamnjoh 1999; Gabriel 1999). It is beyond doubt that this logic contributed to the poor performance of most public and para-public enterprises (Tedga 1990; van de Walle 1994b). Prior to the economic crisis, the Cameroonian government was subsidising parastatal-sector losses to the tune of some FCFA 150 billion a year. Though most of oil revenues were initially kept in secret bank accounts abroad, their primary function was soon to cover parastatal deficits.

From the start of the economic crisis, the World Bank made parastatal reform the cornerstone of its lending conditions and, given growing budgetary constraints, the Biya government officially agreed to cooperate. In May 1987, it appointed a national commission to recommend reforms in the parastatal sector. A year later, the commission reported back to the President, having determined which institutions should be liquidated, sold to the private sector or revived. However, few public enterprises were effectively privatised, only six between 1988 and 1994 (Mama 1996: 175). Van de Walle (1994b: 162) offered the following reasons for the slow pace of privatisation:

> Although the government is proceeding with care on the politically sensitive issue of lay-offs, this does not appear to be the major constraint on rapid implementation of the reform agenda. Rather, intra-elite competition and haggling over the rents freed up by privatisation, along with the lack of technical expertise within the state, served to slow down the process of institutional reform.

Dissatisfied with the government's performance, the World Bank threatened to suspend credit to Cameroon amounting to US$ 75 million in early 1994 if it did not accelerate the process of privatisation. Subsequently, on 15 July, the government announced the privatisation of 15 large public enterprises. Among these were five agro-industrial parastatals, including the CDC whose announced privatisation incited commotion in the country, particularly in the Anglophone region (see Chapter 2).

The government's announcement of the privatisation of this important agro-industrial enterprise was all the more shocking to Anglophones since the CDC:

- had been one of the few public enterprises in Cameroon to perform relatively well until the economic crisis;
- had been able to survive this crisis mainly because the management and workers had agreed to adopt a series of drastic adjustment measures aimed at cost reduction and productivity increase; and
- was on the way to economic recovery following the 50% devaluation of the CFA franc in early 1994 (Konings 1995b).

That the government singled out the CDC for privatisation despite its bright prospects for recovery and immense contributions to regional development was regarded by the Anglophone community as provocation and led to regional protest actions against what was perceived as a further step in the dismantling of the Anglophone colonial economic legacy by the Francophone-dominated state (Konings & Nyamnjoh 1997, 2003).

Unsurprisingly, the most vehement opposition in Anglophone Cameroon came from landowners. As soon as the CDC's privatisation was announced, the Bakweri chiefs and elite mobilised to revive the moribund BLC and adopt a common position regarding its privatisation, which had been planned without any consideration of the Bakweri land problem. Soon afterwards the BLC was renamed the Bakweri Land Claims Committee (BLCC).

On 23 July 1994, the Bakweri chiefs and elite met in Buea under the chairmanship of Paramount Chief S.M.L. Endeley of Buea and Paramount Chief F. Bille Manga Williams of Victoria (Limbe) to discuss the implications of the government's decision. They agreed to oppose in no uncertain terms the announced privatisation on the grounds that CDC lands were Bakweri property and could thus not be sold to non-natives without Bakweri consent. After lengthy and passionate discussions, an *ad-hoc* committee was elected by acclamation to assist the BLCC in preparing a detailed memorandum on the Bakweri position that would be presented to the government and all other interested parties.[8]

Over 500 Bakweri chiefs, dignitaries and elite gathered at the Buea Youth Cultural and Animation Centre on 4 August 1994 and approved the *ad-hoc* committee's memorandum. The Bakweri agreed that if privatisation had to take place at all, it should be on the basis of 'a creative and enlightened partnership between the owners of the land on which the corporation operates and the providers of finance capital without which it would not be possible to run a modern, technologically sophisticated agro-industrial complex like the CDC'.[9] They insisted that any privatisation plan be based on 'terms which recognise the ownership of land as a distinct variable which, together with the cash, make plantation agriculture possible; consequently, landowners deserve ground rent compensation in much the same way as the CDC was liable to pay ground rents for the use of the land'.[10] The memorandum was later presented to the Provincial Governor for onward transmission to President Biya. At the end of this historic meeting, the eminent Bakweri scholar, Prof. Ndiva Kofele-Kale, the secretary of the *ad-hoc* committee, was designated counsel for the Bakweri people with instructions to present their case to the United Nations and other international forums.

The Bakweri case was strongly supported by Anglophone movements. A powerfully worded petition to the head of state, co-signed by the Anglophone movements and Bakweri chiefs, reiterated that the Bakweri had never relinquished ownership of the CDC lands and that the corporation could not be sold without Bakweri consent. It pointed out that the Bakweri had not received any royalties for the use of their lands since the creation of the CDC in 1946. It also stressed that the Bakweri were not inclined to renew the 60-year CDC lease, preferring to repossess the CDC lands after its expiry in 2007 (Konings 1996b: 213).

Concerned with mounting anger in the Anglophone region in general and the Bakweri community in particular, the Biya government decided to send a delegation of high-ranking Anglophone allies to the South West Province to appease the local population. The delegation was led by Chief Ephraim Inoni who was Deputy Secretary General at the Presidency and the Chief of Bakingili, a village located on the territory of a Bakweri sub-group, and met a number of Bakweri representatives in Buea to discuss the land problem. Though speaking on behalf of the government, Chief Inoni appealed to Bakweri representatives not to forget that he was one of them. He acknowledged that there should have been prior contact between the government and the Bakweri before the announcement of the corporation's privatisation but he denied widespread rumours in Anglophone Cameroon that the French and some high-ranking Francophones had masterminded the whole operation. While admitting that the financial situation of the corporation had improved after the 1994 devaluation of the CFA franc, he argued that privatisation would enable the corporation to obtain new capital for the investments needed in production and processing. The Bakweri Paramount Chief, S.M.L. Endeley,[11] who had always been a staunch supporter of the regime until the Bakweri land issue arose, then took the floor. Amid thunderous applause, he declared that he himself, as the custodian of the ancestral lands, and the Bakweri population as a whole, were against the CDC's privatisation. He requested Chief Inoni report this to President Biya:

> We are in a country where we like to cheat ourselves, where government hands decisions through dictatorship (...) We say no, no [to privatisation], go and tell Mr Biya that he cannot afford to go down in history as the man who sold the CDC.[12]

After the government delegation returned to Yaoundé, the government did not undertake any further action regarding the CDC privatisation. This apparent victory for Anglophone resistance turned out to be short-lived and in 1997 rumours of its imminent privatisation became more persistent. In compliance with the agreement with the IMF and the World Bank within the framework of the Enhanced Structural Adjustment Programme (ESAP) in 1997, the privatisation of the CDC was expected to be launched soon. That the government, under severe pressure from the Bretton Woods institutions, was preparing the ground for the privatisation could be concluded from the speeches and interviews of leading government and CDC officials at the opening ceremony of the corporation's golden-jubilee celebrations in Bota-Victoria on 1 December 1997. In his speech, the newly appointed Prime Minister Peter Mafany Musonge, a Bakwerian who had been the CDC's general manager from 1988 to 1997, said:

> Since the traditional international funding agencies no longer finance corporations like CDC, the establishment should be prepared (...) to foster new business relationships to raise new money while the state plays the role of facilitator. (...) Traditional rulers within CDC's areas of operation, workers and other Cameroonians must understand perfectly well and make sure that peace reigns for conclusive investment.[13]

The CDC's chairman, N.N. Mbile, added that 'privatisation should not scare us as we are confident that government will protect the interests of the Cameroonian people, the original landowners, the workers, new investors and the state itself'. The CDC's deputy general manager, Richard Grey, then revealed that the reputable international consultancy firm Coopers and Lybrand had been selected by the World Bank and the government to carry out a study into the privatisation of the CDC that would be completed by 30 June 1998. The Bakweri chiefs who attended the ceremony, notably Chief S.M.L. Endeley of Buea, were frustrated by these statements and revelations and condemned any future privatisation.[14]

The CDC was put up for sale in January 1999. Few protests were heard from the almost dormant Anglophone movements (Konings & Nyamnjoh 2000: 29-30). Their leadership's only activity was to make a strongly worded statement on 10 April 1999 warning prospective CDC buyers to desist from investing in its purchase. Bakweri chiefs and elite, however, quickly rallied. In a meeting with southwestern members of parliament and government, they denounced the privatisation saying that the latter's acceptance of the sale of the CDC 'was tantamount to a betrayal of their people'.[15] The BLCC officially wrote to President Biya on behalf of the Bakweri people on 3 March 1999 requesting that it be included in privatisation negotiations and that compensation be paid for the use of Bakweri lands. When rumours spread that various multinational companies like Fruitiers/Dole, Chiquita and Del Monte were negotiating with individual government officials about the purchase of the whole or parts of the CDC at throwaway prices, the Bakweri in the diaspora once again addressed the head of state on 1 October 1999 in support of the BLCC position.[16]

Since no reply was forthcoming from the presidency, the BLCC, supported by regional organisations of chiefs and the elite, like the South West Chiefs' Conference (SWECC) and the South West Elites Association (SWELA),[17] decided to raise national and international awareness by starting a high-profile public relations campaign on the Internet and writing open letters, petitions and newspaper articles. The BLCC was reconstituted and an interim bureau was set up in the US.

During a BLCC general assembly meeting on 15 April 2000 it was decided that only chiefs could occupy the positions of president and vice-president. (There were four vice-presidents representing each of the subdivisions in the Fako Division of the South West

Province.) Other traditional rulers would constitute the Chiefs' Advisory Council of the Board of Trustees and the modern elite would occupy positions in the secretariat and act as technical advisors. This division of labour was meant to demonstrate that the chiefs were the leaders of the Bakweri communities and capable of mobilising and sensitising their subjects, while the modern elite had the bureaucratic and technical capabilities to operate the secretariat and provide the organisation with any necessary advice.

In May 2000, the BLCC interim bureau in the US opened to establish an effective, active and visible presence within the Bakweri and Cameroonian diaspora and to create permanent lines of communication with all potential CDC buyers, donor agencies, NGOs and foreign governments directly or indirectly involved in the sale of the CDC. BLCC-USA was very vocal and set up its own website.[18] Its first action was to send a memo to the Managing Director of the IMF, Horst Köhler, on 16 June 2000 warning him of growing unrest among the Bakweri and threatening legal action should the privatisation of the CDC be pursued without BLCC involvement:

> As the current impasse in Zimbabwe and Kenya demonstrates, land expropriated from African natives by European colonialists a century ago is the source of much contemporary unrest and instability. All Cameroonians of goodwill bear witness that the Bakweri people have over the years opted for a peaceful resolution of the CDC Bakweri land problem. However, should the privatisation of the CDC go ahead without the imput of the Bakweri on whose land most of the corporation's agro-industrial activities are located, we preserve the right to seek legal redress against the government of the Republic of Cameroon, the IMF, the World Bank as well as all lessees who derive title to the land by whatever means, in any country of the world where such bodies are located.[19]

This was followed by massive pro-BLCC demonstrations in New York and Washington during the United Nations Millennium Summit in September 2000 that was attended by a large Cameroonian delegation led by President Paul Biya. As a result of these demonstrations and a flurry of other pro-BLCC activities, the embarrassed Cameroonian delegation, along with leading donor agencies, were able to gauge the high levels of support for the BLCC within the Cameroonian diaspora in the US.

In a press release on 5 August 2000, the BLCC revealed that it was going to take its campaign for land restitution and compensation a notch higher by seeking consultative status within the United Nations' Economic and Social Council (ECOSOC).[20] It believed that the granting of consultative status would provide it with a global platform to proclaim its struggle for land rights, 'bringing it into contact with other NGOs which claim to represent the interests of indigenous groups from around the world as well as with sympathetic UN members who have championed the cause of dispossessed people on the floor of the General Assembly and at the numerous ECOSOC meetings over the years'.[21] Soon afterwards, on 21 August 2000, the United Nations invited the Counsel of the BLCC, Prof. Ndiva Kofele-Kale, to make a representation on the Bakweri lands issue to the UN Human Rights Commission in Geneva.

Following the government's renewed call for tenders for the CDC in September 2000, the BLCC cautioned prospective buyers in an open letter saying that:

> it is our duty to advise you to think twice before you commit the resources of your shareholders in a venture that is still mired in controversy and whose promised financial and economic rewards may prove to be illusory in the long run.[22]

During the late 1990s it had become increasingly evident that the BLCC was finding it hard to defend Bakweri interests at the national level. This had been particularly the case in 1996 when 'their own son', Peter Mafany Musonge, was appointed prime minister. Without doubt, one of the main reasons for his appointment was that President Biya regarded him, as an ex-CDC general manager and a Bakweri, as the most suitable candidate to handle the delicate issue of CDC privatisation.

The appointment of Musonge initially raised high expectations among the Bakweri. They were convinced that their son would pay particular attention to the land question and take Bakweri interests into consideration in the case of any eventual sale of the CDC. These expectations appear to have had solid foundations because, in his previous position, Musonge had publicly declared in a radio interview in 1994 that any privatisation of the CDC should be 'not only economically effective but also socially equitable'.[23] He expressed his belief that indigenous landowners, workers and investors would be directly involved in this endeavour. Once appointed prime minister however, he came under immense pressure from the IMF and his superior, Paul Biya, to champion the economic advantages of CDC privatisation and to forget about paying compensation to Bakweri landowners. Unable to convince his ethnic group to give up its claim to what could possibly amount to tens of billions of CFA francs after more than 50 years of CDC existence, Musonge was eventually reported to have resorted to intimidation, using the Buea Sub-prefect and the Fako Prefect to that end.

In March 2000, Buea Sub-prefect Aboubakar Njikam banned a BLCC general assembly meeting that he had given his approval for at an earlier stage. When he learnt that compensation was high on the agenda, the prime minister quickly called a halt to the meeting but failed to intimidate the committee that eventually met on 15 April 2000. In June 2000, the Fako Prefect, Jean-Robert Mengue Meka, accused it of being an illegal organisation and the committee was ordered to stop its activities. Two of the newly elected BLCC executives, Chief Peter Moky Efange (President) and Mola Njoh Litumbe (Secretary General), responded by telling Mengue Meka that he was acting illegally by claiming that the BLCC, which was founded in 1946, was an unlawful association. He was reminded that the BLCC was a duly incorporated organisation that had been registered in accordance with the laws of the country and had been received by the South West Governor in 1994 and thus could not now have its legality questioned.[24]

As a result of the high-profile BLCC publicity at home and abroad, the prime minister could no longer ignore the committee and its demands. He invited members to his Yaoundé office and on 4 October 2000, the BLCC leadership met with Musonge, Chief Ephraim Inoni, the Bakweri Deputy General Secretary at the Presidency and a number of other government officials. Musonge conceded at this meeting that the issues of land ownership and the payment of ground rents were legitimate demands but urged that these demands be pursued separately from the issue of privatisation. He argued that a hostile environment was being created by the BLCC protest campaign and was scaring off potential investors.[25]

The BLCC delegation agreed with the Prime Minister that privatisation would be successful only in a peaceful atmosphere but pointed out that the Bakweri protest actions, such as the UN Millennium Summit demonstrations, stemmed from a lack of government response to their pleas and representations. It stressed that Bakweri protest actions would inevitably continue until 'justice, equity, and legitimate rights of the Bakweri were met'. The delegation then reiterated the main BLCC demands that:

- the government recognise that the lands occupied by the CDC were private property as defined by Part II of the 1974 Land Law and that the Bakweri were the legitimate owners of these lands;
- the Bakweri be fully involved in the CDC privatisation negotiations to ensure their interests were effectively protected;
- ground rents be paid into a Bakweri land trust fund; and
- the Bakweri, acting either jointly or individually, be allocated a specific percentage of shares in each of the privatised sectors of the corporation.[26]

While the BLCC was embarking on a dialogue with local and national authorities, it continued to caution potential CDC buyers and the Bretton Woods institutions against any privatisation without the involvement of the landowners. The latter, in turn, put pressure on the Cameroonian government to settle the privatisation imbroglio. In the wake of the reluctance of foreign companies to invest in the CDC due to the unresolved land issue, the government was compelled to reissue the CDC bid for tenders on 1 January 2001 and then again on 1 January 2002.

In October 2002, the BLCC filed a complaint about the land dispute with the African Commission on Human and People's Rights 'on behalf of the Traditional Rulers, Notables and Elites of the indigenous minority peoples of Fako Division against the Government of Cameroon'. Three years later, in February 2006, the commission made a decision on the issue, which was endorsed by the African Union. It ruled that 'the Bakweri had a strong case backed by history and law, that the BLCC had the mandate to speak on behalf of the Bakweri and that the BLCC and the Government of Cameroon should seek an amicable settlement of the land dispute'. It availed its good offices to both parties in order to facilitate such a settlement. Unfortunately, this has yet to come about.

## Conclusion

This chapter highlighted the powerful resistance of Bakweri chiefs to the Cameroonian government's announcement of the privatisation of the CDC. It would be wrong to conclude that Bakweri chiefs are against privatisation *per se*. In fact, their 1994 petition to the head of state clearly stated that:

> In principle, the Bakweri and other Anglophones have no quarrel with the idea of privatisation or sale of companies in which government enjoys majority control since we fully understand the logic behind such an exercise, i.e. the relocation of the management of inefficiently managed parastatals in more efficient hands. We recognise that government, as the controlling shareholder in these companies, has an obligation to the majority shareholders and the Cameroonian taxpayer to ensure that their tax revenues are not wasted in failing parastatals.

The strong opposition by Bakweri chiefs to the privatisation was partly because they saw it as provocation of the Anglophone community. They pointed out that the CDC had the reputation of being one of the few parastatals in Cameroon that had played a significant role in regional development and performed relatively well until the economic crisis. They also claimed ownership of CDC lands. Since the 1940s they had been engaged in a fierce and protracted struggle for the retrieval of the Bakweri lands that were expropriated by the Germans for plantation agriculture. They therefore complained bitterly that they, as the custodians of the Bakweri lands, were never consulted prior to the announcement of the corporation's privatisation and they demanded compensation for any sale or lease of CDC lands to multinational companies.

The opposition of Bakweri chiefs to the establishment and privatisation of the CDC has had important implications for current debates on their position in local society and in the national arena. Geschiere (1993: 165-66) pointed out two reasons for the integration of the chieftaincy, which was more or less a colonial creation, into Bakweri society: chieftaincy was strengthened during British indirect rule and, even more significantly, it became a potential rallying point against the 'strangers', attracted by the plantation economy created by the Germans, who invaded Bakweri territory in large numbers. The persistent struggle of the Bakweri chiefs since the 1940s for justice regarding the expropriated Bakweri lands may have been an even more important factor for integrating chieftaincy into local society. While chiefs in Anglophone Cameroon have been officially transformed into auxiliaries of the state in the aftermath of independence and reunification and most chiefs maintain close links with the ruling party (Geschiere 1993: 166-69; Fisiy 1995: 57-59), my case study demonstrates that Bakweri chiefs cannot be characterised as mere puppets of the regime (van Rouveroy van Nieuwaal 1996: 39). As in other parts of Africa (van Rouveroy van Nieuwaal 1998: 80-87), large-scale state expropriation of the local community's land has been a permanent source of conflict between the state and Bakweri chiefs.

In their long-standing struggle to retrieve ancestral lands and in vehement opposition to the current privatisation of the CDC, Bakweri chiefs have been backed by the Bakweri elite at home and in the diaspora, irrespective of their political affiliation. The elite has placed its bureaucratic and technical competence at the disposal of the BLCC, the legitimate representative of the Bakweri people who are seeking the restoration of their ancestral land rights. They are using modern communication methods, including the Internet, to caution potential investors and the Bretton Woods institutions against any privatisation of the CDC without Bakweri consent and compensation. This has scared off foreign capital and the government has been unable to control such modern resistance.

The Bakweri chiefs have also been supported by newly created Anglophone associations that perceive the Bakweri land issue as part of their struggle to redress the marginalisation and subordination of their region within the Francophone-dominated state.

The combined forces of Bakweri and Anglophone traditional and modern elites have compelled the government to repeatedly postpone the privatisation of the CDC and to take Bakweri interests into consideration in a new privatisation construction.

## Notes

1. See letter from Chief G.M. Endeley to the Resident in charge, Buea, dated 8 June 1946, ref. no. BLC/2/1, in BNA, File Qf/e (1946)1, Bakweri Land Committee.

2. Britain had assumed responsibility for the territory, the so-called Southern Cameroons, under UN Trusteeship after the Second World War. See Konings & Nyamnjoh (2003).

3. Petition of the Bakweri Land Committee to the Right Honourable S.A. Creech Jones MP, Secretary of State for the Colonies, dated 24 August 1946, in BNA, File Qf/e (1946)1, Bakweri Land Committee.

4. Mr Bridges had served as a political officer in the area for a considerable period and had even submitted a detailed intelligence report on the Bakweri. See BNA, File Ag 10, Intelligence Report on Bakweri, Victoria Division, Cameroon Province, by W.M. Bridges, D.C.

5. According to the Bakweri, the 1974 Land Law (Ordinance No. 74-1 of 6 July 1974 to establish rules governing land tenure) does in fact ground Bakweri rights in positive law in its classification of all land tenured into the 'Grund Buch' (the case with all CDC lands) as 'land ... subject to the right of private property'. See BLCC, Open Letter to all Prospective Buyers of CDC Plantations, Buea, 12 October 2000. For the 1974 Land Law, see Republic of Cameroon (1981), *Land Tenure and State Lands*, Yaoundé: Imprimerie Nationale.

6. Republic of Cameroon (1981), *Land Tenure and State Lands*, Yaoundé: Imprimerie Nationale, 81.

7. For the causes and effects of this crisis, see Konings (1996a).

8. See *Fako International*, Vol. 1, No. 2 (January 1995), pp. 14-16.

9. Memorandum of the Bakweri People on the Presidential Decree to privatise or sell the Cameroon Development Corporation, Buea, 27 July 1994.

10. *Ibid.*

11. Chief S.M.L. Endeley is a brother of Dr E.M.L. Endeley and D.M.L. Endeley who were leading figures in the BLC. He is a retired Chief Justice who acted as chairman of the ruling party, the Cameroon People's Democratic Movement (CPDM), in Fako Division and chairman of the CDC before being appointed Paramount Chief of Buea in 1992. For further details of his career, see Gwellem, J.F. (1985), *Cameroon Year Book 1985/86*, Limbe: Gwellem Publications, pp. 113-114.

12. Cited in *Fako International*, Vol. 1, No. 2 (January 1995), p. 16.

13. *The Post*, 5 December 1997, pp. 1-2.

14. *Ibid.*

15. Isaha'a Boh, Cameroon, Bulletin No. 405.

16. See letter from the Bakweri around the World to President Paul Biya of Cameroon, 1 October 1999.

17. For these organisations, see Nyamnjoh & Rowlands (1998: 328-30) and Eyoh (1998: 338-39).

18. http://www.bakwerilands.org. Most of the documents quoted in this article can be found on this website.

19. Letter from Dr Lyombe Eko, Executive Director of BLCC-USA, to Horst Köhler, Managing Director of the IMF, 16 June 2000.

20. Press Release No. blc/us/05/08/00, 'The BLCC to seek consultative status at the UN Economic and Social Council (ECOSOC)'.

21. *Ibid.*

22. BLCC, Open Letter to All Prospective Buyers of CDC Plantations, Buea, 12 October 2000.

23. See *Cameroon Post*, 26 July-2 August 1994, pp. 12-13.

24. BLCC, 'The BLCC refuses to stand down in the face of threats from Fako administrative authorities', Buea, 15 June 2000.

25. Through such manoeuvres, Musonge succeeded in dividing the BLCC into two camps: on the one hand, a majority faction led by its president, Chief Efange, which stood its ground, and, on the other, a minority faction led by the Bakweri Paramount Chief, Sam Endeley, which was more sensitive to Musonge's arguments. The latter accused the new BLCC executive of being too radical and opposed its ongoing Internet campaign on the CDC's privatisation compensation.

26. Report of the meeting of Prime Minister Mafany Musonge with the BLCC Delegation, Yaoundé, 4 October 2000.

# 6

# Privatisation and labour militancy:
# The case of Cameroon's tea estates

## Introduction

Privatisation is an essential part of an overall neo-liberal reform package aimed at creating transparency and accountability in the management of national affairs as well as a favourable environment for opening up African economies to market forces and private-sector development (World Bank 1989, 1992; Sandbrook 2000).

Privatisation calls for a re-evaluation of relations between the public and private sectors in Africa. Under pressure from international donors, governments have been urged to reduce state ownership and enhance private-sector development. International donors tend to attribute the massive growth of state enterprises since independence and their generally poor performance to the bad governance of Africa's neo-patrimonial regimes. They claim that statist conceptions of development have resulted in a widespread politicisation of economic decision-making and rent-seeking behaviour among the parasitic political elite (World Bank 1997; Olukoshi 1998; van de Walle 2001). Privatisation would help cut public-sector inefficiency and waste, solve the problem of rising budgetary deficits, stimulate private-sector development, attract more investment and new technology, and revive economic growth.

There is a growing body of literature on privatisation that discusses the mixed results these practices have had in Africa and the serious problems and controversy they have encountered (cf. Mkandawire 1994; Bennell 1997; Campbell White & Bhatia 1998; Tangri 1999; van de Walle 2001; Pitcher 2002; Rakner 2003). Privatisation problems in Africa are attributed not only to technical and financial constraints but also to the fact that privatisation did not offer the break with the previous dynamics of the post-colonial state that the Bretton Woods institutions and bilateral donors had expected. Cameroon is a clear example of the failure of privatisation to free the parastatal sector of government neo-patrimonial logic (van de Walle 1994b; Walker 1998; Konings 2003b, 2007a). There is considerable evidence that the Biya regime was initially extremely reluctant to sell state-owned enterprises, which it saw as a threat to its patronage politics and the maintenance and consolidation of its power. It was only later that it was prepared to speed up the programme of privatisation. In addition to persistent pressure from international donors, the regime realised that privatisation itself did not necessarily foreclose rent-seeking opportunities for the parasitic bureaucratic and political elite. Indeed, some members benefited from it. For politicians responsible for the privatisation process, privatisation measures have frequently been an opportunity for corrupt practices. Divestiture has not been a transparent process and, in return for the payment of substantial kickbacks, public enterprises have been sold at prices far below their true value amid reports of embezzlement of the proceeds. Moreover, privatisation has not excluded members of the bureaucratic and political elite from occupying top positions in former state-owned enterprises. Some have been re-appointed and others have been newly recruited (Konings 2007a).

The problems of privatisation in Africa are seen by some as also being due to the fierce opposition of civil-society organisations (cf. Olukoshi 1998; Beckman & Sachikonye 2001; Konings 2003a, 2003b, 2007a). Although World Bank studies have recommended the involvement of civil society in neo-liberal economic reforms, arguing that their participation in policy making would ensure ownership, credibility and sustainability of the reform process (World Bank 1992, 1995; Rakner 2001), there is ample evidence that civil-society organisations tend to be excluded from the decision-making process because of their expected resistance to the allegedly harmful effects of externally imposed privatisation schemes on their members. Academics, students and ethno-regional movements have vehemently denounced the sale of national and regional patrimony to western multinationals and nationals closely connected with African regimes (Tangri 1999; Konings 2003b, 2007a). They and various indigenous business groups have criticised the prominent role of foreign companies in the privatisation process as a 'recolonisation of Africa'. Consumer groups have often protested against the poor and/or expensive services delivered by newly privatised enterprises. Undoubtedly, the most public, persistent and organised opposition to privatisation in Africa has come from the labour movement. Trade unions have, on occasion, succeeded in blocking or slowing down the privatisation of specific enterprises or influencing negotiations for a privatisation agreement. At other times and in response to external pressures, governments have simply brushed union opposition aside, leaving a legacy of anger and political tension (Beckman & Sachikonye 2001; Konings 2006).

Remarkably, hardly any detailed studies have been published on the responses of African workers to privatisation in West-Central Africa.[1] This is all the more surprising because privatisations of large, strategic public enterprises in Cameroon and other African countries have often been followed by militant protests by workers against massive lay-offs and deteriorating conditions of service.

This chapter discusses how the privatisation of the CDC's tea estates generated not only persistent regional protest but also protracted strikes by estate workers. I focus on workers in the two privatised tea estates in Anglophone Cameroon, namely the Tole Tea Estate and the Ndu Tea Estate (see Chapter 3).

The chapter is divided into two parts. The first provides evidence that the announced privatisation of the CDC tea estates in October 2002 was fiercely opposed by Anglophone and other ethno-regional organisations, in particular the Bakweri Land Claims Committee (BLCC), all the more so because it turned out to be engineered by a few well-connected members of the regional elite who were conniving with the Cameroonian state. The second part describes the growing militancy of Tole and Ndu workers following a dramatic deterioration in their conditions of service in the aftermath of the privatisation of their estates.

## The privatisation of the CDC tea estates

Attempts to privatise the CDC have been vehemently opposed by Anglophone and South West associations (see Chapters 2 and 5) as well as by other regional civil-society organisations. The most important was the Fako Agricultural Workers Union (FAWU), which is responsible for the representation and defence of CDC workers in Fako Division (Konings 1993a; 1995b). Its president, Cornelius Vewessee, is one of the most prominent union leaders in Cameroon, having played a significant part in achieving a large measure of union autonomy in 1992. He insisted that the CDC could not be privatised without consulting the FAWU, arguing that CDC workers had made personal sacrifices during the economic crisis to assist the corporation's recovery. Moreover, he said the union would resist any mass lay-offs and/or deterioration in workers' conditions of service as a result of privatisation. And finally, the Anglophone press severely criticised the announced privatisation: it has long defended the Anglophone cause and informed the Anglophone population of the issues at stake.

The united Anglophone front was able to prevent the implementation of the corporation's privatisation for some time. However to the consternation of Anglophones in general and the Bakweri in particular, it was announced in October 2002 that the CDC tea estates had been sold to a South African consortium, Brobon Finex PTY Ltd. Brobon Finex would run the tea sector, including the Tole Tea Estate in the Bakweri area, under the name of Cameroon Tea Estates (CTE).

The privatisation agreement between the Cameroonian government and Brobon Finex was on the following terms. The Cameroonian government was to hand over 65% of its shares to Brobon Finex which, in turn, would sell 5% of its shares to its personnel. Brobon Finex was to expand tea production area from about 1,500 to 3,000 ha in fifteen years and invest about FCFA 8 billion over the following ten years. It would also reimburse the FCFA 1.1 billion owed by the CDC tea estates. In addition, it agreed not to lay off any workers, improve existing health, education and accommodation facilities, and continue buying produce from local contract farmers. Finally, and conforming to the government's privatisation policy of agro-industrial enterprises, land would be excluded from the transaction.

At the signing of the agreement on 18 October 2002, the Executive Chairman of Brobon Finex, Derrick Garvie, declared that his company would demonstrate within a few years that the government's act of confidence had not been misplaced and that no effort or expense would be spared in developing Cameroon's tea sector. He guaranteed the jobs of the existing labour force, adding that more workers would be recruited as a result of plans for expansion.[2]

The BLCC expressed its bewilderment at the sale of the CDC tea estates without any consultation or compensation of the landowners in spite of previous deliberations between the committee and the government. The Anglophone secessionist movement, the SCNC, claimed that the Francophone-dominated state had no *locus standi* to privatise, sell or transfer CDC tea estates located within the territorial boundaries of Anglophone Cameroon to South Africans or any other person (Konings 2003b). In March 2000, the unions had warned the government that the 1992 Labour Code provided that workers would be consulted in the event of privatisation as to whether they would prefer to be paid off before negotiating new contracts with the new employer.[3]

The privatisation of the CDC tea estates soon became a national scandal when it emerged that a handful of politically well-connected elites were going to benefit at the expense of the public treasury and the native landowners. From his comments, it became clear that this privatisation was masterminded by John Niba Ngu, a former CDC general manager and minister of agriculture, who is known to be a close friend of President Biya (see Chapter 2). He used both his technical knowledge and his many connections within the regime's highest levels to design the privatisation of the CDC tea estates. While experts had estimated the value of the three tea estates at between FCFA 5 billion and FCFA 10 billion, Ngu managed to bring the price down to FCFA 1.5 billion. Less than three months later, the CTE sold stocks worth FCFA 4.6 billion. In return for his excellent services, the Board of Brobon Finex appointed Ngu as general manager on a monthly salary and benefits amounting to FCFA 4 million. According to Ngu, they allocated him 5% of the CTE's share capital, although this was later contested by the Board of Brobon Finex.

There were also growing doubts about Brobon Finex's takeover when it became clear that the real owner of the CTE was Alhadji Baba Ahmadou Danpullo, an extremely wealthy Mbororo from the North West Province of Anglophone Cameroon who was apparently using Brobon Finex as a front. He is a well-known cattle rancher and businessman in Cameroon with an international network stretching as far as South Africa and also a member of the central committee of the ruling party, the Cameroon People's Democratic Movement (CPDM). Interestingly, Danpullo had previously been involved in another privatisation scandal in Cameroon, namely an attempt to sell the *Société de Développement du Coton* (SODECOTON), a huge parastatal in Northern Cameroon, which was on the same privatisation list as the CDC in 1994. Danpullo was among the small group of politically well-connected elite, most of them originating from Northern Cameroon, who managed to buy the company at a giveaway price. The deal was eventually cancelled by the government following a popular outcry and the intervention of external donors, in particular France and the World Bank (Takougang & Krieger 1998: 169-80). Apparently, Danpullo had put John Niba Ngu, who was looking for a South African financier for his privatisation scheme for the CDC tea estates, in contact with Brobon Finex. Although he was not a signatory to the convention between the Cameroonian government and Brobon Finex, he paid the money for the takeover of the CDC tea estates to the public treasurer, and has since been engaged in other financial transactions on behalf of the CTE.

Investigations by the BLCC in South Africa found that Brobon Finex existed in name only and had no office premises. Its chairman, Derrick Garvie, was indeed known in South African business circles but not in connection with Brobon Finex. This raised suspicions that Brobon Finex was merely a straw company. Some of my informants alleged that Danpullo made use of the Brobon Finex construction because it improved his chance of acquiring the tea estates, being well aware that the government would be inclined to sell large, strategic state enterprises to foreign companies. It enabled him to whitewash part of his ill-gotten capital. After initially being designated by the Brobon Finex Board as a major shareholder, he gradually started to act as chairman of the CTE Board, as the South African Brobon Finex board members became less visible in Cameroon.

In January 2003, the BLCC threatened to sue Brobon Finex in South Africa for trespassing on Bakweri property without the prior consent of its owners. In addition, it called upon the government to revoke the controversial privatisation of the CDC tea estates and to open meaningful discussions with the BLCC with a view to achieving an equitable resolution of the Bakweri land problem.[4] Amid growing evidence of financial malpractice, President Biya instructed the prime minister and the security forces to investigate the matter. The outcome of these investigations has never been made public but it is widely believed that Danpullo had been using his political network to help settle the matter and been engaged in bribing investigators. Moreover, it would appear that President Biya himself has serious allegations to answer about personally authorising the transfer of the CDC tea estates to his friends.

What is more relevant to our discussion here is that the controversial privatisation scheme was going to have nefarious consequences for the Tole and Ndu Tea estate workers whose living and working conditions had already been badly affected by the economic recession prior to privatisation. This gave rise to an unprecedented degree of labour militancy on both estates.

## Growing labour militancy on the Tole Tea Estate

Neither the government nor the CDC's management had felt it necessary to inform the Tole Tea Estate workers of the planned privatisation of their estate so they only came to learn of it through the media. Being aware that privatisations in Cameroon had usually led to retrenchments and a deterioration in workers' conditions of service, they were worried about their future despite assurances given by the new owners on the signing of the privatisation agreement that the existing labour force and their conditions of service would be maintained. Shortly after the estate's privatisation on 18 October 2002, one of the women pluckers expressed the workers' widespread anxieties as follows:

> I am not sure whether we are going to enjoy similar conditions as under the CDC. I am rather afraid that we are going to suffer when the new owners have installed themselves. Nobody appears to be willing to enlighten us on the effects of privatisation and our new status. One simply asks us to wait.[5]

The workers were even more alarmed when the 'real' owner of the CTE, Alhadji Baba Ahmadou Danpullo, decided in November 2002 to transfer 23 managerial staff from his business enterprises in Douala to his new company, probably because he thought they would be more loyal than former CDC staff members. His decision created serious problems on the estate. First, these newly appointed managers were Francophones who all had difficulty communicating with the Anglophone estate managers and workers. And given the deepening Anglophone-Francophone divide in the country (Konings & Nyamnjoh 2003), it was hardly surprising that their appointment was generally seen on the estate as a highly provocative attempt to establish Francophone domination of a former Anglophone enterprise. As one of these Francophone managers put it:

> The Francophones are looked upon here as invaders. The Anglophones have not digested the fact that the tea sector of the CDC has come under the control of French-speaking Cameroonians. One has therefore the impression that they will do everything to chase us from the company.[6]

Second, although lacking any experience in tea production, these newly appointed managers rapidly usurped the functions of the former CDC managerial staff and lorded over them and the workers. This behaviour fuelled existing tensions and feelings of solidarity and militancy among the workers. Without the first CTE general manager's knowledge, these Francophone managers engaged in dubious financial transactions that resulted in a lack of funds to improve estate facilities and workers' conditions of service. Their lack of experience and frequent clashes with Anglophone managers and workers soon led to a serious drop in tea production.

From 29 December 2002 to 4 January 2003, the estate workers staged a first strike against the new CTE management.[7] They asserted that their conditions of service had declined following privatisation. Their social-security contributions had not been transferred to the National Social Security Fund since 1996, medical care was not being provided, ambulances and factory tractors had broken down, sceptic tanks were not being emptied, and wages for November 2002 had not yet been paid to all the field workers. Many workers

154

also protested at the sudden dismissal on 4 January 2003 of the CTE's general manager, John Niba Ngu, and his replacement by his Francophone deputy general manager, Mahamat Alamine Mey. While the Board of Brobon Finex insisted that Ngu had been fired because of his unilateral decision to dismiss all the newly hired, inexperienced and unpopular Francophone managers, the workers claimed that he had been fired because of his plans to improve their conditions of service. At a meeting with some of the Brobon Finex board members on the same day, their shop stewards or staff representatives (Konings 1993a; 1995a) were told not to meddle in the sacking of their former general manager and to ensure workers returned to work, while the CTE management looked into all their problems. The board members ordered the immediate payment of any salary arrears and made the following promises: the CTE would increase workers' salaries by April 2003, raise their conditions of service to the standards prevailing on the tea estates in Kenya and elsewhere, and provide them with toilet and medical facilities as well as protective clothing and boots. A few days later, the new CTE general manager, Mahamat Alamine Mey, signed a protocol agreement with the President of the FAWU, Cornelius Vewessee, reassuring workers that all their acquired rights would be honoured.

On 17 June 2003, estate workers staged another strike in protest at what they termed 'poor working conditions and humanitarian neglect'.[8] They felt particularly aggrieved by the abrupt cancellation of certain allowances and bonuses they had been enjoying under the CDC and the regular lack of medical facilities on the estate. Although an amount of FCFA 650 was deducted from their monthly wages for medical care, they were forced to go to the CDC hospitals where they were charged the same as other non-CDC personnel. Apparently representing the feelings of most estate workers, a 52-year-old widowed tea plucker lamented the fact that:

> The abolition of several allowances has drastically reduced my income. My monthly wage has dropped from FCFA 40,000 to FCFA 22,000. I am not even sure if I will get this little amount. They are always finding pretexts to cut my present wage. One speaks of taxes to be paid, absenteeism, indiscipline and so on. At present, I am torn between resigning and revolt. I would like to leave but I wonder how I could raise my children if I did so.[9]

Despite growing discontent among the workers, the chairman of Brobon Finex, Derrick Garvie, still presented an optimistic picture of the company's future during the celebrations to mark the first anniversary of the CTE on 18 October 2003. He again stressed that one of the principal managerial objectives was 'to make CTE a clear example of the success story of privatisations'.[10]

Soon after these celebrations, the CTE management implemented a controversial reorganisation in December 2003. Staff representatives pointed out how a number of the proposed measures went against the 1992 deregulated Labour Code, and they attributed the absence of any state intervention in the matter to the close links between top government officials and Alhadji Baba Ahmadou Danpullo. The reorganisation started with a 50% slash in workers' salaries and the withdrawal of any remaining allowances. When workers reacted to this dramatic decline in their income by resorting to protracted strike action on 8 January 2004, management used this illegal strike as a pretext for implementing two further measures. It immediately dismissed 268 workers without paying their severance pay, and started recruiting new workers from outside Anglophone Cameroon. Among those dismissed were a number of staff representatives. The CTE's management simply refused to seek authorisation for their dismissal from the Ministry of Labour as required in the Labour Code. It then changed almost the entire labour force – with the exception of 90 workers – from being permanent workers into casual and temporary workers. These measures were accompanied by the introduction of a labour regime that became more and more despotic (Burawoy 1985), the banning of trade unionism on the estate and the bypassing of staff representatives.

Furious about these measures, workers continued to strike until 5 February 2004 when the Minister of Labour, Prof. Robert Nkili, decided to intervene. Immediately after his mediation and the settlement of the dispute, it became evident that management was unwilling to respect his instructions about refraining from 'wrongful terminations of contracts and unacceptable wages and terms of employment'. It started introducing new reorganisation measures that led to a further deterioration in workers' conditions of service. It also notified tea pluckers that their daily task would be increased to 32 kg in the slack season and 45 kg in the peak season. The workers then decided to stay away from work on 10 February. And in retaliation, management announced an additional cut in wages.

Given these developments, the living and working conditions on the estate became so deplorable that workers started complaining that 'the takeover of the tea estate by Brobon Finex had re-introduced slavery in this part of the country'.[11] While CTE management was celebrating the company's second anniversary on 23 October 2004, workers circulated tracts in which they called for the return of John Niba Nga as general manager to save the company from total collapse. They deplored their loss of benefits and the social amenities they had enjoyed under the CDC, the fall in the quality of their tea, and the abandonment of certain sections of the plantation which, they said, had fallen into disuse.[12]

During the course of 2005, workers became increasingly desperate. They regularly appealed to the government to return the estate to the CDC, stressing that Alhadji Baba Ahmadou Danpullo was focusing his attention and capital on his newly constructed 4,000-hectare tea estate in Ndawara in the North West Province which, he boasted, was making use of the latest technology. Irrespective of its 35% stake in the CTE, the government remained silent, apparently unconcerned about the decrease in tea production and workers' declining conditions of service. Feeling abandoned by the government, workers gradually lost faith in any future improvement in their predicament under CTE management. Significantly, while many appeared to no longer be interested in keeping their jobs at any costs, they did not want to resign before all they were owed had been paid out since this would enable them to repay their debts and invest in a new future.[13] Their growing realisation of a common interest in fighting for their accrued rights became a source of solidarity. This was clearly manifest in 2006 when a protracted strike – probably the longest in Cameroon's labour history – paralysed all the estate's activities for almost an entire year.

On 18 January 2006, the workers held a short strike as a warning. They had been informed that the Minister of Labour would be coming on a working visit to Buea and the next day they intercepted him and informed him that the sale of their estate to Brobon Finex had not been a good move. They had been exposed to untold hardships following privatisation, and were unable even to send their children to school. The minister replied that he had refrained from any earlier intervention on their behalf because he had expected their problems to be solved at the company level. He asked them to go back to work while he tried to solve their problems by meeting Prime Minister Ephraim Inoni with a view to reconsidering the privatisation of the CDC tea estates.[14]

Nothing more was heard of the minister after he left Buea and on 26 February 2006 workers announced that they had no other choice than to go on strike due to 'the inhuman working conditions we are subjected to by the CTE management'. They stressed that they would not resume work until they had been paid the following benefits:

> severance payment from CDC to date; accrued leave allowances from 2003 to 2006; good separation bonuses, [their] own 5 per cent shares in the CTE as spelt out in the privatisation agreement; [their] social insurance dues; [their] credit union contributions which were never transferred by the CTE to the credit union; and balances owed to retrenched workers since January 2004.[15]

By the start of this strike, a new spokesman for the workers, Blasius Mosoke, had emerged who acted in close cooperation with existing staff representatives. He was not a worker but a manager, being one of the estate's field assistants. He told me that two major factors were responsible for his siding with the workers during the strike. First, like the workers, he felt he had been badly treated by the newly recruited Francophone managers after privatisation. His relationship with the CTE's management had become particularly strained after he refused to provide the names of the workers involved in the first strike in 2006. Just like them, he had considered resigning after receiving his severance pay. Second, he felt obliged to fight not only for himself but also for the workers because he thought that the core of the estate's labour force was predominantly made up of poorly educated women who were incapable of representing their own interests effectively.[16]

At a crisis meeting in Limbe on 29 March that was attended by representatives of the regional administration, management and workers, the newly appointed French general manager of the CTE,

Jean-Pierre Croze, disclosed that he intended to close the estate for three months during the ongoing strike to replace the machines in the tea factory at a cost of approximately FCFA 3.5 billion. He then offered the workers FCFA 14.9 million that, he said, represented part of their accrued benefits. Staff representatives rejected his offer, however, saying that the workers would prefer the immediate payment of all their benefits.[17]

Not long after this meeting, on 8 April, the strikers started blockading the Tole to Sasse road. This had the intended consequence of forestalling the reopening of some local elitist colleges after the Easter holidays. The workers' argument was simple: if they prevented students from going to school, their parents, who belonged to the cream of the Cameroonian elite, would be likely to bring pressure to bear on the government to meet their demands.[18] Indeed, on 12 April, the Minister of Labour organised another crisis meeting in Buea but in spite of heated discussions, he failed to persuade workers' representatives to accept the CTE management's initial offer of FCFA 14.9 million (with the remainder of their accrued benefits being paid progressively). However in the end, he reached a compromise with both parties agreeing that all the accrued benefits would be paid out three months later. In the meantime, each party would calculate the total amount and then compare their findings with the payment coming in July.[19]

After this agreement, three significant events occurred. First, there was an attempt by CTE owners to continue selling tea stocks during the strike and in the night of 25 April, soldiers tried to remove bags of processed tea from the estate's factory. It soon transpired that Alhadji Baba Ahmadou Danpullo had hired these soldiers to transport the tea to one of his lorries that was parked in Buea. Defying warning shots, incensed workers attacked the soldiers and damaged their truck and, in revenge, soldiers tried to arrest Blasius Mosoke, the estate's field assistant and the workers' spokesman. Workers responded by warning the military that they would not take it lying down if anything happened to Mosoke.[20]

Second, there was an attempt by the Bakweri elite to buy the estate. Claiming that it was extremely worried about the ongoing crisis in one of the region's most important enterprises, the management of the Bakweri transport and shipping company

Fakoship announced on 14 July its intention to take over the Tole Tea Estate. However, this offer was immediately dismissed by the chairman of Brobon Finex, Derrick Garvie, who said that 'as the owner of the estate, his company had the sole right to let it go fallow, dismiss workers, dismantle machines, close it down and sell it without the government or anybody else interfering in its affairs'.[21] Alhadji Baba Ahmadou Danpullo strongly condemned the offer as being another expression of Bakweri opposition to his company. He repeatedly declared that the crisis on the estate was not due to managerial lapses but to the political machinations of the Bakweri elite who continued to incite workers against the management with the aim of undermining the company and serving their own interests.[22]

Third, the most dramatic event was the workers' decision to besiege the CDC's Head Office in Bota-Limbe. They had been frustrated by the government's failure to respect the agreement reached at the crisis meeting on 12 April and while they had made their own calculations of their accrued benefits, the three-month deadline had passed without any government response. On 26 July, between 500 and 800 men, women and children from the Tole Tea Estate occupied the CDC's Head Office, demanding FCFA 2.3 billion in accrued benefits. The FAWU's president aptly described the symbolic meaning of their occupation:

> The protesters presently camped at the CDC Head Office have not behaved violently because they have come back to where they were, to express that the marriage to which they were given, had not been successful because the new husband seems to have another wife in Ndawara [referring to Danpullo's newly created tea estate in that locality] and is not taking care of them. So they have come back to their father. CDC is their father.[23]

Although the provincial governor and the CDC's general manager ordered them to leave, the workers resolved to stay until a definitive solution to their problems had been found. Only the personal intervention of President Biya persuaded the workers to call off their protest action on 4 August, and Prime Minister Ephraim Inoni was asked to mediate. He set up an *ad-hoc* committee composed of government, management and workers' representatives that was presided over by the Minister of Labour in order to calculate the amount owed to the strikers and ensure its prompt payment.

The committee started work on 7 August. According to its own calculations, it did not accept the workers' 'exorbitant' demands of FCFA 2.3 billion and proposed the meagre sum of FCFA 169 million. After recalculation, it agreed to a figure of FCFA 308 million, which the workers still considered far below their expectations. Payment was to take place in the subsequent two weeks but was again postponed. It was only after mounting labour unrest that the regional administration announced it would make payments on 30 August.

However when the workers gathered outside the offices of the Provincial Delegation of Labour in Buea to receive their payments, they were informed that nothing would happen without an accurate list. In response, the workers went on the rampage in Buea, erecting road blocks on the main road to Kumba and Douala and tearing down billboards along the roadside. Clashes between workers and the police led to 30 workers being taken to hospital and a passer-by reportedly being hit by a stray bullet.

A few days later, on 2 September, the regional authorities summoned the workers to collect their payments. Since the authorities proved unwilling to publish a list of beneficiaries and the amount each of them would receive, the workers refused to turn up. There were two reasons why they finally collected the money they were owed on 11 September. First, their leaders had been continuously exposed to death threats by the administration, leaving them with no choice but to comply. Second, the workers' united front had been broken after workers at the Tole Credit Union secretly collected some FCFA 2.2 million.[24] Most of the workers were embittered because they had been hoodwinked into accepting miserly sums and they declared that they were no longer prepared to work on the estate.

A month later, all the workers who had been paid off had – either voluntarily or forcibly – left the Tole Tea Estate.[25] Some returned to their villages of origin, while others moved to neighbouring villages to try to eke out a new existence. Those who still wanted to work on the estate were told by CTE management that they had to apply for new contracts. On 1 October, youths hired by the management on a contract basis started pruning the overgrown tea bushes. Tea picking was expected to restart in the course of 2007.

## Growing labour militancy on the Ndu Tea Estate

Given the CTE takeover of all the former CDC tea estates in October 2002, it is not surprising that the Ndu Tea Estate workers faced similar problems to the Tole Tea Estate workers after the controversial privatisation. These included a drastic deterioration in their living and working conditions, massive lay-offs, frequent violations of the Labour Code, the replacement of competent Anglophone managers with inexperienced Francophones and, above all, constant delays in the payment of the financial benefits that the former and present owners, the CDC and the CTE respectively, owed the workers, such as severance pay, termination benefits, compensation for sums (for social insurance and credit union dues) deducted from workers' wages for over the years without interest and the workers' 5% share in the company as stipulated in the privatisation agreement.

Ndu Tea Estate workers used similar tactics to Tole Tea Estate workers to protest against growing exploitation and subordination in the labour process. Faced with the banning of trade unionism on the estate, they began to resort to informal, collective actions. And when they realised that the CTE management was not going to keep its promise of improving their living and working conditions after privatisation, some workers decided to stop working on the estate.

In 2004 the Ndu workers showed their profound dissatisfaction with the estate's privatisation. In February, they began a sit-in. In response, CTE management sanctioned them in a similar way as the Tole workers: and almost the entire Ndu labour force was transformed from having permanent labour status into contract labour. In presidential elections on 11 October, Ndu workers refused to support the incumbent president, Paul Biya, holding him jointly responsible for the estate's privatisation and its nefarious effects on the workers' living and working conditions. This is evident from a two-page memorandum that was signed by the local elite and the chief of Ndu:

The negative influence on voters for the CPDM in Ndu Subdivision, among others, was the privatisation of the CDC and the irregular lay-off of hundreds of workers of the Ndu Tea Estate by the CTE.[26]

In March 2005, Ndu workers threatened to go on strike again to back their grievances. In a petition to the CTE management, they lamented the fact that they had been reduced to contract workers under extremely rigid conditions on the grounds that they had absconded from work during the previous strike. They also decried the punitive transfer of some staff representatives and the allegedly intentional miscalculations on their pay. They claimed that the management still owed them wages and leave allowances. Curiously, instead of addressing their grievances, management threatened to sanction them for their refusal to use the proper channels for seeking redress.[27]

Inspired by the protracted strike on the Tole Tea Estate in the same year, Ndu workers embarked upon a four-month strike on 28 August 2006, demanding the immediate payment of their financial dues. They stressed that they had waited long enough, having sent numerous petitions to the CTE management and the administration of the Donga-Mantung Division, and announced that they were now prepared to fight to the bitter end, even if it cost them their lives. They cut down hundreds of eucalyptus trees from the CTE fuel plantation and blocked the Grassfields ring road, bringing traffic between Bamenda and Nkambe, the capital of Donga-Mantung Division, to a standstill. They had been informed by reliable sources that the CTE management was planning to bring in workers from the Ndawara Tea Estate in the North West Province in an effort to break their strike and ignore their legitimate demands. Fearing that the situation might degenerate into violence, the divisional administration ordered two trucks of armed soldiers from the Nkambe barracks who used force in a number of clashes that resulted in the hospitalisation of more than 30 workers.[28]

Faced with a deteriorating situation, the Senior District Officer (SDO) for Donga-Mantung Division, Godlive Mboke Ntua, and the District Officer (DO) for the Ndu Subdivision, John Mkong Yosimbom, convened a crisis meeting on 1 September. Their attempts to bring the workers to reason failed as the latter had lost all confidence in the divisional administration and CTE management. They then successfully approached Emmanuel Ngafeeson, the Secretary of State at the Ministry of Justice in charge of the Penitentiary, who was a prominent member of the local elite and popular among the masses, being fondly known as the 'man-at-the-grassroots'.

The following day, Ngafeeson went from Yaoundé to Tatum, a village close to Ndu where he was welcomed by the strikers. He then accompanied them to the CTE Ndu office, a distance of more than five kilometres, where he subsequently addressed them in their local languages, appealing to them to calculate all that was owed to them and to send a delegation to Yaoundé on 4 September to negotiate with the government and the CTE management.[29]

During the meeting on 4 September, the Minister of Labour, Prof. Robert Nkili, tried to solve the problems on the Ndu Tea Estate by setting up a tripartite committee to calculate workers' benefits and define the financial responsibilities of the CTE management and the government. The committee later proposed an amount of about FCFA 181 million.[30] The workers immediately rejected the offer as being way below their expectations. They pointed out that the Tole Tea Estate beneficiaries, who were far fewer in number than they themselves, had been offered a much higher sum. They also vehemently disapproved of the fact that only 565 of the 863 permanent and contract workers were on the list for payment. When the Governor for the North West Province, Koumpa Issa, delivered the money to Ndu on 5 October, he met stiff resistance from the workers who simply refused to accept their benefits.[31]

The divisional administration then called on the Provincial Delegate of Labour for the North West Province, Simon Ade Fru, to mediate in the matter. After a lengthy exchange with the strikers on 11 October, they were advised to collect the money being offered. If any of them disagreed with the calculation of his/her personal benefits, s/he could file a complaint in the law courts.[32]

Soon afterwards, one of the principal workers' spokesmen, Francis Kolle, went to Yaoundé where he handed over a memorandum to the Minister of Labour listing what the workers thought was owed to them. A workers' committee had calculated this to be a sum of over FCFA 2.9 billion.[33]

164

In the meantime, it was discovered that seven men and one woman had betrayed the workers' cause by secretly collecting their dues at the Ndu Subdivisional treasury. On 17 October, striking workers visited the homes of these blacklegs with mock coffins and crosses, performed burial rites on their door steps and inscribed 'may your soul rest in peace' on their doors. They later set fire to the coffins that contained magic objects, and the workers were requested to swear an oath over the ashes while vowing not to collect their money. As a result of this action, the divisional administration stated that the strike's ringleaders were to face trial on charges of life-threatening behaviour. Subsequently, it intensified its tactics of intimidation, bringing pressure to bear on them to stop the strike and accept the amount of financial benefit they had previously rejected. Their refusal to submit was perceived as an act of stubbornness, and the administration regularly threatened to call in troops to crush the strike.[34]

On 23 November, 16 workers' representatives, who had been acting as spokesmen for their colleagues, resigned after the DO for Ndu Subdivision, John Mkong Yorisombom, banned meetings between them and the CTE management. Apparently, the DO's banning order came in the wake of a meeting between workers' representatives and CTE management that almost degenerated into a bloody confrontation.[35] A few weeks later, four of them were arrested and tortured.[36]

Relations between the strikers and the divisional administration became more strained when the workers decided to intensify their strike action until they were paid what they thought rightly belonged to them. On 28 November, a protest march was organised by the striking workers, their families and dependents. This was followed by heavy beehives being brought in to reinforce the road blockade between Bamenda and Nkambe in an attempt to forestall the anticipated arrival of some 1,000 workers from the Ndwara and Djuttitsa tea estates.[37]

The next day, the SDO for Donga-Mantung Division, Godlive Mboke Ntua, issued an ultimatum to the strikers. It was broadcast several times on Donga-Mantung Community Radio and branded the workers as a group of recalcitrant fellows who had refused to be brought to reason and were still confronting the divisional administration. He urged them to collect their dues before re-engaging in further negotiations with the CTE management. He stressed that it was ridiculous to claim, as the workers had previously done, an amount of around FCFA 3 billion while the CTE had only paid FCFA 1.5 billion to purchase the three tea estates.[38]

The strikers, however, turned a deaf ear to the SDO's ultimatum. While continuing to man their road blockade, they marched in the night of 29 November to the houses of the CTE estate manager, Falalou Mohammed, and the Ndu Workers' Club president, Joseph Koni, taking both hostage and forcing them to take part in their nocturnal demonstrations.

Violent clashes took place between the strikers and the forces of law and order on 1 and 2 December. The troops first attempted to protect some eight saw operators who had been charged with cutting up the eucalyptus trees that had been used by the strikers to block the ring road. They subsequently attempted to escort truckloads of workers from Ndawara and Djuttitsa that were on the way to the Ndu Tea Estate. Two workers were killed and several others were injured during these confrontations.[39]

Following these dramatic developments, the Minister of Labour felt once again obliged to intervene to resolve the deepening crisis on the estate. He organised another tripartite meeting in Yaoundé on 6 December. After a long and heated debate, it was agreed that workers would accept that their financial dues had been calculated in conformity with the labour laws and regulations in force. Any amounts that were being contested by the workers were to be re-examined by the SDO for the Donga-Mantung Division, a representative of the Ministry of Labour and the CTE management. Since not all the personal financial benefits owed had been wrongly calculated, workers should begin receiving their dues individually. Although the usual punishment for illegal strike actions as stipulated in the Labour Code was the dismissal of the participant(s), the CTE management agreed to keep on all the workers for the sake of peace. The Minister of Labour then requested that all workers resume work immediately, promising that all outstanding grievances would be handled within a year.[40] While the workers' representatives voiced dissatisfaction with the outcome of the meeting, they eventually felt compelled to agree to it due to the state's persistent intimidating tactics, arbitrary arrests, torture and killings. Payment of the financial dues started on 29 December.[41]

It took some time before work resumed on the Ndu Tea Estate since those workers, who had expressed their willingness to continue working for the CTE had to wait to sign permanent contracts. However many strikers refused to resume work because of the maltreatment they had suffered at the hands of the CTE management. Others feared going back because of the desecration inflicted on the estate by the strikers in the form of sorcery and witchcraft.

In January 2007, the Ndu elite held their first meeting after the crisis on the Ndu Tea Estate. They stressed that bringing in workers from other areas was tantamount to provoking local workers and held that the chiefs' right of cleansing and purifying the land could only be effectively carried out in the presence of the workers who had desecrated the estate. In addition, they called on the administrative authorities to release the financial data on the workers' payments to facilitate reconciliation and to set up an *ad-hoc* committee to review any contested financial data. They successfully persuaded the divisional administration and the CTE management to release detainees and withdraw the 'imported' workers from the estate. However, the divisional administration ignored their request to remove the forces of law and order from the estate in order to 'facilitate dialogue and enable the workers to resume work'.[42]

## Conclusion

This study of the privatisation of the CDC estates in Anglophone Cameroon illustrates how externally imposed privatisation schemes have often been opposed by African governments, civil-society organisations and workers alike. Cameroonian government officials have regularly attempted to postpone and manipulate the implementation of schemes that challenge the stabilising and uniting patronage systems in the weak nation state, undermine their limited popular legitimacy and provoke ethno-regional and workers' protests. Although heavy dependence on western donors for continued financial assistance eventually forced them to comply, they attempted to sell state corporations, like the CDC, to foreign companies and nationals closely allied with the regime at giveaway prices in return for considerable kickbacks.

Having been excluded from the decision-making process, civil-society organisations in Anglophone Cameroon strongly contested attempts to privatise the CDC. Ethno-regional organisations feared losing control of their ancestral lands and regional economic heritage, whilst trade unions feared retrenchments and a deterioration in workers' conditions of service.

There is ample evidence that the most militant opposition to the privatisation of the CDC estates came from the workers. Chapter 3 explained the main reasons for their remarkable solidarity and militancy in spite of their internal divisions. It would be wrong to conclude that the Tole and Ndu workers' militant actions against the privatisation of the CDC derived from their opposition to privatisation *per se*. Their leaders told me that workers would support privatisation if it was expected to improve the company's efficiency and workers' conditions of service. They stressed that workers had become vehemently opposed to the privatisation of the CDC for the following reasons:

- They disapproved of the CDC's privatisation because the CDC continued to have the reputation of being one of the few relatively well-managed parastatals. This helps explain their frequent demands during the disastrous privatisation exercise for a return to the mother company.
- They strongly condemned the secretive and corrupt nature of the CDC privatisation as well as the blatant absence of any consultation of workers and trade unions in the process.
- Above all, they quickly discovered that the new owners' promise to safeguard and even improve workers' rights and benefits was not going to be respected. Confronted with unbearable living and working conditions after privatisation, they gradually lost interest in keeping their jobs at any cost and resumed informal collective actions. Determined to receive all their accrued benefits before resigning, they engaged in protracted strike actions that paralysed all the estate's activities.

In sharp contrast to popular resistance to neo-liberal reforms in some African countries (cf. Zeilig 2002), Tole and Ndu workers received little support from civil-society organisations in the region that claimed to be equally opposed to the privatisation of the CDC, in particular the trade unions and various Anglophone associations. Management banned trade unionism from the estates and the Anglophone associations seemed to be first and foremost preoccupied with their own specific grievances. Given these circumstances, the militant actions of the Tole and Ndu workers were bound to remain local expressions of anger and outrage.

There was only one notable example in Cameroon of a broader coalition of popular forces against privatisation practices. This occurred after the takeover of *La Société Nationale d'Electricité* (Sonel) in 2001 by the American multinational AES-Sirocco, which dismally failed to keep its promise of guaranteeing an uninterrupted supply of electricity. Various parts of the country suffered from electricity rationing and regular power cuts, which resulted in a reduction in economic output and hardship for consumers. This, together with excessive increases in the price of electricity and massive lay-offs, led to strikes and boycotts by workers and numerous demonstrations and court cases by consumers. Although workers and consumers eventually failed to achieve the departure of the Americans, they were able to gain important concessions from the privatised company, including the recruitment of new workers, better conditions of service, increased investments in regular power supplies and the replacement of American top managers by Cameroonians (Konings 2007a).

## Notes

1. There are more detailed studies on workers' responses to privatisation in the southern part of Africa. See Larmer (2005, 2007), Pitcher 2002) and Zeilig (2002).

2. See *The Herald*, 20 October 2002.

3. See *The Post*, 8 August 2006.

4. For all the BLCC actions described in this study, see the BLCC website: http://www.bakwerilands.org. See also *The Herald*, 8 and 22 January 2003.

5. Interview with a woman picker on the Tole Tea Estate, 21 November 2002.

6. Interview with a Francophone CTE manager at the Tole Tea Estate, 13 December 2002.

7. Interview with Mathias Anyacheck, staff representative at the Tole Tea Estate, 29 November 2003. For press reports on this strike, see *The Herald*, 6 January 2003 and *Le Messager*, 9 January 2003.

8. Interview with staff representatives at the Tole Tea Estate, 29 October 2003. For a report of this strike, see *The Herald*, 18 June 2003.

9. Interview with a tea picker at the Tole Tea Estate, 29 October 2003.

10. See *The Post*, 20 October 2003.

11. *The Post*, 13 September 2004.

12. *The Post*, 25 October 2004; *The Herald*, 1 November 2004.

13. *The Post*, 13 September 2005.

14. *The Post*, 25 January 2006.

15. *The Post*, 17 March 2007.

16. Interview with Blasius Mosoke at the Tole Tea Estate, 15 March 2006. See also *The Post*, 25 September 2006.

17. *Le Messager*, 30 March 2006; and *Cameroon Tribune*, 12 April 2006.

18. *The Post*, 29 April 2006 and 16 August 2006; and *Cameroon Tribune*, 12 April 2006.

19. *The Post*, 19 April 2006.

20. *The Post*, 1 May 2006.

21. *The Post*, 8 August 2006.

22. *The Post*, 8 August and 12 September 2006.

23. *The Post*, 8 August 2006.

24. *The Post*, 15 September 2006.

25. *The Post*, 20 October 2006.

26. *Herald Today*, 7 November 2004.

27. *The Herald*, 9-10 March 2005, p. 3.

28. *The Post*, 30 September 2006.

29. *Ibid*; and *Le Messager*, 5 September 2006.

30. *Le Messager*, 9 October 2006; and *The Post*, 12 October 2006.

31. *The Post*, 12 October 2006.

32. *The Post*, 19 October 2006.

33. *Ibid*.

34. *The Post*, 3 November 2006.

35. *The Post*, 26 November 2006.

36. *The Post*, 17 December 2006.

37. *The Post*, 30 November 2006.

38. *The Post*, 3 December 2006.

39. *Ibid*.

40. *The Post*, 16 December 2006 and 6 January 2007; and *La Nouvelle Expression*, 8 December 2006.

41. *The Post*, 6 January 2007.

42. *The Post*, 13 January 2007.

# 7

# CDC smallholder development and the agro-industrial crisis

## Introduction

In some post-colonial states there has been a shift from plantation production to smallholder production. This is clearly the case in Kenya where the area devoted to tea by smallholders increased by about 250% during the 1970s, while the area under tea on estates displayed only a slight increase (cf. Swainson 1985). This shift is quite remarkable as it had often been assumed that large-scale, 'modern' estates were more likely to meet the imperatives of increased output and capital accumulation than 'archaic', low-production peasant agriculture. One of the main reasons for this shift seems to be that a growing number of the predominantly foreign-dominated agro-industrial enterprises have been determined to withdraw from plantation production in response to the changing political and economic situation in the post-colonial era. Confronted in newly independent states with difficulties over the ownership of land and problems concerning recruitment and controlling an increasingly costly labour force, they usually prefer to abandon their risky plantation operations and concentrate instead on potentially more lucrative activities like supplying the technical, managerial and marketing skills required to produce, process and sell plantation products (Kirk 1987; Konings 1993a). Consequently, these enterprises are opting for contract farming schemes as an attractive alternative to plantation production (cf. Glover 1984; Goldsmith 1985; Clapp 1988).

Contract farming is a way of organising agricultural production whereby smallholders or out-growers supply produce to agro-industrial enterprises in accordance with the conditions specified in a written or oral contract. These enterprises, in turn, may supply inputs, credit and technical advice as well as undertaking processing and marketing (cf. Minot 1986). A growing number of governments in developing countries and international aid and lending organisations such as COMDEV and the World Bank are actively supporting these schemes, which they see as an important contribution to the local peasantry's (further) integration into the capitalist system and a way of helping increase in their productivity and raise their standard of living (cf. Stryker 1979; Payer 1980; van de Laar 1980; Williams 1981; Ellman 1986). Watts (1986: 4-5) estimates that more than 60 contract farming schemes involving 16 commodities are currently operating in Africa.

Cameroon constitutes a notable exception to this current trend. The government has regularly stated that the established agro-industrial enterprises should play an important intermediary role in the further integration of the local peasantry into the capitalist mode of production:

> The systematic integration of the peasantry into the agro-industrial chain will result in the diversification of its production and the modernisation of its production techniques. It will give rise to the establishment of a class of well-to-do and dynamic farmers, committed to their jobs, and anxious to extend and improve their activities. It may also create gainful employment for the rural youth and motivate them to stay in the rural areas.[1]

In practice, however, it has continued to stimulate the expansion of agro-industrial and, of late, medium-sized plantations without paying any serious attention to the creation of contract farming schemes associated with agro-industrial enterprises (Konings 1993a). The CDC is one of the few (plantation-based) agro-industrial enterprises in Cameroon that have been encouraged by the government to set up various forms of contract farming schemes since its foundation in 1946/47. In 1968 it was transformed into a 'development corporation' by the government (Tchala Abina 1989) and charged with the responsibility of 'assisting smallholders or groups of them engaged in the cultivation of crops similar to those cultivated by itself in the collection area of the mills it managed'.[2] In 1973 President Ahidjo reminded the CDC's management of the role it was expected to play in the 'encadrement' of the peasantry near its estates:

The CDC is an important agro-industrial complex. It must stand out as an example to, and stimulate progress within, the population in the vicinity of its plantations. The local people, in turn, should aspire to establish satellite smallholdings around these plantations where they could learn and implement modern farming methods and techniques.[3]

And in 1977/78, the government ordered the corporation to implement a limited contract farming scheme that had been planned by the corporation's international financiers, particularly the World Bank.

There are different views in the literature of the development potential of contract farming schemes. Modernisation theorists tend to be strong advocates of contract farming, seeing it as a significant trajectory of capital accumulation in the rural areas as it effectively combines agro-industry's management capacity, capital resources, modern technology and marketing facilities with the smallholders' control of land and labour (cf. Morrissy 1974; Kusterer 1981, 1982; Williams & Karen 1984). Morrissy (1974) claimed that contract farming could lead to the development of a stable and politically conservative class of well-to-do farmers in the rural areas. Dependency theorists, on the contrary, are highly critical of contract farming and view it as one of those evil schemes devised by foreign capital and a *comprador* elite that will inevitably result in a deepening dependency of developing countries on the capitalist core and an increasing exploitation and immiseration of the rural poor (cf. Feder 1977a, 1977b; Lappé & Collins 1977; Dinham & Hines 1983). Scholars who have studied contract farming schemes in Kenya have attempted to create a synthesis between the modernisation and dependency perspectives (cf. Buch-Hansen & Marcusen 1982; Cowen 1981; Currie & Ray 1986). They assert that contract farming can give rise to a growing subsumption of the peasantry to capital and state, and still produce the conditions for the emergence of either a rich or middle peasantry.

These conflicting views can be helpful in evaluating the impact of the CDC's various smallholder schemes but they also have some serious shortcomings. First of all, they tend to concentrate on the relations of exchange between the two parties, ignoring the process of production itself. This largely explains why they fail to discuss one of the most essential preconditions for capital accumulation in contract farming schemes: the establishment of managerial control over the labour process. Agro-industrial enterprises try to procure a reliable supply of high-quality and relatively cheap agricultural commodities. This objective is unlikely to be achieved unless management is capable of gaining control of the processes of production and exchange. And secondly, these theories treat smallholders as the passive victims or beneficiaries of capital and state and deny them an active role in shaping their own destiny. I will instead show that (i) CDC smallholders have never resigned themselves to their control and exploitation in the labour process, and (ii) even intensified their modes of resistance during the agro-industrial crisis when their chances of capital accumulation were seriously threatened.

This chapter evaluates the role of CDC smallholders in two separate periods. The first was when the old scheme was in operation from the corporation's foundation in 1946/47 until the World Bank's introduction of a new scheme in 1977/78. The second period was that of the new scheme from 1977/78 until 1994/95 when the corporation began to recover from its economic crisis.

## Smallholder development at the CDC, 1946/47-1977/78

The first attempts to plan and execute a smallholder scheme attached to the CDC were made soon after the corporation's foundation in 1946/47. This scheme, which was closely connected to the Bakweri land problem, was proposed by W.M. Bridges, one of the British administrators in the Southern Cameroons (see Chapter 5). However, his proposals were never implemented as the Bakweri Land Committee (BLC) refused to cooperate with the government and the CDC management until its claims regarding CDC lands had been recognised.[4]

Another attempt followed in the wake of the expansion of banana production in the area in the early 1950s (Bederman 1971). Initially, its chances of success appeared bleak. Although the former German owners used to purchase bananas grown on smallholdings near their estates and export them along with their own produce, the CDC management refused to give in to frequent requests for such assistance on the part of local producers. According to Epale (1978: 76-77), it tended to justify its unfavourable response on the following grounds: (i) the previously limited size of peasant banana production; (ii) the absence of any strong organisation among producers that could act as a broker between the corporation and producers in the process of exchange, and (iii) its fear that encouraging the production of peasant cash crops might aggravate the already existing shortage of locally produced foodstuffs, a problem which was responsible for persistent labour unrest on the corporation's own estates. Underlying these official reasons was the belief prevalent in government and management circles that Bakweri peasants were lazy, unproductive and incapable of taking entrepreneurial initiatives (Courade 1981/82).

This conflict between the CDC management and the smallholders was finally settled following the personal intervention of Dr E.M.L. Endeley, one of the outstanding Bakweri and nationalist leaders and a member of the CDC Board of Directors at the time (Chiabi 1982). The latter was eventually able to enlist the support of the government and the CDC management for a bold plan that aimed at an increased commercialisation of peasant banana production. To this end, he founded the Bakweri Co-operative Union of Farmers (BCUF) in August 1952 and concluded a market agreement with the corporation (cf. Ardener 1958; Epale 1978). Under the terms of that agreement, the CDC was prohibited from making profit on transactions with the BCUF but it was allowed to recover handling charges from the cooperative. Due to uncertainty about the quality of the cooperative's bananas, it was agreed that the CDC would pay the BCUF, on delivery of its crop, two-thirds of the price that the corporation itself had obtained for its carefully graded fruit. However, if the cooperative's supplies turned out to be of satisfactory quality, the difference, less handling charges, was to be paid out by the corporation to the cooperative in the form of an annual bonus, which would serve as working capital for the BCUF's further expansion. The corporation marketed BCUF supplies between 1952 and 1957, when it was compelled to hand over the business to Elders & Fyffes due to its inability to handle the growing supplies of produce (cf. Heinzen 1984). During this period, the scheme gave rise to rapid capital accumulation among Bakweri banana producers. It proved without any doubt that the local peasantry was capable of raising production and undertaking entrepreneurial activities (see Ardener 1970; Geschiere 1988).

A renewed attempt to plan and execute a smallholders' scheme attached to the CDC was made after reunification in 1961. In 1964, the CDC management invited a mission from COMDEV headed by R.J.M. Swynnerton to draft a long-term development plan for the corporation. In its report, it advised the corporation to set up a variety of smallholder rubber, oil palm and tea schemes and to extend its role in smallholder development from exchange to production: the regular supply of inputs, credit and technical advice as well as strict supervision of the labour process (Swynnerton *et al.* 1964; see also Epale 1985: 183-85). COMDEV played a pioneering role in promoting this so-called nucleus/core-satellite contract farming model in developing countries (cf. Rendell 1976; Ellman 1986) and Swynnerton himself was prominent in introducing it in several countries, including Kenya (cf. Sorrenson 1967; Heyer 1981).

The 1964 Swynnerton Mission Report proposed that the CDC not only establish smallholder schemes attached to its own estates and factories but that it should also assist in the setting-up of 'nucleus satellite' schemes in remoter areas. It also recommended the installation of a Smallholder Development Authority by the West Cameroonian government that would be responsible for the planning and execution of smallholder schemes in the territory. Its arguments for the encouragement of smallholder development sound familiar to anyone acquainted with the modernisation theory on contract farming:

> CDC and the government would in this way secure further development of land at present lying idle and they would create a type of *middle-class farmer* growing crops and earning incomes at a level well above the general level of farming in West Cameroon. This should act as an example and incentive to the large number of peasant farmers whose farming is at present relatively unproductive.[5]

Apparently, it preferred recruiting potential participants for the scheme from among the more privileged sections of the rural population: 'selection of settlers should be based on their being married men, preferably having had some education and some previous experience with the crop and having some initial capital'.[6]

In October 1964, a special committee of West Cameroonian government representatives and the CDC management discussed the Swynnerton Mission Report's recommendations. It claimed that the proposed smallholder schemes would ensure the emergence of an agrarian middle class that could contribute to political stability:

> It stressed that the stability of the country would require the evolution of an independent middle class. The present situation when a white-collar civil service was emerging was considered to be unsatisfactory. The projected Smallholder Scheme would ensure the emergence of an agrarian middle class and was therefore commendable.[7]

In 1965 the West Cameroonian government appointed a Smallholder Development Committee under the chairmanship of V.C. Nchami, then Permanent Secretary to the Ministry of Development and Internal Economic Planning, pending the formation of a Smallholder Development Authority (SDA). Between 1965 and 1967/68 this committee tried to implement one of the smallholder schemes recommended by the Swynnerton Mission Report, the Mbonge Smallholder Rubber Scheme, and set up the Smallholder Development Authority.[8] Unfortunately, these projects had to be postponed indefinitely when the federal government refused to grant the financial support needed.[9] By then the federal government had come to the conclusion that an expansion of agro-industrial estate production was more likely to meet the imperatives of increased agricultural output and capital accumulation than smallholder development (Konings 1993a: 28-31).

It is interesting to observe that, despite the indefinite postponement of the Swynnerton Mission's proposals, the CDC became increasingly involved in smallholder development. By 1967/ 68 its assistance was requested for a smallholder oil palm and rubber scheme that had been initiated by the producers themselves and come into existence during the rapid decline of banana production after the achievement of independence and reunification (cf. Bederman 1971). On the BCUF's advice, a number of banana growers started to diversify production and invest their accumulated capital in crops like rubber and oil palms. The only advice they received on crop cultivation was from the government of West Cameroon, in particular the Departments of Agriculture and Co-operatives. When some of the established oil palm and rubber farms reached maturity in 1967/68, these departments arrived at an agreement with the CDC management that the corporation would transport, process and market the smallholders' produce (for their output, see Table 7.1).[10]

The vast majority of these smallholders were peasants who grew oil palms and rubber in addition to other crops and their holdings tended to be quite small. It is estimated that the approximately 3,000 members of the South West Province Oil Palm Smallholders' Co-operative cultivated no more than a total area of 4,000 hectares.[11] They predominantly used family labour but for heavy farm operations, like land development, they either called on mutual work groups called *njangis* (cf. Kleis 1975; DeLancey 1977) or employed casual labour. Their farms were scattered across the South West Province and the CDC management found it an arduous, expensive and time-consuming undertaking to provide them with effective assistance in the form of inputs, technical advice and transport.[12]

In addition to these small producers, there were a few bigger producers who owned farms varying from about 10 ha to 150 ha in size. The largest among them belonged to various sections of the Anglophone elite including well-known politicians, chiefs, top civil servants, CDC managers and directors, and businessmen such as Dr E.M.L. Endeley, E.K. Martin, E.A. Mbiwan, Chief V. Mukete and Chief S.O. Ebanja. They tended to be absentee farmers who left the day-to-day running of their farms to farm managers, usually their own sons. They employed permanent and casual workers, with the actual number depending on the size of their farms. Generally speaking, they maintained their farms better than small producers and sold higher quality produce to the CDC.

Table 7.1 *Output of CDC estates and smallholders, 1971-1995 (M.T.)*

| YEAR | CDC RUBBER | | CDC PALM OIL | | CDC PALM KERNELS | |
|------|--------|-------------|--------|-------------|--------|-------------|
|      | Estate | Small-holder | Estate | Small-holder | Estate | Small-holder |
| 1971 | 8,231  | 64    | 10,129 | 63    | 2,457 | 19  |
| 1972 | 8,894  | 106   | 11,611 | 72    | 3,007 | 22  |
| 1973 | 9,738  | 122   | 13,094 | 41    | 3,233 | 13  |
| 1974 | 10,205 | 172   | 18,286 | 516   | 4,617 | 154 |
| 1975 | 10,154 | 169   | 18,488 | 747   | 3,955 | 162 |
| 1976 | 10,545 | 151   | 21,618 | 507   | 4,294 | 101 |
| 1977 | 11,631 | 146   | 22,263 | 264   | 3,602 | 42  |
| 1978 | 12,062 | 183   | 24,565 | 469   | 3,557 | 67  |
| 1979 | 11,460 | 207   | 18,886 | 285   | 2,825 | 38  |
| 1980 | 12,413 | 243   | 21,453 | 443   | 3,261 | 70  |
| 1981 | 12,831 | 221   | 23,315 | 544   | 3,231 | 78  |
| 1982 | 12,182 | 180   | 22,000 | 501   | 2,479 | 64  |
| 1983 | 11,575 | 152   | 20,671 | 515   | 3,528 | 77  |
| 1984 | 11,409 | 313   | 17,914 | 579   | 3,307 | 95  |
| 1985 | 13,262 | 434   | 22,735 | 929   | 3,841 | 151 |
| 1986 | 13,860 | 350   | 26,520 | 1,691 | 4,453 | 289 |
| 1987 | 16,694 | 298   | 25,155 | 1,546 | 4,914 | 303 |
| 1988 | 17,851 | 354   | 21,428 | 2,283 | 4,252 | 454 |
| 1989 | 19,227 | 711   | 20,062 | 1,464 | 4,126 | 296 |
| 1990 | 18,944 | 749   | 21,373 | 1,414 | 4,122 | 271 |
| 1991 | 19,157 | 734   | 18,080 | 1,286 | 3,565 | 253 |
| 1992 | 23,249 | 975   | 14,335 | 1,238 | 2,887 | 247 |
| 1993 | 22,682 | 924   | 21,354 | 1,394 | 4,490 | 297 |
| 1994 | 24,197 | 1,283 | 12,897 | 1,407 | 2,500 | 282 |
| 1995 | 22,590 | 2,148 | 7,821  | 1,177 | 1,437 | 225 |

*Source*: CDC Annual Reports and Accounts, 1971-1995

Relations between bigger and smaller producers were not always without conflict. The bigger producers managed to appropriate vast lands in areas suitable for oil-palm production with the aid of the traditional authorities and the state but at the expense of the local peasantry. There was one famous case in 1966 when E.A. Mbiwan, the former general manager at the West Cameroon Electricity Corporation, acquired a vast area of land from the Victoria Traditional Council in Batoke, a village on the West Coast. In 1968, peasant cultivators were subsequently driven from the land and, in spite of relentless peasant protest, Mbiwan started his Bonanza Estate on this land growing various crops, including 135 ha of oil palms.[13] Nevertheless it would appear that these internal contradictions did not prevent the smallholders from pursuing *common* interests, namely achieving more assistance and, above all, a higher producer price from the corporation. It is therefore not surprising that smaller producers were willing to join a regional cooperative formed and led by big producers. The South West Province Oil Palm Smallholders' Co-operative was founded in the early 1970s and claimed to represent and defend the interests of all smallholders against the CDC management and the state.

From the very start, there was conflict between the CDC management and producers about producer prices. Both the larger and smaller producers constantly claimed that their incomes were not high enough to compensate for increasing production and transport costs. As the CDC management declined to guarantee smallholders regular transport facilities,[14] most of them experienced serious difficulties in transporting their produce to the CDC's mills. Hire charges of private transport often proved to be exorbitant and delays in procuring transport resulted in considerable losses among perishable fruit crops.[15] Smallholders were obliged to pay at least CDC rates to hire labour and even the largest producers were often unable to pay their workers, including Chief Victor Mukete, who became the largest smallholder in the South West Province during his time as Chairman of the CDC. His workers, estimated to number about 400 in 1982, frequently resorted to strike action in protest at delays in the payment of wages.[16] The following case study of the former chairman of the South West Province Oil Palm Smallholders' Co-operative, Chief Ebanja, illustrates the predicament facing larger smallholders.

# Case No. 7.1 *A large oil-palm producer and cooperative leader*

Chief Ebanja served as a senior civil servant in the Governor's Office in Buea before becoming the Paramount Chief of the Balong. He lives in Mukonje in Meme Division and owns several farms, one of which is a relatively large oil palm plantation in Malende, a Balong village near Muyuka in Fako Division.

He acquired the land in Malende in 1961. Belonging to the Balong royal family and as a civil servant, he was allocated more than 40 ha of forest land in this village in spite of a serious shortage of land there. He first grew food crops and vegetables but then switched to oil palm cultivation. Between 1970 and 1980 he planted 25 ha of oil palms with the help of family labour and nine permanent workers. His eldest son, who lives in Malende, manages the farm.

In 1975 he decided to sell his produce to the CDC. His farm was subsequently surveyed by CDC technical staff who also gave him technical advice during his first three harvests. However, he remained responsible for transporting his produce to the nearest CDC mill, the Mondoni mill, some 30 km from Malende.

His oil palms have not been very profitable so far. In fact, he incurred a loss of about FCFA 1 million, between 1971 and 1980 which he attributed to high production and transportation costs, and low yields and prices. He used savings from when he was a senior civil servant to cover this loss.

While President of the South West Province Oil Palm Smallholders' Co-operative, he forwarded several petitions to the CDC's management in which he complained about its lack of assistance to smallholders and the low remuneration it offered for their labour. He claimed that the CDC management has victimised him because he champions the smallholders' cause. The corporation seized part of his land, denied him transport facilities and regularly rejected his produce.[17] Along with the large majority of smallholders, he often 'regrets having embarked on oil palm cultivation in answer to government directives'.[18]

Dissatisfied with the producer price offered by the corporation, smallholders have frequently engaged in collective informal protest actions. The South West Province Oil Palm Smallholders' Co-operative has petitioned the state and the CDC management, complaining bitterly about its members' predicament and demanding an increase in producer prices. Its leadership has sometimes been victimised for these actions, as the case study of Chief Ebanja demonstrates.

The cooperative's leaders tried to capitalise on their long-established contacts within the regional state apparatus. When the regional authorities were informed of the precarious situation of the smallholders, they tried to mediate on their behalf. However the CDC management refused to give in to their requests to negotiate with smallholders on producer prices. This is evident from the following report written by the economic adviser to the Governor of the South West Province in 1979:

> The Oil Palm Smallholders have for a long time been fighting a battle with the CDC on the price they receive for their palm nuts which they consider low at any given moment. In studying this problem we have often found them justified and have pleaded with the CDC to review their stand. The rate of price increases from the CDC has been at such piece meal that it has never seemed to satisfy the smallholders as they claim that they can hardly break even. On the other hand, the CDC has proved to be rather dictatorial, admitting no dialogue whatsoever in their dealings implying that either the smallholders take it or leave it. Thus defeating the provisions whereby they pledged to assist the small farmers around their plantations.[19]

The CDC management continued to claim that its smallholder and price policies were backed by the government and that it was paying producers a fair price. For example, at a meeting with the Governor of the South West Province on 7 July 1975, the CDC General Manager, J.N. Ngu stated that:

> the corporation had to operate in accordance with the terms of reference defined by the government. It was required to cooperate with government's policy of smallholder development.

184

Consequently, it was not out to make any profit on the smallholders but to pay them the full value of their oil after deducting necessary expenses. On the other hand, it had to operate on commercial lines and not to dash out or lose money unnecessarily. Therefore, it would not increase any prices to the smallholders unless it was economically possible.[20]

And again, on 27 July 1983, he wrote the following to the Secretary of the South West Province Oil Palm Smallholders' Co-operative:

> While I sympathise with the difficulties you are facing in running your various plantations, it is not possible for the corporation to pay you more money than it realises from the processing and marketing of your produce. We produce each year a statement of the actual amount the corporation realises on the marketing of both CDC and smallholder produce and the price you are paid is the *actual average price obtained for local and export sale of palm produce*, less processing, administrative and depreciation costs.[21]

As soon as it became clear that the CDC management was simply ignoring the cooperative's demands, smallholders resorted to a variety of informal actions in protest. They neglected farm maintenance, refused to make any further investments in expanded production, and supplied low-quality produce to the corporation's factories. Some even stopped delivering produce to the corporation, processing the palm fruit themselves in the traditional way – an undertaking that is quite tedious and results in low extraction rates (cf. Tjeega 1973) – and selling the oil at the local markets. A few completely withdrew from the scheme. CDC management, in turn, interpreted these actions as evidence of the smallholders' lack of entrepreneurship and their unwillingness to follow its instructions concerning production and exchange. For this reason, it decided to exclude these smallholders from a new scheme that was to be implemented within the framework of a CDC development programme financed by the Cameroonian government, the World Bank, COMDEV and the Central Fund for Economic Cooperation (CCCE), the so-called CAMDEV II project (1978-1982) (see

Konings 1993a: 42-44). This scheme was planned by the World Bank to strengthen management control of the processes of production and exchange. It should, however, be noted that the previous scheme continued to operate alongside the new scheme.

## Smallholder development at the CDC, 1977/78-1994/95

In its 1977 Appraisal Report of the CAMDEV II project,[22] the World Bank recommended the corporation take a more active role in smallholder development. It advocated the introduction of a smallholder scheme based on the 1964 Swynnerton Mission Report's contract farming model, with considerable managerial control of the processes of production and exchange. However, contrary to the report, it insisted on focusing on rural low-income groups rather than on richer and more progressive peasants.

The report proposed that the corporation assist in setting-up about 1,000 ha of smallholder rubber and 1,000 ha of smallholder oil palms during the CAMDEV II period (1978-1982). The programme was to be funded by the financiers of the CAMDEV II project as follows: the Cameroonian government was to contribute US$ 1 million, the World Bank US$ 1.1 million; and COMDEV and CCCE US$ 0.6 million each. The allocated funds were to be channelled through the National Fund for Rural Development (FONADER) to the CDC, with the latter acting as the transmitting agent between FONADER and the scheme's participants. The CDC was also charged with setting up a Smallholders' Unit that would manage the scheme.

Any candidate who wanted to join the scheme was requested to sign a contract with the CDC,[23] which laid down the conditions for participation and the obligations of the contracting parties. It aimed at correcting the shortcomings of the old scheme and enhancing managerial control over the processes of production and exchange.

The most important conditions for participation were that candidates have Cameroonian nationality and derive at least 75% of their income from farming. They had to be between 25 and 40 years of age and fit enough physically to set up a farm, although older persons who had access to (family) labour might also qualify. As stipulated in the contract, they had to own land that was suitable for either oil palm or rubber cultivation within a 30 km radius of a CDC oil mill or rubber factory and that was less than 500 m from a road accessible to CDC vehicles. There also had to be a land-use right of a minimum of 24 years. And finally, they had to have the corporation's official approval for participation in the scheme.

The mutual obligations of the two contracting parties were as follows. Participants in the scheme should (i) carry out punctually all instructions given by the CDC management in the labour process, (ii) attend all meetings called by the CDC management for training and farm management purposes, (iii) sell all their produce to the corporation, and (iv) settle 'scrupulously' all their debts with the corporation. The CDC's management, in turn, would provide participants with the necessary inputs, technical advice and supervision. These services were to be offered on credit and had to be repaid in instalments after the plants had started to produce. Repayment was to be deducted from the participants' sales to the corporation. In addition, CDC management had to transport participants' output for a fixed price to the factories and process it. Producers were to be paid monthly for their deliveries.

The contract was for a period of 27 years from the year when the land was first cleared. The ultimate sanction for non-compliance with the terms of the contract was the seizure of the farm of any defaulting debtor by FONADER, the scheme's creditor. Following the repayment of all debts incurred, participants were to receive a land certificate from the Survey Department for the area under cultivation.

The scheme's participants were prohibited from developing more than 1 to 2 ha of land in the first year on the assumption that this would be the maximum they could reasonably handle. Depending on their performance, however, they might later be encouraged to expand this to a total of 5 ha of oil palms and 4 ha of rubber, respectively. The World Bank believed this scheme would help create a stable middle peasantry: the amount of land to be cultivated with modern production techniques would be sufficient to provide participants with a higher income than non-participants, thus making them more liable to management control. During the initial maturation period, producers were to receive a non-refundable cash grant of FCFA 56,900 for oil palms and FCFA 108,106 for rubber as compensation for their labour input.[24]

Compared to the old scheme, the new scheme would appear to be a more promising effort on the part of the 'development coalition' (Bates 1981) – the Cameroonian post-colonial state, international finance capital and agro-industry – to incorporate the local peasantry into the capitalist system and subsume it to the imperatives of increased output and capital accumulation. It allowed CDC management to greatly extend its control over the both the means of production and the processes of production and exchange. These and similar schemes have resulted in a substantial loss of peasant autonomy and the virtual emergence of a peculiar form of proletarianisation: they transform the producer into a kind of task worker for agro-industry on his own land (cf. Bernstein 1979; Konings 1986a, 1986b). As Clapp (1988: 16) observed in this respect:

> Contract farming is a form of disguised proletarianisation: it secures the farmer's land and labour, while leaving him/her with formal title to both. The control exercised by the company is indirect but effective; the farmer's control is legal but illusory. In this sense s/he is a 'propertied labourer' – on the one hand a landlord, and on the other a labourer who cares for corporate plants.

The new scheme greatly benefits the corporation with its potential to supply agricultural commodities to the corporation's oil mills and rubber factories at relatively little cost and on a regular basis. On the one hand, almost all the production costs are transferred to the producers because inputs and agricultural services are provided on credit and have to be repaid with interest after delivery of a crop. On the other hand, the corporation is exempted from controlling and paying a large wage-labour force. Moreover, it shifts some of the production risks to the producers as they bear the brunt of poor harvests and price fluctuations on national and international markets. And finally, the new scheme has provided management with the opportunity to present itself as a champion of regional development and establish a group of local allies among those who are directly involved in smallholder schemes (cf. Bates 1981).

Management has always claimed that the new scheme would benefit producers as well. It initially emphasised that the scheme would allow them to diversify their production and obtain inputs, credit facilities, technical advice, a guaranteed market, a regular monthly income throughout the year and substantial improvements in their living standards compared to those of non-participants. Wyrley-Birch *et al.* (1982: 90) estimated the annual net income of participants in the oil palm scheme in 1982 at FCFA 250,000 per hectare of mature palms. This income compared favourably with the wage levels of skilled and unskilled CDC workers, which were estimated at an annual rate of FCFA 240,000 and FCFA 180,000 respectively, and the average peasant income of approximately FCFA 100,000-150,000. Without doubt, if these estimates were correct, any participant with a few hectares of oil palms was likely to become a member of the middle peasantry.

A public announcement was made in the *Cameroon Tribune* of 19 July 1978 that peasants in the vicinity of CDC estates and factories could apply to participate in the scheme. Samuel Ndum, a technical adviser to the Ministry of Agriculture, was subsequently seconded to the CDC to head the newly established Smallholders' Department at Tiko and assumed his duties on 27 November 1978. He immediately held meetings with the more than 100 candidates, over 90% of whom were full-time peasant cultivators who had applied for the scheme. At these meetings it emerged that the scheme was 'poorly understood'. Some applicants had been eager to apply because they thought that participation would facilitate obtaining loans and cash grants but when they realised that loans were to be in the form of inputs and technical advice and that the cash grants were only to be allocated after the completion of certain tasks, they often withdrew their applications (see Table 7.2).

Following an inspection of the remaining applicants' farm lands, approved candidates were registered and organised in groups similar to the traditional *njangi* work groups to promote cooperation on certain arduous farm activities. However, it was also hoped that these groups would function as organs of control over the membership. It was decided that any legal action was only to be considered after the group had failed to discipline and correct the actions of defaulting members. Each group was asked to elect a president, secretary and treasurer. The groups were to be reorganised in the future into a cooperative that could present the interests of all participants to the project management.[25]

Table 7.2 *CDC smallholders' development scheme, 1978/79-1994/95*

| YEAR | AREA UNDER CULTIVATION (HA) | | | NUMBER OF SMALLHOLDERS | | | TOTAL GRANTS & LOANS (FCFA) |
|---|---|---|---|---|---|---|---|
| | Oil palm | Rubber | Total | Oil palm | Rubber | | Total |
| 1978/79 | 25 | 57 | 82 | 15 | 37 | 52 | 11,851,785 |
| 1979/80 | 170 | 214 | 384 | 101 | 136 | 237 | 37,656,609 |
| 1980/81 | 350 | 430 | 780 | 143 | 190 | 333 | 60,631,644 |
| 1981/82 | 383 | 528 | 911 | n.k. | n.k. | 378 | 21,572,000 |
| 1982/83 | 383 | 526 | 909 | n.k. | n.k. | 378 | 19,000,000 |
| 1983/84 | 383 | 526 | 909 | n.k. | n.k. | 378 | 26,000,000 |
| 1984/85 | 467 | 527 | 994 | 147 | 224 | 371 | 7,500,000 |
| 1985/86 | 557 | 737 | 1,294 | 187 | 245 | 432 | 9,700,000 |
| 1986/87 | 557 | 737 | 1,294 | 187 | 245 | 432 | 17,000,000 |
| 1987/88 | 557 | 730 | 1,287 | 186 | 245 | 431 | 12,800,000 |
| 1988/89 | 557 | 730 | 1,287 | 186 | 245 | 431 | 4,700,000 |
| 1989/90 | 557 | 730 | 1,287 | 186 | 245 | 431 | 8,600,000 |
| 1990/91 | 557 | 730 | 1,287 | 186 | 245 | 431 | |
| 1991/92 | 750 | 730 | 1,480 | 187 | 245 | 432 | |
| 1992/93 | 750 | 730 | 1,480 | 187 | 245 | 432 | |
| 1993/94 | 1,405 | 1,990 | 3,395 | 187 | 245 | 432 | |
| 1994/95 | 1,832 | 1,990 | 3,822 | 187 | 245 | 432 | |

*Source:* CDC Smallholders' Development Scheme, Annual Report: Summary 1980/81, in File MINEP/ED/SWP/A/554, Small Palm Holders Scheme; CDC Annual Reports and Accounts, 1978-1995.

Despite all the plans and organisation, the scheme never got off the ground and its performance in the CAMDEV II period (1978-1982) did not meet expectations. By 1982 it had attracted fewer than 378 participants (see Table 7.2) and had failed to reach its cultivation targets: only 38.3% of the planned 1,000 ha of oil palms and 52.8% of the anticipated 1,000 ha of rubber had been achieved. In addition, a large proportion of the cultivated area had been poorly maintained. These disappointing results can be attributed to a number of important factors:[26]

(i) *The restrictions imposed on cultivation.* From an efficiency angle, the CDC's management could be justified in restricting cultivation to lands within a 30 km radius of a CDC mill or factory and close to a passable road. However, this drastically reduced the area available for cultivation and these restrictions were further reinforced in 1982 when the CDC decided to change 'passable' roads to 'tarred' roads.

(ii) *Regular delays in the delivery of agricultural inputs.* There were delays in delivering inputs as the corporation often gave priority to its own estates. For example, in May 1979, participants in the scheme had to postpone planting because the CDC refused to supply any seedlings to the scheme before all its estates had been served. Following this setback, the project started considering the possibility of setting up its own oil palm and rubber nurseries to reduce its dependence on CDC supplies. In the 1983/84 crop year, it finally succeeded in establishing a small oil palm nursery at Tiko.[27]

(iii) *Serious land shortages in the area.* There was a shortage of land because of the very presence of the CDC's estates and the increased settlement of immigrants in the area. Land prices have been constantly on the increase: 1 ha of land sold in 1985/86 for about FCFA 250,000-350,000. As a result, the scheme tended to attract the section of the rural population that was privileged enough to own its (reserve) lands or capital resources, rather than the target group, namely the rural poor. This seems to be substantiated by a survey that I carried out among smallholders in the Balong area of Muyuka Subdivision in 1985/86 when I found that the large majority of participants were the male heads of immigrant families (90%), 65% of whom originated from the Grassfields. This is not surprising if one takes into account the fact that these elders have become the largest and richest peasants in the area. Their almost exclusive participation in the scheme has exacerbated contradictions in the area. There is, first of all, the conflict between the Balong and immigrants about control over land. The Balong have become very resentful of the large-scale immigrant occupation of their ancestral lands, which has given rise to numerous disputes about land rights and has led to serious confrontations between the groups. The Chief of Malende has become one of the main leaders of local opposition. Being at the same time the president of the local smallholders' group, he has refused to supply land to various large-scale Bamileke farmers for rubber cultivation and barred them from joining the scheme. During my interviews, I discovered that some immigrants had joined the scheme with a view to settling and reinforcing their rights to land rather than to developing oil palm and rubber farms.[28] And secondly, there is the conflict between the elders on the one hand and young men and women on the other. The elders do not usually allocate land to young men and women who want to join the scheme but instead employ all the available household members on their own rubber and oil palm farms. This is a continuous source of friction as the young men are anxious to earn an income of their own and the women prefer to work on their own food farms (cf. Carney 1987). Some of the women were very annoyed when their husbands started to create rubber farms on part of their food farms.

(iv) *The obstruction of the scheme by local chiefs.* Quite a number of chiefs demanded large sums of money before signing the required land-use attestations, even though they knew very well that the applicants were land owners in their villagers. Between 1978 and 1980 the scheme seems to have lost 80 potential candidates because of this bottleneck.[29]

(v) *Participants' financial strains.* All the smallholders interviewed complained that the financial assistance offered by the project management did not cover the costs of developing, maintaining, and expanding their farms. The majority (75%) hired labour from time to time. However, the cash grants they received were not sufficient to cover their own labour input during a farm's development, let alone for employing expensive labour. They were often forced to invest their savings in the development and expansion of their farms and to raise loans.

(vi) *Relatively low producer prices.* Initially, the scheme attracted peasants who expected to earn good monthly incomes from rubber and oil palm cultivation. However when producer

192

prices remained far below expectations, potential candidates became hesitant about joining the scheme. Those who had already joined became frustrated but found it difficult to withdraw from the scheme as they had to pay back their loans and lacked the capital necessary to invest in other crops. This general frustration among smallholders is manifest in the following case study.

## Case No. 7.2 *A participant in the new scheme*

This participant is one of many former CDC workers who joined the scheme. He is 45 years old and from Menchum Division in the North West Province. He worked as a rubber tapper on various CDC estates for 15 years. In 1978 he decided to resign in order to join the new scheme. He acquired 2 ha of land from the Chief of Malende and started to develop a rubber farm. He had saved about FCFA 500,000 during his time at the CDC but the amount left after he bought the land was not sufficient to cover the costs of developing his rubber farm. Still, he was able to raise some capital for investment purposes from three sources: his receipt of cash grants from the project management, his regular employment as a casual worker on local cocoa and coffee farms, and his membership of a local rotating credit association (*njangi*).

When he first started tapping in 1985, he was confronted with a drastic fall in the price of rubber. His monthly income has, therefore, never been sufficient to support his family. He deeply regrets resigning from the CDC and joining the scheme. During his time at the CDC, he enjoyed a higher monthly income and a number of benefits including free accommodation and medical care. He claims that the CDC exploits smallholders since it offers low returns on his substantial investments in the scheme and his labour. Moreover, he sees himself as a 'prisoner' of the scheme who is unable to escape because of his investments and debts.

Following an evaluation of the scheme in 1982, international financiers expressed concern about its lack of headway during the CAMDEV II period (1978-1982).[30] Nevertheless, they did not lose faith in the scheme's viability and even recommended expanding the scheme during the subsequent CAMDEV II Oil Palm and

Rubber Consolidation Project between 1982/83 and 1986/87. An additional 500 ha of smallholder oil palms and 1,000 ha of smallholder rubber was planned at an estimated cost of FCFA 1,159 million.

The adverse climate conditions between 1982 and 1984 hindered the planned expansion of the scheme.[31] The number of participants even declined during the 1984/85 crop year from 378 to 371 due to 'abandonments' (see Table 7.2). Dissatisfied with the scheme's slow progress and the deplorable conditions of a number of the participants' farms, the newly appointed expatriate project manager recommended concentrating on expanding the cultivated area by the most committed participants and progressive new recruits with lands adjacent to the existing farms, and developing relatively large lands on project costs. Similar to the tenant purchase schemes proposed by the 1964 Swynnerton Mission Report, these project lands were later to be subdivided into blocks of five ha maximum and sold on credit to selected smallholders.[32] He then presented a new smallholder development programme covering the 1985/86-1987/88 period that aimed at expanding 700 ha of rubber: 500 ha on project account in the village of Ikiliwindi in the Kumba-Mamfe area and 200 ha by committed participants and new recruits. An expansion of 550 ha of oil palms was also planned: 300 ha on project account in the Bakweri village of Ikata near Muyuka, and 250 ha by committed participants and new recruits.

However the severe crisis that affected the CDC from 1986 onwards formed a formidable obstacle to this initiative, and to smallholder development in general. It frustrated any hopes of a substantial expansion of the scheme and the creation of a stable middle peasantry. During the crisis, CDC management found it hard to assist smallholders and, even worse, could not avoid reducing producer prices, especially in the oil palm sector.

Like the participants in the old scheme, members of the new scheme have continued to protest individually and collectively against the fluctuating, and often low, producer prices. For example, in 1986, smallholders in Muyuka Subdivision sent a strongly worded petition to the CDC General Manager protesting at the drastic 50% cut in producer prices during the crisis in the domestic agro-industrial oil palm sector (see Chapter 2). In the petition they stated that:

They believed that the Smallholders' Development Scheme created by the government and placed under the CDC was aimed at uplifting the living standards of the peasant farming families in Cameroon. But the recent slash in the price of their produce had come to them as a surprise... It would appear that they were becoming victims of price cuts in agricultural produce in a country where salaries of workers are regularly increased and the prices of other crops are increased annually with high bonus.[33]

They also demanded the introduction of a price stabilisation fund for rubber and palm oil production.

In addition to collective actions, members also resorted to informal actions to protest against their control and exploitation in the labour process. First of all, they declined to adhere strictly to the production rules set by management. For example, contrary to the scheme's regulations, a substantial number of oil palm smallholders decided to grow food crops on their own oil palm farms to compensate for the depletion of their capital reserves. Such practices were difficult for management to control. In 1985 the project management complained:

> Eighty-five hectares of palms were planted in 1984/85. Although it was stipulated at the outset that no intercropping would be allowed and the leguminous cover crops must be established, this in many cases was not done by the farmers of whom it had not been demanded previously. The only sanctions left were to (i) withhold delivery of planting material and (ii) withhold the payment of cash grants. If palm seedlings were not delivered, there was the risk that the project would be left with substantial quantity of such seedlings in the nursery and in consequence it was decided to go ahead with the planting and to withhold the payment of cash grants until these two conditions had been met.[34]

Second, they tended to neglect farm maintenance and increasingly withdrew from the scheme. The 1994 CDC Annual Report mentioned that 77 of the 432 smallholders were 'inactive' (45 in rubber and 32 in oil palms). It also reported that 16 oil palm growers had started felling their trees for tapping palm wine.

And third, they, and especially oil palm growers, tried to evade the terms of exchange imposed by the corporation by either selling their fruit at the local market or processing them at local mills.[35] Of course, such activities were aimed at realising a higher rate of return on their labour. Contrary to oil palm growers, rubber growers are more locked into exchange relations as they lack processing and marketing facilities.

Rendell (1976: 219) rightly observed that informal protest actions are more likely to occur if smallholders are not fully dependent on income derived from participation in the scheme. He asserted that the tea contract farming schemes created by the Commonwealth Development Corporation in Uganda and Mali performed below expectation because the growing of other cash crops made smallholders less dependent on tea for income, less committed to it in periods when prices were low, and less willing to subordinate themselves to the management's authority and discipline in the labour process. There is no doubt that CDC smallholders' informal protest actions were also prompted by the fact that the scheme's participants had additional sources of income too, with most producing other cash crops such as cocoa and coffee.

Fortunately, the situation started to improve in 1994. Increasing world market prices allowed the CDC's management to pay its smallholders higher prices, which, in turn, motivated smallholders to increase output.[36]

## Conclusion

This chapter presents a serious challenge to modernisation theorists who assumed that the creation of contract farming schemes would inevitably result in the maximisation of capital accumulation and the emergence of a stable middle peasantry. In fact, I have demonstrated that the various CDC smallholder schemes have been largely unsuccessful, particularly during the corporation's unprecedented economic crisis. I have also highlighted some of the main reasons for their relative failure.

There was, first of all, the rather ambiguous attitude of the government and CDC management towards smallholder development. In its policy statements, the government regularly expressed its firm commitment to the agro-industrial 'encadrement' of the local peasantry.[37] In practice, however, it seems to have been more interested in the expansion of agro-industrial estates and medium-sized plantations, mainly for the possibilities that the modernisation strategy offers the political elite for private capital accumulation. Its ambiguous attitude towards smallholder development may have been reinforced by the relative failure of the few contract farming schemes that were implemented under pressure from the international financiers of agro-industrial expansion, particularly the World Bank. This failure should not, however, be attributed to the local peasantry's inherent traditionalism, lack of entrepreneurship or unwillingness to join the scheme, but rather to the serious problems that participants faced from the very start of contract farming schemes. In the absence of any determined and consistent smallholder policy, CDC management continued to render assistance only reluctantly to smallholder schemes. It has tried to remain faithful to its historical mission of estate development and to look upon smallholder development as a matter of secondary importance. And, even more importantly, it has never been challenged as to its priorities. The government seems to have supported its smallholder and price policies, and the corporation has never been dependent on the supply of smallholder produce, which has always only accounted for a tiny proportion of total CDC output (see Table 7.1).

Secondly, there has been, as the dependency theorists have correctly observed, a precarious dependence on commodity prices on domestic and international markets. The banana scheme flourished in the days before independence, primarily because of a trade preference for the agricultural commodities of Commonwealth countries in the United Kingdom, but it collapsed following the withdrawal of preferential treatment after independence and reunification (cf. Epale 1985: 190-91). Unlike the banana scheme, the rubber and oil palm schemes never experienced a real boom period as they immediately became subject to fluctuating, and often low, prices. The sharp fall in commodity prices on the world market in the 1980s brought both the CDC and smallholders to the verge of bankruptcy.

And finally, there has been the problem of establishing control over these schemes. Feeling exploited, participants have continued to oppose managerial efforts to gain control over the processes of production and exchange. They have been regularly engaged in a variety of collective and informal modes of resistance that have seriously impeded the progress of the schemes, notably during the corporation's economic crisis. These forms of protest, which have been largely ignored by both the modernisation and dependencia-theorists, have been manifest in their common struggle against the low producer prices offered by the corporation, their defiance of management authority over the labour process reflected in their persistent violation of production rules and refusal to maintain their farms, and their withdrawal from relations of exchange and, in the last resort, from the scheme itself.

## Notes

1. République Unie du Cameroun (1980), *Bilan Diagnostic du Secteur Agricole de 1960 à 1980,* Yaoundé: Ministère de l'Agriculture, 97-98.

2. See Law no. 68/LF/9 of 11 June 1968.

3. Quoted in Fongang (1981/82: 18).

4. See BNA, File Qf/e (1946) 1, Bakweri Land Committee, and BNA, File Qf/e (1951) 1, Examination of Petitions from the Bakweri Land Committee.

5. Swynnerton *et al.* (1964: 37).

6. *Ibid.,* p. 54.

7. Minutes of a Meeting of the Committee on the Future of the CDC held at the office of the Financial Secretary on 3 October 1964, in BNA, File Qd/a (1962) 1, Correspondence with CDC.

8. See BNA, File Se/a (1966) 1, Smallholder Development Committee.

9. *Ibid.*

10. See letter from G.A. Eyong, Manager Bonanza Estates, Victoria, to General Manager CDC, Bota, dated 27 August 1973, in File MINEP/ ED/SWP/A/554, Small Palm Holders' Scheme.

11. See Petition of the South West Province Oil Palm Smallholders' Co-operative, Victoria, to Minister of Commercial and Industrial Development, Yaoundé, dated 12 January 1975, in *ibid.*

12. See, for instance, Report of the Smallholders' Oil Palm Scheme Meeting held in the Divisional Office, Victoria, on 11 January 1974, in *ibid.*

13. See Petition of Strangers of Batoke, Native West Coast, to the Permanent Secretary, Ministry of Lands and Survey, Buea, dated 6 June 1968, in BNA, File Qd/a (1969) 1, Surrender of Land by CDC at Bakingili.

14. See letter from General Manager CDC to Secretary South West Province Oil Palm Smallholders' Co-operative, c/o Bonanza Estate, Limbe, dated 27 July 1983, in File MINEP/ED/SWP/A/554, Small Palm Holders' Scheme.

15. See letter from South West Province Oil Palm Smallholders' Co-operative, c/o Bonanza Estate, Limbe to General Manager CDC, Bota, dated 22 July 1983, in *ibid.*

16. See File MTPS/SWP/BU.95/S.43/vol. 1, Complaints from Mukete Plantations, Kumba.

17. See letter from Ebanja and Sons, Malende to the Chairman of the CDC, dated 9 March 1981, in File MINEP/ED/SWP/A/554, Small Palm Holders' Scheme.

18. See letter from South West Province Oil Palm Smallholders' Co-operatives to General Manager CDC, dated 28 August 1979, in *ibid.*

19. See report of Dr (Mrs) Terisia Elad, Economic Adviser to the Governor of the South West Province on price paid to oil palm smallholders by CDC, dated 6 July 1979, in *ibid.*

20. See minutes of a meeting held in the Governor's Office, Buea, on 17 July 1975 to discuss the price of palm fruit paid to smallholders, in *ibid.*

21. See letter from General Manager CDC, to Secretary South West Province Oil Palm Smallholders' Co-operative, c/o Bonanza Estate, Limbe, 27 July 1983, in *ibid.*

22. World Bank, 'Cameroon: Appraisal of a Second CAMDEV Project, Report No. 1676-CM', Washington DC, December 1977.

23. See CDC, Conditions of the contract governing relations between the CDC and smallholder plantation farmers; and CDC, Contract for smallholder's oil palm/rubber plantations.

24. Cash grants have been revised by project management over the years. For example, the total cash grant for rubber cultivation rose to FCFA 149,923 in 1985.

25. Manager Smallholders' Development Scheme, Tiko, to General Manager CDC, 27 September 1979, Progress Report of the Smallholders' Development Scheme, 1 January-30 June 1979, in File MINEP/ED/SWP/A/554, Small Palm Holders' Scheme.

26. See Ministère de l'Agriculture, Direction des Études et Projets, *Développement Rural Intégré, Rapport Principal,* Yaoundé, September 1984; and Project Manager CDC Smallholders' Development Scheme, Notes for Visiting Agents M/S Hall and Pigot, Tiko, 1985, ref. no. SDT/AD/3.

27. CDC Annual Report and Accounts 1984, pp. 20-21.

28. See also Manager Smallholders' Development Scheme, Tiko, Smallholder Rubber Plantations, 1979, in File MINEP/ED/SWP/A/554, Small Palm Holders' Scheme; and van de Belt (1981).

29. See Report of the Manager Smallholders' Development Scheme, Tiko, to the Chief of the Economic Division for the South West Province, dated 6 October 1980, in File MINEP/ED/SWP/A/554, Small Palm Holders' Scheme.

30. See République Unie du Cameroun et Commonwealth Development Corporation, 'Accord de Prêt relatif à Projet de Consolidation de CAMDEV II', Yaoundé, 22 April 1982.

31. CDC Annual Report and Accounts 1984, pp. 20-21.

32. See Project Manager CDC Smallholders' Development Scheme, Tiko, Notes for Visiting Agents M/S Hall and Pigot, 1985, ref. no. SDT/AD/3.

33. *Cameroon Outlook,* 28 June 1986.

34. Project Management CDC Smallholders' Development Scheme, Tiko, Notes for Visiting Agents M/S Hall and Pigot, 1985, ref. no. SDT/AD/3.

35. CDC Annual Report and Accounts 1994.

36. *Ibid.,* 1995.

37. See, for instance, République du Cameroun, 'Sixième Plan Quinquennal de Développement Économique, Social et Culturel, 1986-1991', Yaoundé, Ministère du Plan et de l'Aménagement du Territoire, 1986.

# 8

# Pamol's contract farmers and cooperatives: Their development in response to the agro-industrial crisis

## Introduction

Like the CDC, Pamol has played a pioneering role among the agro-industrial enterprises in Cameroon regarding contract farming. Soon after independence and reunification, it began a contract farming scheme near its oil palm estates in response to government requests to agro-industrial enterprises to play an intermediary role in regional development.

This chapter shows how the Pamol contract farming scheme was characterised by weak managerial control and supervision over the labour process and a large degree of social differentiation. A small group of large producers with close links to management and the state formed the core group of Pamol's contract farmers, producing by far the largest and highest-quality output. They have proved, however, to be more dependent on the company's transport and milling facilities than smaller producers who are often capable of processing their limited amounts of produce themselves if management fails to buy it for one reason or another.

In this chapter I argue that large producers felt more threatened than the smaller ones during Pamol's crisis and liquidation. They then decided to form a cooperative, claiming that it was going to protect not only their own interests but also those of smaller producers. However, it soon emerged that this cooperative lacked the bargaining power required to hold the management to the terms of the contract in a situation of severe marketing and liquidity problems. Faced with growing dissatisfaction among members who began looking for alternative milling facilities, the cooperative's executive board tried to establish a larger measure of autonomy for the cooperative *vis-à-vis* the company by setting up transport and milling facilities of its own.

The first part of this chapter describes the emergence and development of Pamol's contract farming scheme up until the start of the company's crisis. And in the second part, I assess the role played by the newly established cooperative in defending its members' interests during Pamol's financial crisis and liquidation.

## The emergence and development of Pamol's contract farming scheme

Unilever was already seriously contemplating the implementation of contract farming schemes in Africa by the end of the Second World War. In a memorandum to the Nigerian colonial administration in 1944 (Fieldhouse 1994: 211-12), the United Africa Company (UAC), Unilever's most important subsidiary in Africa, proposed establishing oil palm contract farming schemes in Nigeria and British Cameroon based on the highly successful Gezira settler cotton scheme in Sudan (Gaitskell 1959). However after extensive discussions, no more was ever heard of this proposal.

It was not until the early 1960s that Pamol made a renewed attempt to implement contract farming schemes in response to the federal government's urgent request to existing agro-industrial enterprises to play an intermediary role in setting up contract farming schemes near their estates.[1] During his 'get to know the people tour' in December 1963, J.N. Lafon, the Secretary of State for Local Government in the Federated State of West Cameroon, discussed the possibility of company assistance to smallholder oil palm producers in Ndian Division with divisional authorities and Pamol's management.[2] Pamol assured the Secretary of State that the company was ready 'to assist the local population in the cultivation of this permanent crop of long-lasting value'. All the participants had high expectations for future Pamol contract farming schemes:

> The opportunity to establish such projects is favourable as Pamol has got good plant material, will provide advice freely, and is willing to buy the produce. Good land is available around the estates. All factors are present to make smallholder projects a success provided that the communities have sufficient interest.[3]

Following these discussions, a meeting was arranged with representatives from villages close to the Pamol estates. Mr Evans, the Pamol management's representative, explained the purpose of contract farming schemes and the village representatives hailed the introduction of such schemes, saying that 'they saw these schemes as excellent opportunities for economic development'. They added that they were in favour of the communal farming of oil palms and that the proceeds of their communal efforts would be used to set up village development projects. Both parties then agreed on their mutual obligations in the establishment of communal farms.[4] Communal farming was undertaken not only by villages near the Pamol estates but also by various schools and churches.

Despite initial enthusiasm, communal farming soon ran into difficulties. First, there were conflicts between communal farmers and the owners of selected plots. For instance, the Divisional Officer of Ekondo Titi Subdivision reported on the plot selected by Lobe village as follows:

> This plot is the old Native Authority School site with kolanut trees, palms and mangoes. It is said to belong to the family of Ajia Mambo. Strangers had been given plots on this land to cultivate farms of cassava. On selection of this plot, the natives cut down stands of cassava and destroyed some young palms. The family sued the town to the Native Court asking them to quit and pay damages. The work came to a standstill. A settlement was finally reached with the family by the District Officer.[5]

Communal ownership also gave rise to internal conflicts among communal farmers. Some hard-working farmers felt frustrated by those who either refused to work or were lazy, which resulted in a lack of farm maintenance. Asked to intervene, the Director of Agriculture recommended dividing communal farms into individual plots, claiming that this was the only way to produce satisfactory results. His recommendation was rejected, however, on the ground that communal land could not be owned by individuals. The communities concerned then agreed that communal farming would be made compulsory and that an annual fine of FCFA 1,000 would be imposed on anyone failing to work on these farms. This resolution proved ineffective.[6]

Alongside these communal farms, one can also see the emergence of an increasing number of individual farmers (see Table 8.1). In contrast to other schemes in Cameroon and elsewhere,[7] the Pamol scheme has the following three main characteristics.

Table 8.1 *Pamol contract farmers: Number, cultivated area and output, 1980-1993*

| YEAR | NUMBER | CULTIVATED AREA (HA) | OUTPUT (M.T. of FFB)[1] |
|------|--------|----------------------|--------------------------|
| 1980 | 231 | 1,979 | 5,904 |
| 1981 | 246 | 2,144 | 8,420 |
| 1982 | 268 | 2,323 | 9,187 |
| 1983 | 282 | 2,409 | 6,625 |
| 1984 | 301 | 2,487 | 9,911 |
| 1985 | 313 | 2,700 | 7,993 |
| 1986 | 322 | 2,779 | 10,234 |
| 1987 | 349 | 2,946 | 5,682 |
| 1988 | 345 | 2,946 | 2,821 |
| 1989 | 345 | | 8,525 |
| 1990 | 349 | 3,689 | 8,730 |
| 1991 | 350 | 4,077 | 6,599 |
| 1992 | | | 8,522 |
| 1993 | | | 4,723 |

*Source:* Data supplied by Pamol Head Office, Lobe.
*Note 1:* FFB stands for Fresh Fruit Bunches.

First, the vast majority (90%) of the scheme's participants were immigrants, 65% of whom came from the North West Province. They were mostly Pamol workers and managerial staff who had bought land from local peasants during their working lives and then settled in neighbouring villages when they retired. In the past, this never posed a problem: land was not in short supply in this sparsely populated area and was extremely cheap. Local villagers welcomed any outsider who wanted to settle in their community, provided s/he respected local customs and authority. It was not until the liberalisation process that the regime and its South West allies began to exploit and exacerbate the divisions between 'indigenous' people and 'strangers' in the South West Province for political ends. Many immigrants, especially from the North West, belong to the country's main opposition party, the North West-based Social Democratic Front (SDF). As a result, some local villagers have become resentful of the large-scale occupation of their ancestral lands by immigrants and the almost exclusive participation of immigrants in the scheme.

Second, the contract between the company and the scheme's participants is quite 'loose', with little managerial control over participants' production (and exchange). Pamol usually supplies participants with seeds and technical advice, often even free of charge to boost production, but there is hardly any on-going managerial control and supervision of the labour process. Since the company is often unable to transport participants' produce to its mills, especially during the rainy season, it cannot force them to sell their produce to Pamol alone. Moreover, participants have full legal authority over their land and do not have to adhere to the terms of the contract in order to retain their plots. The company's principal sanctions are to refuse to process low-quality produce, and to expel participants from the scheme if they regularly sell part or all of their produce on the open market.

Third, there is a high degree of social differentiation among the scheme's participants, especially because the company has never set any limits on the area under cultivation. Approximately 60% of participants have small farms, varying in size from less than 1 ha to 5 ha. The majority are Pamol workers who grow oil palms in their spare time. Given their familiarity with agro-industrial oil palm cultivation, it is understandable that the management has never devoted much time or energy to extension services and regular supervision. The remainder of the small producers are local peasants who are simultaneously engaged in cocoa, coffee and food cultivation. Generally speaking, the latter have shown little interest in joining the scheme, partly because they lack sufficient capital since the cultivation of oil palms yields no income in the first four years. This financial aspect, together with the high demand for locally produced foodstuffs, encourages food production instead, which offers quick returns. With few exceptions, maintenance levels on oil palm farms are thus inadequate.

These small producers predominantly make use of family labour, but for heavy farm operations, such as land development, they either call upon mutual work groups called *njangis* (DeLancey 1977) or employ casual labour. Chronic labour problems are another factor accounting for poor maintenance practices. Small producers cannot afford to pay casual labour on a regular basis but their own sons tend to leave the isolated and marginalised Ndian Division and migrate to the coastal towns in search of employment. They therefore mostly have to rely on female labour. Women are traditionally not entitled to land – which is why very few women participate in the scheme – but are responsible for food production. Work on their household's oil palm farm places an additional burden on women's extensive productive and reproductive responsibilities, while the proceeds from such cultivation go to the male head. Although male heads are traditionally not obliged to reward women for their additional labour input, they usually try to avoid potential conflicts by giving them a share of the proceeds in the form of presents or a small sum of money.

Small producers account for only a very limited proportion of contract farmers' total output. They are therefore of little importance to the company. This is manifest in management policies towards contract farming: they usually give the lowest priority to small producers in the allocation of inputs, technical advice and transport. On the other hand, small producers see oil palm cultivation as a supplementary source of income, since they already enjoy other income from wage labour or agricultural production. Not fully dependent on oil palm cultivation, they tend to be less committed to it when prices are low, and less willing to subordinate themselves to managerial control over the labour process. Owing to their relatively limited output, they are able to process at least part of their output themselves if management is unable, for whatever reason, to provide transport for their produce. They process it either in the traditional way or with the help of small presses, and then consume part of it themselves and sell the remainder at the local market.

Approximately 25% of participants have medium-sized farms, cultivating between 5 ha and 10 ha. This middle stratum consists mainly of clerical and supervisory staff at Pamol and richer local peasants who appear to be more interested than small producers in expanding production. These producers often employ a few permanent and casual workers in addition to family labour. This group is not, however, very stable as members either succeed in joining the group of large producers or, particularly in times of crisis, may find themselves sliding into the category of small producers.

Approximately 15% of the participants are large producers cultivating between 10 ha and 100 ha. They are mainly former managerial staff at Pamol, local chiefs, civil servants and businessmen, and have usually maintained close relations with Pamol management and the state apparatus, and some even have important positions in the ruling party. A few are absentee farmers who have left the actual running of their farms to farm managers, usually their sons. Large producers employ a number of permanent and casual workers depending on the size of the farm but often have trouble hiring steady, efficient and reliable workers. These contract farmers cannot compete in their labour recruitment efforts with the Pamol estates that offer higher wages and better social amenities and benefits. Moreover, the company strictly forbids contract farmers from hiring estate workers on a casual basis at peak production periods, with breaches of this rule being punished by eviction from the scheme.[8] Generally speaking, the large producers maintain their farms better than the small ones and sell higher-quality produce to the company.

Two former northwestern managerial staff members, A.N. Gana and A.Ḅ. Nzams, belong to the group of successful, pioneering contract farmers. After retiring from the company in 1964, they each bought 100 ha of land from the local chiefs and gradually expanded their oil palm farms. In 1984, Gana was cultivating 50 ha of oil palms at Lipenja and employed about 30 workers. He sold 464 tonnes of fresh fruit to the company that year for a total of FCFA 11.5 million.[9] He was also engaged in business and animal husbandry. With more than 50 workers, Nzams has been cultivating almost 100 ha at Lobe. His farm has attracted numerous high-ranking national and foreign visitors as it shows what contract farmers can accomplish if they follow technical advice on fertiliser and maintenance.

For Pamol management, the large producers are the most important group of contract farmers, as they supply by far the largest and best-quality produce. They are consequently given privileges when it comes to the allocation of inputs, technical advice and transport facilities, a position that is strengthened by the close contacts between large producers and management and state. These contacts are also beneficial for large producers in securing substantial bank loans for expanded production. Despite this privileged position, they nevertheless appear to be more vulnerable than small producers as they lack the means to process their substantial output and are thus more dependent on Pamol for transport and milling facilities than small producers are. It is little wonder then that, having made considerable investments in the scheme, they felt the most threatened when management could no longer provide these facilities when the company's financial problems started and it subsequently went into liquidation. They then took the initiative of setting up a cooperative. While they claimed it would defend the interests of all contract farmers, they were primarily concerned with protecting their own interests.

## Contract farmers' cooperatives and Pamol's crisis and liquidation

Even at the start of the crisis in 1980, large producers were already giving serious consideration to forming a cooperative. They feared that Pamol would no longer be able to provide services to contract farmers or to compensate them for their rising production costs by regularly increasing the producer price. They became more determined to form a cooperative when the management actually refused to discuss their demands for a review of the producer price in early 1980. In this particular case, they felt strongly that this demand was justified, since Pamol's price of FCFA 11,000 per tonne compared unfavourably with the neighbouring CDC that was paying FCFA 22,000. The management, for its part, claimed that it was offering its farmers a fair price because they had lower production costs than the CDC farmers.[10] Interestingly, some large producers had already suggested that the new cooperative should aim at constructing a mill of its own in the longer term and take over transporting produce from its members' farms to the mill. They perceived the cooperative as a means both of strengthening their bargaining position with management and reducing their dependence on the company for transport and processing facilities.

Since cooperatives were then still subordinated to state control, the large producers approached the state for approval and to register their cooperative. The request was granted in March 1980 and led to the inauguration of the Ndian Division Oil Palm Smallholders' Cooperative. Pamol management did not oppose this newly created cooperative, seeing it as presenting a channel for passing information on to contract farmers, an auxiliary body of control over the contract farmers' production and exchange, and an intermediary organ for settling disputes between contract farmers and the company. The management did, however, express misgivings about the motives behind the cooperative as it felt that bigger farmers would obviously dominate the cooperative and would be 'more concerned with following their own interests to a conclusion than the interests of the cooperative society as a whole'. It also warned that, after investing so heavily over the years in establishing a viable contract farming scheme near its estates, the company would never allow the newly created cooperative to construct milling facilities of its own.[11]

The activities of the newly created cooperative were largely restricted to contract farmers around the Ndian Estate. However it proved incapable of defending its members' interests when Pamol's deepening crisis threatened the very survival of the contract farming scheme. In June 1984 and again in April 1986, Pamol's management was obliged to announce that the company could no longer purchase produce from contract farmers due to marketing and liquidity problems. It was in this precarious period, that the large producers near the Lobe Estate decided, on 4 September 1986, to form a cooperative of their own: the Ekondo Titi Oil Palm Smallholder Cooperative Society Ltd (Ekoscoop Ltd). Its leadership was likewise monopolised by big farmers and small producers were never given the opportunity to participate in the decision-making process. None of them were ever invited to attend the cooperative's regular meetings and although they sometimes resented their inferior position in the cooperative, they never seem to have challenged its leadership. Small producers often maintain a clientelistic relationship with large producers, who request certain favours for them with the management and the state. They, in return, provide the large producers with labour services. They usually acknowledge the superior bargaining power of the large producers and benefit from the cooperative's achievements, such as increased producer prices.

Soon after it was established, the power of the new cooperative was put to the test. Pamol's management informed the executive board on 23 May 1987 that it could no longer guarantee payment for produce supplied by contract farmers and suggested two alternatives:

- Contract farmers could try to deliver their produce to SOCAPALM and the CDC. Since these parastatals were desperately short of cash, it would be in the farmers' interests not to supply fruit before obtaining prior confirmation of payment. This option, of course, would involve extremely high transport costs since these parastatals' mills were a long way from Ndian Division and the connecting roads were usually in bad shape.
- Contract farmers could continue delivering their produce to Pamol and they would be paid as soon as cash became available.[12]
- Since the management was not prepared to negotiate on this issue, the cooperative's leadership tried to make use of its contacts in the state apparatus. An emergency board meeting at Ekoscoop on 19 June 1987 resolved to send a delegation to Yaoundé to argue for immediate government intervention on the contract farmers' behalf. The cooperative's problems took on an even greater urgency eight days later when Pamol's management decided to stop purchasing produce from contract farmers altogether. The Minister of Agriculture, J.B. Yonke, then intervened, appealing to management to do everything possible to buy the farmers' fruit, but Pamol simply ignored this appeal.[13] The Ekoscoop board thus had no other option but to advise its members to sell to the CDC's Mondoni Oil Mill. However, most contract farmers refused to do so in view of the high transport costs involved. Since the large producers were capable of processing only a tiny proportion of their produce themselves, the remainder of their perishable crops was left to rot, which resulted in major financial losses.

Following Pamol's liquidation, the newly appointed liquidator told the Ekoscoop executive that he would not start purchasing produce from contract farmers until there were signs of the company's recovery. In these circumstances, some of the larger producers with the necessary capital resources began to invest in mechanical presses to process their own and others' produce. Increasingly, even people without oil palm farms were coming to own milling facilities. They bought fruit from contract farmers, Pamol workers and local villagers who were involved in large-scale theft of company produce.

It was not until 23-24 June 1988 that the liquidator, C.G. Mure, arranged a meeting of Pamol contract farmers to announce that the company would distribute oil palm seedlings to registered contract farmers free of charge, pay all their arrears and start purchasing fruit from them on 1 July 1988. Significantly, he informed them that the company had drawn up a new contract farming policy on the advice of the Commonwealth Development Corporation (COMDEV), which at that time was showing great interest in taking over the company. Pamol was going to focus on contract farming. Production would therefore be reorganised to such an extent that by the early 21st century, 60% of produce would be supplied by contract farmers and only 40% by the company's estates. To achieve this, the company would make a special effort to bring an increasing number of local peasants into the scheme. Furthermore, contract farmers would be offered shares in the company after reorganisation.[14] In line with this new policy, Itoe Sylvestor Imbea was appointed special projects manager as of 1 April 1989. Imbea, who hailed from Dikome Balue in Ndian Division and was thus well acquainted with the local situation, would be responsible for local peasants' participation in the contract farming scheme and for providing them with technical advice.

Contract farming activities, which had been at a virtual standstill since 1987, were once again being promoted. In 1989/90, the company supplied over 33,000 oil palm seedlings free of charge to contract farmers and started offering technical advice again. The results of these new efforts were, however, disappointing as very few peasants joined the scheme. This was mainly due to continuing transport problems and the fall in producer prices from FCFA 24,000 to FCFA 20,000 per tonne in Ekondo Titi Subdivision. Between 1989 and 1992 the number of participants in the scheme only rose from 345 to 350. Contract farmers produced about 9,000 tonnes of FFB worth FCFA 225 million in 1990 (see Table 8.1).

From 1990 onwards, relations between Ekoscoop Ltd and management began to deteriorate again. Imbea, the newly appointed special projects manager, was dismissed for allegedly not managing the contract farming scheme efficiently and there was less focus on contract farming after COMDEV's withdrawal of its takeover bid, which manifested itself in the liquidator investing all available financial resources in the replanting of the estates. The low producer price weakened the Ekoscoop board's control over its members who, understandably, were starting to look for alternative processing facilities and markets for their produce. There were also persistent transport problems, especially during the rainy season, and a regular shortage of oil palm seedlings. Above all, the company was not paying its contract farmers on a regular basis.

On 25 January 1991, the Annual General Meeting of Ekoscoop Ltd was held at Bekora, and was attended by the liquidator and several managers. The cooperative's board and members recounted their numerous problems at the meeting and the liquidator appeared annoyed by the cooperative's criticism of the scheme. He announced that the oil palm seedlings would now be sold at FCFA 500 each, since he had noticed that most farmers were not attaching any value to these seedlings if they were supplied free of charge. Moreover, he berated cooperative members for selling their produce to alternative markets in spite of the various forms of (free) assistance provided by the company. He explained that the irregular payments were to be blamed on the company's liquidity problems, which were caused by a renewed undercutting of prices by the two major agro-industrial parastatals. However, he stressed that liquidity problems were not confined to Pamol but had become a common phenomenon in Cameroon during the economic crisis and he warned that if the theft of fruit continued, the company would stop buying produce from contract farmers. He then informed his audience that the producer price would be increased from FCFA 20,000 to FCFA 25,000 with effect from 1 February 1991.[15]

There were no apparent improvements in the contract farmers' situation after this meeting. On the contrary, the company's deepening crisis prevented management from paying the contract farmers more regularly and providing them with assistance. Experiencing difficulties in surviving, the large producers approached the cooperative's board, exhorting it to bring more pressure to bear on Pamol to adhere to the terms of the contract. The board, in turn, claimed it lacked the bargaining power to improve the farmers' situation as long as the marketing and liquidity problems affecting the agro-industrial oil palm sector remained. Dissatisfied with the responses from Pamol's management and the cooperative's board, a rapidly growing number of contract farmers began selling at least part of their produce to the new group of local press owners who were able to pay them promptly.

To regain the loyalty of its members, the board decided to implement previous plans to establish a larger measure of autonomy for the cooperative *vis-à-vis* the company. This move was facilitated by the enactment of a new cooperative law by Parliament on 14 February 1992 that reflected the country's ongoing liberalisation process. It freed the existing cooperatives from state control and gave them more leeway for autonomous action. In its pursuit of autonomy, the board took the following measures:[16]

- it attempted to create milling facilities of its own. Land was acquired from the Chief of Bongongo I, one of the bigger contract farmers, and the board procured two mechanical presses and applied for foreign assistance to help set up a mill;
- it attempted to solve the chronic transport problems by buying a tractor and a four-wheel drive vehicle from Pamol; and
- it began buying seeds to establish nurseries of its own.

Obviously, this drive for autonomy formed a potential challenge to Pamol's substantial investments in its contract farming scheme as well as to its market monopoly. Although management had previously warned the cooperative that the company would never allow it to engage in milling activities of its own, it nevertheless adopted an attitude of wait and see. It found it difficult to prohibit the cooperative outright from implementing its new measures because the company had failed to provide the necessary assistance to contract farmers and to pay them regularly. In addition, it soon became clear that the cooperative would not be able, at least in the short term, to realise its plans. For instance, its various requests for international funding for a mill have not yet yielded any results. Moreover, its newly procured means of transport have proved not only insufficient in coping with its members' output but also unsuitable for local road conditions in the rainy season. Its members, and in particular the big producers, thus continue to be largely dependent on the company for transport and milling services.

The cooperative's very survival has remained precarious ever since. The two-month labour strike in 1993 brought untold hardship to members as no produce was bought at all by the company during this period. Following the appointment of a local management team after the strike, the company started purchasing produce again but payments remained irregular until 1994. In that year, the 50% devaluation of the CFA franc opened up brighter prospects for an economic recovery.

## Conclusion

This chapter has documented the pioneering but pivotal role Pamol has played in developing contract farming in Ndian Division. This role is all the more significant if one considers that, unlike the agro-industrial parastatals, the company never received any financial assistance from the post-colonial state for it.

I have tried to show how a group of large contract producers began organising into cooperatives when deteriorating market conditions for palm oil endangered Pamol's continued existence, and thus producers' opportunities for capital accumulation. The company's economic crisis, however, soon exposed the cooperative's weakness, namely the large producers' high degree of dependence on the company for transport, processing and marketing. When management was no longer able to provide these services, the cooperative lacked the power to compel it to abide by the terms of the contract. Increasingly disillusioned with the cooperative board's performance, the large producers were, for the first time, obliged to seek alternative processing and marketing facilities. Such informal protest actions by contract farmers have been widespread in Africa and elsewhere (Konings 1993b; Little & Watts 1994).

After Pamol went into liquidation in 1987, there were some initial indications that the cooperative's bargaining position would improve. The liquidator informed its executive that he intended to shift from estate production to smallholder production, which would have considerably boosted the cooperative's membership. As was already the case in the Kenya Tea Development Authority (KTDA) (Lamb & Muller 1982), the cooperative's board was to be represented in Pamol's management, and cooperative members would own shares in the company. Unfortunately, nothing ever came of all this, and the period of relative harmony and cooperation was brief.

Unable to pressurise management into improving its members' situation during the deepening crisis, the large producers eventually forced the cooperative's board to pursue a greater measure of autonomy in relation to the company by developing nurseries and transport and milling facilities of its own. The cooperative's new policies, however, never posed any serious challenge to the company's market monopoly as the cooperative failed to implement its autonomy measures, at least in the short term. It is therefore little wonder that a growing number of large producers began to circumvent the cooperative once again, either investing in mechanical presses themselves or selling some or all of their produce to a new group of press owners who had grown up in the area during the company crisis, and who were capable of paying promptly.

The relatively poor performance of the Pamol cooperative is by no means exceptional among the handful of cooperatives that exist in contracting schemes in the developing world. Clapp (1994: 82) has concluded that 'cooperatives may coordinate the interests of large growers when they coincide with the company's, but when conflict arises between growers and company, they have been largely helpless'. One of the rare examples of relative success in Africa is the KTDA cooperative in Kenya, which wields considerable power by virtue of its vast membership. According to Grosh (1994: 254), the KTDA cooperative has, for this very reason, continued to be strongly represented at various levels in the KTDA governance structure, and the parastatal has modified its practices over time in response to the cooperative's priorities.

# Notes

1. République Unie du Cameroun (1980), *Bilan Diagnostic du Secteur Agricole de 1960 à 1980,* Yaoundé: Ministère de l'Agriculture, 97-98.

2. See letter from District Officer, Ekondo Titi Subdivision, to Honourable J.N. Lafon, dated 6 July 1964, in BNA, File Cd (1963) 1, Administrative Reorganisation: Ekondo Titi Sub-District.

3. See *Pamol News,* 1 January 1969, p. 2.

4. See letter from District Officer, Ekondo-Titi Subdivision, to Honourable J.N. Lafon, dated 8 July 1964, in BNA, File Cd (1963) 1, Administrative Reorganisation: Ekondo Titi Sub-District.

5. *Ibid.*

6. Economic and Social Report of Ekondo Titi Quarter Ending, 30 September 1970, in BNA, File Cd (1964) 2, Periodical Intelligence Report: Ekondo Titi.

7. For instance, a recently created contract farming scheme associated with the CDC has a more homogeneous contract farming group and strict managerial control over participants' production and exchange. See Chapter 7.

8. See letter from W.N. Kimbeng, Manager of Lobe Estate, to all smallholders, dated 10 November 1980, in File G 4002/49, Vol. 2, Pamol Cameroon Ltd – General Correspondence.

9. See letter from District Officer, Ekondo Titi, to the Honourable Minister of Finance, Yaoundé, dated 6 November 1985, in *ibid.*

10. Minutes of the General Meeting of Oil Palm Smallholders in Ndian Division, dated 18 April 1980, in File MINEP/ED/SWP/A/54, Small Palm Holders Scheme.

11. See letter from D.J. Lucking, Managing Director of Pamol, to T.A.N. Elad, Provincial Head of Economic Division, Buea, dated 11 July 1980, in File ECOPLAN/516, Plantations Pamol du Cameroun Ltd.

12. See letter from B.J.R. Mack, Managing Director of Pamol, to Senior Divisional Officer, Mundemba, dated 23 May 1987, in File G 4002/49, Vol. 2, Pamol Cameroon Ltd – General Correspondence.

13. See letter from J.B. Yonke, Minister of Agriculture, Yaoundé, to Pamol, Douala, dated 26 June 1987, in *ibid.*

14. See letter from C.G. Mure, Liquidator of Pamol, to Senior District Officer, Mundemba, dated 22 June 1988, in *ibid.*

15. Minutes of the Ekondo Titi Oil Palm Smallholder Cooperative Ltd (Ekoscoop Ltd) Annual General Meeting held at Bekora on 25 January 1991, Archives of Ekoscoop Ltd, Lobe.

16. See Opening Address by the President of Ekondo Titi Oil Palm Cooperative Society (Ekoscoop), Chief Esoh Itoh, at the Annual General Meeting held at Bekora on 18 September 1993, Archives of Ekoscoop Ltd, Lobe.

# References

ABRAHAMSEN, R. (2000), *Disciplining democracy: Development discourse and good governance in Africa*, London/New York: Zed Books.

ADESINA, J.O. (1989), 'Worker consciousness and shopfloor struggles: A case study of Nigerian refinery workers', *Labour, Capital and Society* 22 (2): 288-345.

ADESINA, J.O. (1994), *Labour in the explanation of an African crisis*, Dakar: CODESRIA.

AGIER, M., J. COPANS & A. MORICE, eds, (1987), *Classes ouvrières d'Afrique noire*, Paris: Karthala/ORSTOM.

AKWETEY, E.O. (1994), *Trade unions and democratization: A comparative study of Zambia and Ghana*, Stockholm: University of Stockholm.

ALL ANGLOPHONE CONFERENCE (1993), *The Buea declaration, 2-3 April 1993*, Limbe: Nooremac Press.

AMIN, S. (1974), *Accumulation on a world scale: A critique of the theory of underdevelopment*, New York/London: Monthly Review Press.

AMIN, S. (1976), *Unequal development: An essay on the social formations of peripheral capitalism*, New York/London: Monthly Review Press.

AMIN, S. & K. VERGOPOULOS (1974), *La question paysanne et le capitalisme*, Paris: Anthropos.

ANANABA, W. (1979), *The trade union movement in Africa: Promise and performance*, London: C. Hurst & Co.

ARDENER, E. (1956), *Coastal Bantu of the Cameroons*, London: International African Institute.

ARDENER, E. (1962), *Divorce and fertility: An African study*, London: Oxford University Press.

ARDENER, E. (1967), 'The nature of the reunification of Cameroon'. In: A. Hazlewood, ed., *African integration and disintegration: Case studies in economic and political union*, London: Oxford University Press, 285-337.

ARDENER, E. (1970), 'Witchcraft, economics, and the continuity of belief'. In: M. Douglas, ed., *Witchcraft confessions and accusations*, London: Tavistock.

ARDENER, E. (1996), *Kingdom on Mount Cameroon: Studies in the history of the Cameroon coast 1500-1970*, Providence/Oxford: Berghahn Books, Cameroon Studies, vol.1.

ARDENER, E., S. ARDENER & W.A. WARMINGTON (1960), *Plantation and village in the Cameroons*, London: Oxford University Press.

ARDENER, S.G. (1958), 'Banana co-operatives in Southern Cameroons'. In: *Conference Proceedings*, Ibadan: Nigerian Institute of Social and Economic Research, 10-25.

AYINA, J.P. (1983), 'L'Assistance des compagnies françaises aux sociétés agro-industrielles au Cameroun: Les cas de la C.F.D.T. à la SODECOTON et de la SOMDIAA à la SOSUCAM et à la CAMSUCO', Thèse de Doctorat de Troisième Cycle, University of Yaoundé: IRIC.

BAGCHI, A.K. (1982), *The political economy of underdevelopment*, Cambridge: Cambridge University Press.

BANAJI, J. (1977), 'Modes of production in a materialist conception of history', *Capital and Class* 2 (3): 1-44.

BANGURA, Y. (1991), 'Steyr-Nigeria: The recession and workers' struggles in the vehicle assembly plant'. In: I. Brandell, ed., *Workers in Third-World industrialization*, London: Macmillan, 177-196.

BANGURA, Y. & B. BECKMAN (1993), 'African workers and structural adjustment: A Nigerian case-study'. In: A.O. Olukoshi, ed., *The politics of structural adjustment in Nigeria*, London: James Currey, 75-91.

BARBIER, J.-C., G. COURADE & J. TISSANDIER (1980), *Complexes agro-industriels au Cameroun*, Paris: ORSTOM.

BARKER, J., ed. (1984), *The politics of agriculture in tropical Africa*, Beverly Hills: Sage.

BATES, R.H. (1971), *Unions, parties and political development: A study of mineworkers in Zambia*, New Haven: Yale University.

BATES, R.H. (1981), *Markets and states in tropical Africa: The political basis of agricultural policies*, Berkeley/Los Angeles: University of California Press.

BAYART, J.-F. (1979), *L'État au Cameroun*, Paris: Presses de la Fondation Nationale des Sciences Politiques.

BAYART, J.-F. (1981), 'Le politique par le bas en Afrique noire', *Politique Africaine* 1: 53-82.

BAYART, J.-F. (1983), 'La revanche des sociétés africaines', *Politique Africaine* 11: 95-128.

BAYART, J.-F. (1989), *L'État en Afrique: La politique du ventre*, Paris: Fayard.

BECKFORD, G.L. (1972), *Persistent poverty: Underdevelopment in plantation economies of the Third World*, New York/London: Oxford University Press.

BECKMAN, B. (1985), 'Bakolori: Peasants versus the state and capital', *Nigerian Journal of Political Science* 4: 76-104.

BECKMAN, B. & L.M. SACHIKONYE, eds, (2001), *Labour regimes and liberalization: The restructuring of state-society relations in Africa*, Harare: University of Zimbabwe Publications.

BEDERMAN, S.H. (1968), *The Cameroon Development Corporation: Partner in national growth*, Victoria-Bota: CDC.

BEDERMAN, S.H. (1971), 'The demise of the commercial banana industry in West Cameroon', *Journal of Geography* 70 (4): 230-234.

BENJAMIN, J. (1972), *Les Camerounais occidentaux: La minorité dans un état bicommunautaire*, Montréal: Les Presses de l'Université de Montréal.

BENN, D.M. (1974), 'The theory of plantation economy and society: A methodological critique', *Journal of Commonwealth and Comparative Politics* 12 (3): 249-260.

BENNELL, P. (1997), 'Privatization in Sub-Saharan Africa: Progress and prospects during the 1990s', *World Development* 25 (11): 1795-1803.

BERLAN, J.-P., J.-P. BERTRAND, L. LEPPER & P. DE VRIES (1978), *Unilever: Une multinationale discrète*, Paris: Les Éditions du Cerf.

BERNSTEIN, H. (1979), 'African peasantries: A theoretical framework', *Journal of Peasant Studies* 6 (4): 421-443.

BERNSTEIN, H. & M. PRITT (1974), 'Book review: Plantations and modes of exploitation', *Journal of Peasant Studies* 1 (4): 514-526.

BOEKE, J.H. (1953), *Economics and economic policy of dual societies*, New York: Institute of Pacific Relations.

BOESEN, J. (1979), 'On peasantry and the "modes of production debate"', *Review of African Political Economy* 15-16: 154-161.

BOLTON, D. (1985), *Nationalization: A road to socialism?*, London: Zed Books.

BRATTON, M. (1989), 'Beyond the state: Civil society and associational life in Africa', *World Politics* 41 (3): 407-429.

BRATTON, M. (1994), 'Civil society and political transitions in Africa'. In: J.W. Harbeson, D. Rothchild & N. Chazan, eds, *Civil society and the state in Africa*, Boulder, CO: Lynne Rienner, 51-81.

BRAVERMAN, H. (1974), *Labour and monopoly capital: The degradation of work in the twentieth century*, New York/London: Monthly Review Press.

BRETT, E.A. (1973), *Colonialism and underdevelopment in East Africa: The politics of economic change*, London: Heinemann.

BRYCESON, D. (1980), 'The proletarianisation of women in Tanzania', *Review of African Political Economy* 17: 4-27.

BUCH-HANSEN, M. & H. MARCUSEN (1982), 'Contract farming and the peasantry: Cases from Western Kenya', *Review of African Political Economy* 23: 9-36.

BURAWOY, M. (1979), *Manufacturing consent: Changes in the labour process under monopoly capitalism*, Chicago: University of Chicago Press.

BURAWOY, M. (1985), *The politics of production: Factory regimes under capitalism and socialism*, London: Verso.

CALLAGHY, T. & J. RAVENHILL, eds (1993), *Hemmed in: Responses to Africa's economic decline*, New York: Columbia University Press.

CAMPBELL WHITE, O. & A. BHATIA (1998), *Privatization in Africa*, Washington, DC: World Bank.

CARNEY, J.A. (1987), 'Struggles over crop rights and labour within contract farming households in a Gambian irrigated rice project', *Journal of Peasant Studies* 15 (3): 334-350.

CHABAL, P. & J.-P. DALOZ (1999), *Africa works: Disorder as political instrument*, Oxford: James Currey.

CHAUNCEY, G. Jr. (1981), 'The locus of reproduction: Women's labour in the Zambian Copperbelt 1927-1953', *Journal of Southern African Studies* 7 (2): 135-164.

CHEM-LANGHËË, B. (1976), 'The Kamerun plebiscites 1959-1961: Perceptions and strategies', Ph.D. Thesis, University of British Columbia.

CHEM-LANGHËË, B. (1995), 'The road to the unitary state of Cameroon, 1959-1972', *Paideuma* 41: 17-25.

CHIABI, E.M.L. (1982), 'Background to nationalism in Anglophone Cameroon: 1916-1954', Ph.D. Thesis, University of California.

CHILVER, E.M. (1971), 'Paramountcy and protection in the Cameroons: The Bali and the Germans, 1889-1913'. In: P. Gifford & W.R. Louis, eds, *Britain and Germany in Africa: Imperial rivalry and colonial rule*, New Haven: Yale University Press, 479-511.

CHILVER, E.M. & P.M. KABERRY (1967), *Traditional Bamenda: The precolonial history and ethnography of the Bamenda Grassfields*, Buea: Ministry of Primary Education and Social Welfare/West Cameroon Antiquities Commission.

CLAPP, R.A.J. (1988), 'Representing reciprocity, reproducing domination: Ideology and the labour process in Latin American contract farming', *Journal of Peasant Studies* 16 (1): 5-40.

CLAPP, R.A.J. (1994), 'The moral economy of the contract'. In: P. Little & M. Watts, eds, *Living under contract: Contract farming and agrarian transformation in Africa*, Madison, WI: University of Wisconsin Press, 78-94.

CLARENCE-SMITH, W.G. (1989), 'From plantation to peasant production in German Cameroun'. In: P. Geschiere & P. Konings, eds, *Proceedings/ contributions of the conference on the political economy of Cameroon – Historical perspectives, Leiden, June 1988*, Leiden: African Studies Centre, Research Report (2 vols), 483-502.

CLARENCE-SMITH, W.G. (1993), 'Plantation versus smallholder production of cocoa: The legacy of the German period in Cameroon'. In: P. Geschiere & P. Konings, eds, *Itinéraires d'accumulation au Cameroun*, Paris: Karthala, 187-216.

CLARKE, D.G. (1977), *Agricultural and plantation workers in Rhodesia*, Gwelo: Mambo Press.

COHEN, R. (1980), 'Resistance and hidden forms of consciousness amongst African workers', *Review of African Political Economy* 19: 8-22.

COLLIER, P. & D. LAL (1986), *Labour and poverty in Kenya 1900-1980*, Oxford: Clarendon Press.

COOPER, F. (1981), 'Africa and the world economy', *African Studies Review* 24 (2): 1-86.

COOPER, F. (1986), *On the African waterfront: Urban disorder and the transformation of work in colonial Mombasa*, New Haven/London: Yale Univertsity Press.

COURADE, G. (1978), 'Les plantations industrielles d'Unilever au Cameroun (Plantations Pamol du Cameroun Ltd) ou la croissance d'une firme multinationale dans une région marginale', *Cahiers de l'ONAREST* 1 (2): 91-159.

COURADE, G. (1981/82), 'Marginalité volontaire ou imposée: Le cas des Bakweri (Kpe) du Mont Cameroun', *Cahier ORSTOM, sér. Sci. Hum.* 18 (3): 357-388.

COURADE, G. (1984), 'Des complexes qui coûtent cher: La priorité agro-industrielle dans l'agriculture camerounaise', *Politique Africaine* 14: 75-91.

COURTENAY, P.P. (1965), *Plantation agriculture*, London: G. Bell & Co.

COWEN, M. (1981), 'Community production in Kenya's Central Province'. In: J. Heyer, P. Roberts & G. Williams, eds, *Rural development in tropical Africa*, London: Macmillan, 121-144.

CRISP, J. (1984), *The story of an African working class: Ghanaian miners' struggles*, London: Zed Books.

CURRIE, K. & L. RAY (1986), 'On the class location of contract farmers in the Kenyan economy', *Economy and Society* 15: 445-475.

DADDIEH, C. (1994), 'Contract farming and palm oil production in Côte d'Ivoire and Ghana'. In: P. Little & M. Watts, eds, *Living under contract: Contract farming and agrarian transformation in Africa*, Madison, WI: University of Wisconsin Press, 188-215.

DELANCEY, M.W. (1973), 'Changes in social attitudes and political knowledge among migrants to plantations in West Cameroon', Ph.D. Thesis, Indiana University.

DELANCEY, M.W. (1974), 'Plantation and migration in the Mount Cameroon region'. In: H.F. Illy, ed., *Kamerun: Struktur und Probleme der sozio-ökonomischen Entwicklung*, Mainz: Hase und Koehler Verlag, 181-236.

DELANCEY, M.W. (1977), 'Credit for the common man in Cameroon', *Journal of Modern African Studies* 15 (2): 316-322.

DELANCEY, M.W. (1989), *Cameroon: Dependence and independence*, Boulder/ San Francisco: Westview Press.

DE LA VEGA, B. (1971), 'La plantation de thé de Tole (Cameroun occidentale), Travail d'études et de recherches', University of Bordeaux: Institute of Geography.

DE SILVA, S.B.D. (1982), *The political economy of underdevelopment*, London: Routledge & Kegan Paul.

DINHAM, B. & C. HINES (1983), *Agribusiness in Africa: A study of the impact of big business in Africa's food and agricultural production*, London: Earth Resources Research.

EBUNE, J.B. (1992), *The growth of political parties in Southern Cameroons 1916-1960*, Yaoundé: CEPER.

EDWARDS, R. (1979), *Contested terrain: The transformation of the workplace in the twentieth century*, London: Heinemann.

ELLMAN, A. (1986), 'Nucleus estates and smallholders outgrower schemes', Paper presented at the IDS Workshop 'People in Plantations: Means or Ends', Sussex: IDS, 26-27 September.

ELSON, D. & R. PEARSON (1984), '"Nimble fingers make cheap workers": An analysis of women's employment in Third World export manufacturing'. In: P. Waterman, ed., *For a new labour internationalism*, The Hague: Ileri, 120-141.

EPALE, S.J. (1978), 'The mobilization of capital in a rural milieu: The example of the Bakweri of the South-West Province of Cameroon', *Rural Africana* 2 (n.s.): 69-88.

EPALE, S.J. (1985), *Plantations and development in Western Cameroon*, New York: Vantage Press.

EPSTEIN, A.L. (1958), *Politics in an urban African community*, Manchester: Manchester University Press.

EYOH, D. (1998), 'Through the prism of a local tragedy: Political liberalisation, regionalism and elite struggles for power in Cameroon', *Africa* 68 (3): 338-359.

EYONGETAH, T. & R. BRAIN (1974), *A history of the Cameroon*, Harlow, Essex: Longman.

EZUMAH, N.K. & E.G. FONSAH (2004), 'Women in the banana industry: A case study of Tiko Banana Plantation, South West Province, Cameroon'. In: J. Endeley, S. Ardener, R. Goodridge & N. Lyonga, eds, *New Gender Studies from Cameroon and the Caribbean, Vol. 1*, Oxford: African Books Collective, 79-93.

FEDER, E. (1977a), *Strawberry imperialism: An enquiry into the mechanisms of dependency in Mexican agriculture*, The Hague: Institute of Social Studies.

FEDER, E. (1977b), 'Capitalism's last-ditch effort to save under-developed agriculture: International agribusiness, the World Bank, and the rural poor', *Journal of Contemporary Asia* 7 (1): 56-78.

FIELDHOUSE, D.K. (1978), *Unilever overseas: The anatomy of a multinational, 1895-1965*, London: Croom Helm.

FIELDHOUSE, D.K. (1994), *Merchant capital and economic decolonization: The United Africa Company 1929-1989*, Oxford: Clarendon Press.

FISIY, C.F. (1992), *Power and privilege in the administration of law: Land law reforms and social differentiation in Cameroon*, Leiden: African Studies Centre, Research Report no. 48.

FISIY, C.F. (1995), 'Chieftaincy in the modern state: An institution at the crossroads of democratic change', *Paideuma* 41: 49-61.

FOEKEN, D. & N. TELLEGEN (1994), *Tied to the land: Living conditions of labourers on large farms in Trans Nzoia District, Kenya*, Aldershot: Avebury.

FONGANG, M. (1981/82), 'Case study: The Cameroon Development Corporation and the smallholders' scheme', Buea: RPAID/WA Student Report.

FONSAH, E.G. (1993), 'Economics of banana production and marketing in Cameroon', Ph.D. thesis, University of Nigeria, Nsukka.

FONSAH, E.G. & A.S.D.N. CHIDEBELU (1995), *Economics of banana production and marketing in the tropics: A case study of Cameroon*, London: Minerva Press.

FORGE, J.W. (1981), *The one and indivisible Cameroon*, Lund: University of Lund, Department of Politics.

FRANK, A.G. (1967), *Capitalism and underdevelopment in Latin America*, New York/London: Monthly Review Press.

FRANK, A.G. (1969), *Latin America: Underdevelopment and revolution*, New York/London: Monthly Review Press.

FREUND, B. (1981), *Capital and labour in the Nigerian tin mines,* Harlow, Essex: Longman.

FREUND, B. (1984), 'Labor and labor history in Africa: A review of the literature', *African Studies Review* 27 (2): 1-58.

FREUND, B. (1988), *The African worker,* Cambridge: Cambridge University Press.

FRIEDMAN, A. (1977), *Industry and labour: Class struggle at work and monopoly capitalism,* London: Macmillan.

GABRIEL, J.M. (1999), 'Cameroon's neopatrimonial dilemma', *Journal of Contemporary African Studies* 17 (2): 173-196.

GAILLARD, Ph. (1992), 'Pluralisme et régionalisme dans la politique camerounaise', *Afrique 2000* 11: 97-109.

GAITSKELL, A. (1959), *Gezira: A story of development in the Sudan,* London: Faber & Faber.

GESCHIERE, P. (1978), 'The articulation of different modes of production: Old and new inequalities in Maka villages (South-East Cameroon)'. In: R. Buijtenhuijs & P. Geschiere, eds, *Social stratification and class formation, African Perspectives 1978/2,* Leiden: African Studies Centre, 45-69.

GESCHIERE, P. (1985), 'Applications of the lineage mode of production in African studies', *Canadian Journal of African Studies* 19 (1): 80-91.

GESCHIERE, P. (1988), 'Witchcraft and cash crops, transformations of witchcraft beliefs and their implications to development in two Cameroonian societies', Paper presented at the World Congress for Rural Sociology, Bologna, 25-30 June.

GESCHIERE, P. (1989), 'Moderne mythen: Cultuur en ontwikkeling in Afrika', Inaugural Lecture, University of Leiden.

GESCHIERE, P. (1993), 'Chiefs and colonial rule in Cameroon: Inventing chieftaincy French and British style', *Africa* 63 (2): 151-175.

GESCHIERE, P. (1995), *Sorcellerie et politique en Afrique: La viande des autres,* Paris: Karthala.

GESCHIERE, P. (2009), 'Von Gravenreuth and Buea as a site of history: Early colonial violence on Mount Cameroon'. In: I. Fowler & V.G. Fanso, eds, *Encounter, transformation, and identity: Peoples of the Western Cameroon borderlands 1891-2000,* Oxford: Berghahn Books, Cameroon Studies, Vol. 8, 69-93.

GESCHIERE, P. & F.B. NYAMNJOH (2000), 'Capitalism and autochthony: The seesaw of mobility and exclusion', *Public Culture* 12 (2): 423-452.

GIBBON, P., ed. (1993), *Social change and economic reform in Africa*, Uppsala: Nordiska Afrikainstitutet.

GIBBON P., ed. (1995), *Structural adjustment and the working poor in Zimbabwe: Studies on labour, women informal sector workers and health*, Uppsala: Nordiska Afrikainstitutet.

GIBBON, P. (1997), 'Prawns and piranhas: The political economy of a Tanzanian private sector marketing chain', *Journal of Peasant Studies* 24 (4): 1-86.

GLOVER, D.J. (1984), 'Contract farming and smallholder outgrower schemes in less-developed countries', *World Development* 12 (11): 1143-1157.

GLOVER, D.J. & K. KUSTERER (1990), *Small farmers, big business: Contract farming and rural development*, London: Macmillan.

GOHEEN, M. (1993), 'Les champs appartiennent aux hommes, les récoltes aux femmes: Accumulation dans la région de Nso'. In: P. Geschiere & P. Konings, eds, *Itinéraires d'accumulation au Cameroun*, Paris: Karthala, 241-271.

GOHEEN, M. (1996), *Men own the fields, women own the crops: Gender and power in the Cameroon Grassfields*, Madison, WI: University of Wisconsin Press

GOLDSMITH, A. (1985), 'The private sector and rural development: Can agri-business help the small farmer?', *World Development* 13 (10/11): 1125-1138.

GOLDTHORPE, J.E. (1985), *The sociology of the Third World: Disparity and development*, Cambridge: Cambridge University Press.

GOODMAN, D. & M. REDCLIFT (1981), *From peasant to proletarian: Capitalist development and agrarian transitions*, Oxford: Basil Blackwell.

GORDON, R.J. (1977), *Mines, masters and migrants: Life in a Namibian compound*, Johannesburg: Ravan Press.

GRAHAM, E. & I. FLOERING (1984), *The modern plantations in the Third World*, London/Sydney: Croom Helm.

GRAVES, A. & P. RICHARDSON (1980), 'Plantations in the political economy of colonial sugar production: Natal and Queensland, 1860-1914', *Journal of Southern African Studies* 6: 214-229.

GROSH, B. (1994), 'Contract farming in Africa: An application of the new institutional economics', *Journal of African Economics* 3 (2): 231-261.

GROSH, B. & R.S. MAKANDALA, eds (1994), *State-owned enterprises in Africa*, Boulder/London: Lynne Rienner.

HALLDÉN, E. (1968), *The culture policy of the Basel mission in the Cameroons 1886-1905*, Uppsala: University of Uppsala, Studia Ethnographica Uppsaliensia 31.

HASHIM, Y. (1994), 'The state and trade unions in Africa: A study in macro-corporatism', Ph.D. Thesis, The Hague: Institute of Social Studies.

HEINZEN, B.J. (1984), 'The United Brands Company in Cameroon: A study of the tension between local and international imperatives', Ph.D. Thesis, University of London.

HERBST, J. (1991), 'Labour in Ghana under structural adjustment: The politics of acquiescence'. In: D. Rothchild, ed., *Ghana: The political economy of recovery*, Boulder, CO: Lynne Rienner, 173-192.

HEYER, J. (1981), 'Agricultural development policy in Kenya from the colonial period to 1975'. In: J. Heyer, P. Roberts & G. Williams, eds, *Rural development in tropical Africa*, London: Macmillan, 90-120.

HYDEN, G. (1980), *Beyond ujamaa in Tanzania: Underdevelopment and an uncaptured peasantry*, London/Ibadan/Nairobi: Heinemann.

HYMAN, R. (1971), *Marxism and the sociology of trade unionism*, London: Pluto Press.

JAIN, S. & R. REDDOCK, eds (1998), *Women plantation workers: International experiences*, Oxford/New York: Berg.

JEFFRIES, M.D.W. (1962), 'The Wiya tribe', *African Studies* 21 (2): 83-104.

JEFFRIES, R. (1978), *Class, power and ideology in Ghana: The railwaymen of Sekondi*, Cambridge: Cambridge University Press.

JOHNSON, W.R. (1970), *The Cameroon federation: Political integration in a fragmentary society*, Princeton, NJ: Princeton University Press.

JONES, W.O. (1968), 'Plantations'. In: D.L. Sills, ed., *International Encyclopedia of the Social Sciences*, Vol. 12, 154-159.

JUA, N. (1991), 'Cameroon: Jump-starting an economic crisis', *Africa Insight* 21 (1): 162-170.

JUA, N. & P. KONINGS (2004), 'Occupation of public space: Anglophone nationalism in Cameroon', *Cahiers d'Études Africaines* XLIV (175): 609-633.

KABERRY, P.M. (1952), *Women of the Grassfields: A study of the economic position of women in Bamenda, British Cameroons*, London: HMSO.

KAPTUE, L. (1986), *Travail et main-d'oeuvre au Cameroun sous régime français 1916-1952*, Paris: L'Harmattan.

KEMP, C. & A. LITTLE (1987), 'Editorial introduction', *IDS Bulletin* (Sussex) 18 (2): 2-17.

KENDRICK, R. (1979), 'Survey of industrial relations in Cameroon'. In: U.G. Damachi, H.D. Seibel & L. Trachtman, eds, *Industrial relations in Africa*, London: Macmillan, 73-103.

KIRK, C. (1987), 'Contracting out: Plantations, smallholders and transnational enterprise', *IDS Bulletin* (Sussex) 18 (2): 45-51.

KLEIS, G.W. (1975), 'Network and ethnicity in an Igbo migrant community', Ph.D. Thesis, Michegan State University.

KOFELE-KALE, N., ed. (1980), *An African experiment in nation building: The bilingual Cameroon Republic since reunification*, Boulder, CO: Westview Press.

KOFELE-KALE, N. (1981), *Tribesmen and patriots: Political culture in a poly-ethnic African state*, Washington, DC: University Press of America.

KOFELE-KALE, N. (1986), 'Ethnicity, regionalism and political power: A post-mortem of Ahidjo's Cameroon'. In: M.G. Schatzberg & I.W. Zartman, eds, *The political economy of Cameroon*, New York: Praeger, 53-82.

KONINGS, P. (1986a), *The state and rural class formation in Ghana: A comparative analysis*, London/Boston: Kegan Paul International.

KONINGS, P. (1986b), 'L'État, l'agro-industrie et la paysannerie au Cameroun', *Politique Africaine* 22: 120-137.

KONINGS, P. (1989), 'La liquidation des plantations Unilever et les conflits intra-ethniques dans le Cameroun anglophone', *Politique Africaine* 35: 132-137.

KONINGS, P. (1993a), *Labour resistance in Cameroon: Managerial strategies and labour resistance in the agro-industrial plantations of the Cameroon Development Corporation*, London: James Currey.

KONINGS, P. (1993b), 'Contract farming and capital accumulation in Cameroon: The case of the CDC smallholder schemes'. In: P. Geschiere & P. Konings, eds, *Itinéraires d'accumulation au Cameroun*, Paris: Karthala, 217-239.

KONINGS, P. (1995a), *Gender and class in the tea estates of Cameroon*, Aldershot: Avebury, African Studies Centre Leiden Research Series no. 5.

KONINGS, P. (1995b), Plantation labour and economic crisis in Cameroon', *Development and Change* 26 (3): 525-549.

KONINGS, P. (1996a), 'The post-colonial state and economic and political reforms in Cameroon'. In: A.E. Fernández Jilberto & A. Mommen, eds, *Liberalization in the developing world: Institutional and economic changes in Latin America, Africa and Asia*, London/New York: Routledge, 244-265.

KONINGS, P. (1996b), 'Privatisation of agro-industrial parastatals and Anglophone opposition in Cameroon', *Journal of Commonwealth and Comparative Politics* 34 (3): 199-217.

KONINGS, P. (1996c), 'Chieftaincy, labour control and capitalist development in Cameroon', *Journal of Legal Pluralism and Unofficial Law* 37-38: 329-346.

KONINGS, P. (1998a), *Unilever estates in crisis and the power of organizations in Cameroon*, Hamburg: LIT Verlag.

KONINGS, P. (1998b), 'Unilever, contract farmers and co-operatives in Cameroon: Crisis and response', *Journal of Peasant Studies* 26 (1): 112-138.

KONINGS, P. (1998c), 'Women plantation workers and economic crisis in Cameroon'. In: S. Jain & R. Reddock, eds, *Women plantation workers: International experiences*, Oxford/New York: Berg, 151-165.

KONINGS, P. (1999), 'The "Anglophone problem" and chieftaincy in Anglophone Cameroon'. In: E.A.B. van Rouveroy van Nieuwaal & R. van Dijk, eds, *African chieftaincy in a new socio-political landscape*, Hamburg: LIT Verlag, 181-206.

KONINGS, P. (2000), 'Trade unions and democratisation in Africa'. In: P. Konings, W. van Binsbergen & G. Hesseling, eds, *Trajectoires de libération en Afrique contemporaine,* Paris: Karthala, 166-183.

KONINGS, P. (2001), 'Mobility and exclusion: Conflicts between autochthons and allochthons during political liberalization in Cameroon'. In: M. de Bruijn, R. van Dijk & D. Foeken, eds, *Mobile Africa: Changing patterns of movements in Africa and beyond,* Leiden: Brill, 169-194.

KONINGS, P. (2002), 'Structural adjustment and trade unions in Africa: The case of Ghana'. In: A.E. Fernández Jilberto & M. Riethof, eds, *Labour relations in development,* London/New York: Routledge, 311-336.

KONINGS, P. (2003a), 'Chieftaincy and privatisation in Anglophone Cameroon'. In: W. van Binsbergen, ed., *The dynamics of power and the rule of law: Essays on Africa and beyond,* Münster: LIT Verlag, 79-99.

KONINGS, P. (2003b), 'Privatisation and ethno-regional protest in Cameroon', *Afrika Spectrum* 38 (1): 5-26.

KONINGS, P. (2004a), 'Opposition and social-democratic change in Africa; The Social Democratic Front in Cameroon', *Commonwealth and Comparative Politics* 42 (3): 289-311.

KONINGS, P. (2004b), 'Good governance, privatisation and ethno-regional conflict in Cameroon'. In: J. Demmers, A.E. Fernández Jilberto & B. Hogenboom, eds, *Good governance in the era of global neoliberalism: Conflict and depolitisation in Latin America, Eastern Europe, Asia and Africa,* London/New York: Routledge, 306-330.

KONINGS, P. (2005), 'The Anglophone Cameroon-Nigeria boundary: Opportunities and conflicts', *African Affairs* 104 (415): 275-301.

KONINGS, P. (2006), 'African trade unions and the challenge of globalisation: A comparative study of Ghana and Cameroon'. In: C. Phelan, ed., *The future of organised labour: Global perspectives,* Oxford/Bern: Peter Lang, 361-395.

KONINGS, P. (2007a), 'The neoliberalising African state and private capital accumulation: The case of Cameroon'. In: A.E. Fernández Jilberto & B. Hogenboom, eds, *Big business and economic development: Conglomerates and economic groups in developing countries and transition economies under globalisation,* London/New York: Routledge, 251-273.

KONINGS, P. (2007b), 'Trade unionism in Cameroon: From crisis to revitalisation?', In: C. Phelan, ed., *Trade union revitalisation: Trends and prospects in 34 countries,* Oxford/Bern: Peter Lang, 431-443.

KONINGS, P. (2008), 'Autochthony and ethnic cleansing in the post-colony: The 1966 Tombel disturbances', *International Journal of African Historical Studies* 41 (2): 203-222.

KONINGS, P. (2009a), 'The history of trade unionism in Cameroon'. In: C. Phelan, ed., *Trade unionism since 1945; Towards a global history, Volume 1: Western Europe, Eastern Europe, Africa and the Middle East,* Oxford/Bern: Peter Lang, 315-341.

KONINGS, P. (2009b), *Neoliberal bandwagonism: Civil society and the politics of belonging in Anglophone Cameroon,* Bamenda/Leiden: Langaa/ASC.

KONINGS, P. (2010), 'Occupational change, structural adjustment and trade union identity in Africa: The case of Cameroonian plantation workers'. In: D. Bryceson, ed., *How Africa Works: Occupational change, identity and morality,* Rugby, Warwickshire: Practical Action Publishing.

KONINGS, P. & F.B. NYAMNJOH (1997), 'The Anglophone problem in Cameroon', *Journal of Modern African Studies* 35 (2): 207-229.

KONINGS, P. & F.B. NYAMNJOH (2000), 'Construction and deconstruction: Anglophones or autochtones?', *The African Anthropologist* 7 (1): 207-229.

KONINGS, P. & F.B. NYAMNJOH (2003), *Negotiating an Anglophone identity: A study of the politics of recognition and representation in Cameroon,* Leiden: Brill.

KRIEGER, M. (1994), 'Cameroon's democratic crossroads, 1990-4', *Journal of Modern African Studies* 32 (4): 605-628.

KURIAN, R. (1982), *Women workers in the Sri Lanka plantation sector,* Geneva: ILO.

KURIAN, R. (1989), 'State, capital and labour in the plantation industry in Sri Lanka 1834-1984', Ph.D. Thesis, University of Amsterdam.

KUSTERER, K. (1981), 'The social impact of agribusiness: A case study of ALCOSA in Guatemala', Washington, DC: USAID.

KUSTERER, K. (1982), 'The social impact of agribusiness: A case study of asparagus canning in Peru', Washington, DC: USAID.

LACLAU, E. (1971), 'Feudalism and capitalism in Latin America', *New Left Review* 67: 19-38.

LAMB, G. & L. MULLER (1982), 'Control, accountability, and incentives in a successful development institution: The Kenya Tea Development Authority', Staff Working Paper 550, Washington, DC: World Bank.

LAPPÉ, F. & J. COLLINS (1977), *Food first: The myth of scarcity*, Boston: Houghton Mifflin.

LARMER, M. (2005), 'Reaction and resistance to neo-liberalism in Zambia', *Review of African Political Economy* 103: 29-45.

LARMER, M. (2007), *Mineworkers in Zambia: Labour and political change in post-colonial Africa*, London/New York: Tauris Academic Studies.

LEITNER, K. (1976), 'The situation of agricultural workers in Kenya', *Review of African Political Economy* 6: 34-50.

LENTZ, C. & V. ERLMANN (1989), 'A working class in formation?': Crisis and strategies of survival among Dagara mine workers in Ghana', *Cahiers d'Études Africaines* 29 (1): 69-111.

LE VINE, V.T. (1964), *The Cameroons: From mandate to independence*, Berkeley/Los Angeles: University of California Press.

LE VINE, V.T. (1971), *The Cameroon Federal Republic*, Ithaca, NY: Cornell University Press.

LEWIS, W.A. (1954), 'Economic development with unlimited supplies of labour', *The Manchester School* 22: 139-191.

LEYS, C. (1975), *Underdevelopment in Kenya: The political economy of neo-colonialism*, London: Heinemann.

LITTLE, P.D. (1994), 'Contract farming and the development question'. In: P.D. Little & M.J. Watts, eds, *Living under contract: Contract farming and agrarian transformation in Sub-Saharan Africa*, Madison, WI: University of Wisconsin Press, 216-247.

LITTLE, P.D. & M.J. WATTS, eds, (1994), *Living under contract: Contract farming and agrarian transformation in Sub-Saharan Africa*, Madison, WI: University of Wisconsin Press.

LOEWENSON, R. (1992), *Modern plantation agriculture: Corporate wealth and labour squalor*, London: Zed Books.

LONG, N. (1977), *An introduction to the sociology of rural development*, London: Tavistock Publications.

LUBECK, P. (1986), *Islam and urban labor in Northern Nigeria: The making of a Muslim working class*, Cambridge: Cambridge University Press.

MAMA, T., ed., (1996), *Crise économique et politique de déréglementation au Cameroun*, Paris: L'Harmattan.

MARCUSSEN, H.S. & J.E. TORP (1982), *The internationalization of capital: The prospects for the Third World*, London/New Jersey: Zed Books.

MATUTE, D.L. (1990), *Facing Mount Fako: An ethnographic study of the Bakweri of Cameroon*, Milwaukee: Omni Press.

MBAKE, S. NJIA (1975), 'Traditional authority among the Bakweri', Thesis for Postgraduate Diploma in History, University of Yaoundé.

MBILE, N.N. (2000), *Cameroon political story: Memories of an authentic eye witness*, Limbe: Presbyterian Printing Press.

MBUAGBAW, T.E., R. BRAIN & R. PALMER (1987), *A history of the Cameroon*, Harlow, Essex: Longman.

MEEBELO, H.S. (1986), *African proletarians and colonial capitalism*, Lusaka: Kenneth Kaunda Foundation.

MEHLER, A. (1993), *Kamerun in der Ära Biya*, Hamburg: Institut für Afrika-Kunde.

MEILLASSOUX, C. (1972), 'From reproduction to production', *Economy and Society* 1 (1): 93-105.

MEILLASSOUX, C. (1975), *Femmes, greniers et capitaux*, Paris: Maspero.

MEILLASSOUX, C. (1977), *Terrains et théories*, Paris: Maspero.

MIES, M. (1986), *Patriarchy and accumulation on a world scale*, London: Zed Books.

MILLEN, B.H. (1963), *The political role of labor in developing countries*, Washington: The Brookings Institution.

MINOT, N.W. (1986), 'Contract farming and its effect on small farmers in less developed countries', Michegan State University, Working Paper no. 31.

MKANDAWIRE, T. (1994), 'The political economy of privatisation in Africa'. In: G.A. Cornia & G.K. Helleiner, eds, *From adjustment to development in Africa: Conflict, controversy, convergence, consensus?*, New York: St. Martin's Press, 192-213.

MOLUA, H.N. (1985), 'The Bakweri land problem, 1884-1961: A case study', M.A. Thesis, University of Ibadan.

MORRISSY, D. (1974), *Agricultural modernization through production contracting*, New York: Praeger.

NDONGKO, W.A. (1975), *Planning for economic development in a federal state: The case of Cameroon, 1960-1971*, Munich: Weltforum Verlag.

NDONGKO, W.A. (1985), *Reflexions on the economic policies and development of Cameroon*, Yaoundé: MESRES/ISH.

NDZANA, V. OMBE (1987), *Agriculture, pétrole et politique au Cameroun: Sortir de la crise?*, Paris: L'Harmattan.

NGEND, J. (1982), 'Les plantations de cannes à sucre de Mbandjock et leur influence régionale', Thèse de Doctorat de Troisième Cycle, University of Bordeaux.

NKWI, P.N. & F.B. NYAMNJOH, eds (1997), *Regional balance and national integration in Cameroon: Lessons learnt and the uncertain future*, Yaoundé/Leiden: ICASSRT Monograph no. 1.

NKWI, P.N. & J.-P. WARNIER (1982), *Elements for a history of the Western Grassfields*, Yaoundé: SOPECAM.

NKWI, W.G. (2006), 'Elites, ethno-regional competition in Cameroon, and the Southwest Elites Association (SWELA), 1991-1997', *African Study Monographs* 27 (3): 123-143.

NYAMNJOH, F.B. (1999), 'Cameroon: A country united by ethnic ambition and difference, *African Affairs* 98 (390): 101-118.

NYAMNJOH, F.B. (2005), *Africa's media, democracy and the politics of belonging*, London/New York: Zed Books.

NYAMNJOH, F.B. & M. ROWLANDS (1998), 'Elite associations and the politics of belonging in Cameroon', *Africa* 68 (3): 320-337.

OBBO, C. (1980), *African women: Their struggles for economic independence*, London: Zedd Books.

OLOYEDE, O. (1992), 'Surviving an economic recession: "Game play" in a Nigerian factory', *Review of African Political Economy* 55: 44-56.

OLUKOSHI, A. (1998), *The elusive prince of Denmark: Structural adjustment and the crisis of governance in Africa*, Uppsala: Nordiska Afrikainstitutet, Research Report no. 104.

OLOKOSHI, A.O. & I. AREMU (1988), 'Structural adjustment and labour subordination in Nigeria: The dissolution of the Nigeria Labour Congress re-visited', *Review of African Political Economy* 43: 99-111.

OXAAL, I. (1975), 'The dependency economist as grassroots politician in the Caribbean'. In: I. Oxaal, T. Barnett & D. Booth, eds, *Beyond the sociology of development: Economy and society in Latin America and Africa*, London/Boston: Routledge & Kegan Paul, 28-49.

PAIGE, J. (1975), *Agrarian revolution: Social movements and export agriculture in the underdeveloped world*, New York: Free Press.

PARPART, J.L. (1983), *Labour and capital in the African Copperbelt*, Philadelphia: Temple University Press.

PARPART, J.L. (1986), 'Class and gender in the Copperbelt: Women in Northern Rhodesian copper mining communities'. In: C. Robertson & I. Berger, eds, *Women and class in Africa*, New York/London: Africana Publishing Company, 141-160.

PARPART, J.L. (1988), 'Women, work and collective labour action in Africa'. In: R. Southall, ed., *Labour and unions in Asia and Africa*, Basingstoke: Macmillan, 238-255.

PAYER, C. (1980), 'The World Bank and the small farmers', *Monthly Review* 36 (6): 30-47.

PERRINGS, C. (1979), *Black mineworkers in Central Africa*, London: Heinemann.

PITCHER, M.A. (2002), *Transforming Mozambique: The politics of privatization, 1975-2000*, Cambridge: Cambridge University Press.

PITTIN, R. (1984), 'Gender and class in a Nigerian industrial setting', *Review of African Political Economy* 31: 71-81.

PORTER, G. & K. PHILLIPS-HOWARD (1995), 'Farmers, labourers and the company: Exploring relationships on a Transkei contract farming scheme', *Journal of Development Studies* 32 (1): 55-73.

PORTER, G. & K. PHILLIPS-HOWARD (1997), 'Comparing contracts: An evaluation of contract farming schemes in Africa', *World Development* 25 (2): 227-238.

PROBST, P. & B. BÜHLER (1990), 'Patterns of control in medicine, politics, and social change amongst the Wimbum, Cameroon Grassfields, *Anthropos* 85 (4-6): 447-454.

PRYOR, F.L. (1982), 'Review article: The plantation economy as an economic system', *Journal of Comparative Economics* 6 (3): 288-317.

RAKNER, L. (2001) 'The pluralist paradox: The decline of economic interest groups in Zambia in the 1990s', *Development and Change* 32 (3): 521-543.

RAKNER, L. (2003), *Political and economic liberalisation in Zambia 1991-2001*, Uppsala: Nordic Africa Institute.

RENDELL, W. sir (1976), *The history of the Commonwealth Development Corporation 1948-1972*, London: Heinemann.

REY, P.-P. (1971), *Colonialisme, néo-colonialisme et transition au capitalisme: Exemple de la 'Comilog' au Congo-Brazzaville*, Paris: Maspero.

REY, P.-P. (1973), *Les alliances de classes*, Paris: Maspero.

REY, P.-P. (1976), *Capitalisme négrier, la marche des paysans vers le prolétariat*, Paris: Maspero.

REY, P.-P. (1979), 'Class contradictions in lineage societies', *Critique of Anthropology* 4 (13-14): 41-60.

ROTE, R. (1986), *A taste of bitterness: The political economy of tea plantations in Sri Lanka*, Amsterdam: Free University Press.

ROWLANDS, M. (1993), 'Accumulation and the cultural politics of identity in the Grassfields'. In: P. Geschiere & P. Konings, eds, *Itinéraires d'accumulation au Cameroun*, Paris: Karthala, 71-97.

RUDIN, H.R. (1938), *Germans in the Cameroons 1884-1914: A case study in modern imperialism*, New Haven: Yale University Press.

RÜGER, A. (1960), 'Die Entstehung und Lage der Arbeiterklasse unter dem deutschen Kolonialregime in Kamerun (1895-1905)'. In: H. Stoecker, ed., *Kamerun unter deutscher Kolonialherrschaft*, Berlin: Rütten & Loening, 151-242.

RUEL, M.J. (1960), 'The Banyang of Mamfe Division'. In: E. Ardener, S. Ardener & W.A. Warmington, *Plantation and village in the Cameroons*, London: Oxford University Press, 230-247.

SAFA, H.I. (1979), 'Class consciousness among working class women in Latin America: A case study in Puerto Rico'. In: R. Cohen, P.C.W. Gutkind & P. Brazier, eds, *Peasants and proletarians: The struggles of Third World workers*, London: Hutchinson & Co, 441-459.

SAJHAU, J.-P. (1986), 'Employment, wages and living conditions in a changing industry: Plantations', *International Labour Review* 125 (1): 71-85.

SAJHAU, J.-P. & J. VON MURALT (1987), *Plantations and plantation workers*, Geneva: ILO.

SANDBROOK, R. (1975), *Proletarians and African capitalism: The Kenyan case 1960-1972*, Cambridge: Cambridge University Press.

SANDBROOK, R. (1982), *The politics of basic needs: Urban aspects of assaulting poverty in Africa*, London/Ibadan/Nairobi: Heinemann.

SANDBROOK, R. (1985), *The politics of Africa's economic stagnation*, Cambridge: Cambridge University Press.

SANDBROOK, R. (2000), *Closing the circle: Democratization and development in Africa*, Toronto: Between the Lines.

SANDBROOK, R. & R. COHEN, eds (1975), *The development of an African working class*, London: Longman.

SELLERS, S. (1984), 'Blohorn in the Ivory Coast: A microcosm of Unilever on the banks of a lagoon', *Unilever Magazine* 51: 7-11.

SHADEED, Z.A. (1979), 'Union leaders, worker organization and strikes: Karachi 1969-72', *Development and Change* 10 (2): 181-204.

SIMUTANYI, N.R. (1992), 'Trade unions and the democratization process in Zambia', Paper presented at the Seventh General Assembly of CODESRIA, Dakar, 10-12 February.

SORRENSON, M. (1967), *Land reforms in the Kikuyu country*, Oxford: Oxford University Press.

SOUTHALL, R., ed. (1988), *Trade unions and the new industrialisation of the Third World*, London: Zed Books.

STARK, F. (1976), 'Federalism in Cameroon: The shadow and the reality', *Canadian Journal of African Studies* 10 (3): 423-442.

STEEVES, J. (1975), 'The politics and administration of agricultural development in Kenya: The KTDA', Ph.D. Thesis, University of Toronto.

STICHTER, S.B. & J.L. PARPART, eds (1988), *Patriarchy and class: African women in the home and the workplace*, Boulder, CO: Westview Press.

STRYKER, R. (1979), 'The World Bank and agricultural development', *World Development* 7 (3): 325-336.

SWAINSON, N. (1985), 'Public policy in the development of export crops: Pineapples and tea in Kenya', *IDS Bulletin* (Sussex) 17 (1): 39-46.

SWYNNERTON, R.J.M., K.D.S. BALDWIN & W.J.R. COX (1964), *Report of the agricultural mission*, Victoria-Bota: CDC.

TAKOUGANG, J. (1993), 'The demise of Biya's new deal in Cameroon, 1982-1992', *Africa Insight* 23 (2): 91-101.

TAKOUGANG, J. (1994), 'Chief Johannes Manga Williams and the making of a "native" colonial autocrat among the Bakweri of the Southern Cameroons', *Transafrican Journal of History* 23: 9-31.

TAKOUGANG, J. & M. KRIEGER (1998), *African state and society in the 1990s: Cameroon's political crossroads*, Boulder, CO: Westview Press.

TANGRI, R. (1999), *The politics of patronage in Africa: Parastatals, privatisation and private enterprise*, Oxford: James Currey.

TCHALA ABINA, F. (1989), 'De l'indépendance à la dépendance: Étude de l'évolution des relations sociales de production dans le secteur agricole camerounais de 1960 à 1987'. In: P. Geschiere & P. Konings, eds, *Proceedings/contributions of the conference on the political economy of Cameroon – Historical perspectives, Leiden, June 1988*, Leiden: African Studies Centre, Research Report no. 35 (2 vols), 249-277.

TEDGA, P.-J.M. (1990), *Entreprises publiques, état et crise au Cameroun*, Paris: L'Harmattan.

TERRAY, E. (1969), *Le marxisme devant les sociétés 'primitives': Deux études*, Paris: Maspero.

TERRAY, E. (1975), 'Classes and class consciousness in Abron kingdom of Gyaman'. In: M. Bloch, ed., *Marxist analysis and social anthropology*, London: Malaby Press, 85-113.

TERRAY, E. (1979), 'On exploitation: Elements of an autocritique', *Critique of Anthropology* 4 (13-14): 29-41.

TJEEGA, P. (1973), 'Les types d'exploitation de la palmeraie à huile dans la région d'Esaka-Dingombi', Yaoundé: ORSTOM.

THOMPSON, E.T. (1975), *Plantation societies, race relations, and the South: The Regimentation of populations*, Durham, NC: Duke University Press.

THOMPSON, P. (1983), *The nature of work: An introduction to debates on the labour process*, London: Macmillan.

TIFFEN, M. & M. MORTIMORE (1990), *Theory and practice in plantation agriculture: An economic review*, London: Overseas Development Institute.

VAIL, L. & L. WHITE (1980), *Capitalism and colonialism in Mozambique: A study of Quelemane District*, Minneapolis: University of Minnesota Press.

VAN BINSBERGEN, W.M.J. (1993), 'Kazanga: Ethnicité en Afrique entre état et tradition', *Africa Focus* 9 (1-2): 16-41.

VAN BINSBERGEN, W.M.J. & P. GESCHIERE, eds (1985), *Old modes of production and capitalist encroachment: Anthropological explorations in Africa*, London/Boston: Kegan Paul International.

VAN DE BELT, H. (1981), 'Socio-economic characteristics of "outgrowers" linked to industrial oil-palm plantations: The case of Dibombari, Cameroon'. In: H. van de Belt *et al.*, eds, *Essays in rural sociology: In honour of R.A.J. van Lier*, Wageningen: Agricultural University, 1-23.

VAN DE LAAR, A. (1980), *The World Bank and the poor*, The Hague: Martinus Nijhoff.

VAN DE WALLE, N. (1993), 'The politics of nonreform in Cameroon'. In: T.M. Callaghy & J. Ravenhill, eds, *Hemmed in: Responses to Africa's economic decline*, New York: Columbia University Press, 357-397.

VAN DE WALLE, N. (1994a), 'Neopatrimonialism and democracy in Africa, with an illustration from Cameroon'. In: J.A. Widner, ed., *Economic change and political liberalization in Sub-Saharan Africa*, Baltimore: John Hopkins University Press, 129-157.

VAN DE WALLE, N. (1994b), 'The politics of public enterprise reform in Cameroon'. In: B. Grosh & R.S. Makandala, eds, *State-owned enterprises in Africa*, Boulder/London: Lynne Rienner, 151-174.

VAN DE WALLE, N. (2001), *African economies and the politics of permanent crisis, 1979-1999*, Cambridge: Cambridge University Press.

VAN ONSELEN, C. (1976), *Chibaro: African mine labour in Southern Rhodesia, 1900-1933*, London: Pluto Press.

VAN ROUVEROY VAN NIEUWAAL, E.A.B. (1987), 'Chiefs and African states: Some introductory notes and an extensive bibliography on African chieftaincy', *Journal of Legal Pluralism* 25-26: 1-46.

VAN ROUVEROY VAN NIEUWAAL, E.A.B. (1996), 'State and chiefs: Are chiefs mere puppets?'. In: E.A.B. van Rouveroy van Nieuwaal & D.I. Ray, eds, *The new relevance of traditional authorities to Africa's future*, *Journal of Legal Pluralism and Unofficial Law* 37-38: 39-78.

VAN ROUVEROY VAN NIEUWAAL, E.A.B. (1998), 'Law and protest in Africa: Resistance to legal innovation'. In: E.A.B. van Rouveroy van Nieuwaal & W. Zips, eds, *Sovereignty, legitimacy, and power in West Africa: Perspectives from legal anthropology,* Hamburg: LIT Verlag, 70-116.

VAN ROUVEROY VAN NIEUWAAL, E.A.B. & D.I. RAY, eds (1996), *The new relevance of traditional authorities to Africa's future, Journal of Legal Pluralism and Unofficial Law* 37-38.

VAN ROUVEROY VAN NIEUWAAL, E.A.B. & R. VAN DIJK, eds (1999), *African chieftaincy in a new socio-political landscape,* Hamburg: LIT Verlag.

VAN ZWANENBERG, R.M.A. (1975), *Colonial capitalism and labour in Kenya 1919-1939,* Nairobi: East African Publishing House.

VARMA, B.N. (1980), *The sociology and politics of development: A theoretical study,* London: Routledge & Kegan Paul.

VON MURALT, J. & J.-P. SAJHAU (1987), 'Plantations and basic needs: The changing international and national setting', *IDS Bulletin* (Sussex) 18 (2): 9-14.

WALKER, C., ed. (1982), *Women and gender in Southern Africa to 1945,* Cape Town: David Philips/London: James Currey.

WALKER, S.T. (1998), 'Both pretense and promise: The political economy of privatization in Africa', Ph.D. Thesis, Indiana University.

WARMINGTON, W.A. (1960), *A West African trade union,* Oxford: Oxford University Press.

WARNIER, J.-P. (2009), *Régner au Cameroun: Le roi-pot,* Paris: Karthala.

WATERMAN, P. (1983), 'Aristocrats and plebeians in African trade unions?: Lagos port and dock workers organisation and struggle', Ph.D. Thesis, Catholic University of Nijmegen.

WATTS, M. (1986), *Contract farming in Sub-Saharan Africa,* Binghampton: Institute for Development Anthropology (2 vols).

WATTS, M. (1994), 'Life under contract: Contract farming, agrarian restructuring, and flexible accumulation'. In: P. Little & M. Watts, eds, *Living under contract: Contract farming and agrarian transformation in Africa,* Madison, WI: University of Wisconsin Press, 21-77.

WELLS, F.A. & W.A. WARMINGTON (1962), *Studies in industrialisation: Nigeria and the Cameroons,* London: Oxford University Press.

WILLIAMS, G. (1981), 'The World Bank and the peasant problem'. In: J. Heyer, P. Roberts & G. Williams, eds, *Rural development in tropical Africa*, London: Macmillan, 16-51.

WILLIAMS, S. & R. KAREN (1984), *Agribusiness and the small-scale farmer: A dynamic partnership for development*, Boulder, CO: Westview Press.

WILSON, Ch. (1954), *The history of Unilever: A study in economic growth and social change*, London: Cassel (2 vols.).

WILSON, Ch. (1968), *Unilever 1945-1965: Challenge and response in the post-war industrial revolution*, London: Cassell.

WOLF, E.R. (1982), *Europe and the people without history*, Berkeley/Los Angeles: University of California Press.

WOLPE, H. (1972), 'Capitalism and cheap labour in South Africa: From segregation to apartheid', *Economy and Society* 1 (4): 425-456.

WOLPE, H., ed. (1980), *The articulation of modes of production: Essays from 'Economy and Society'*, London: Routledge & Kegan Paul.

WORLD BANK (1989), *Sub-Saharan Africa: From crisis to sustainable growth*, Washington, DC: World Bank.

WORLD BANK (1992), *Governance and development*, Washington, DC: World Bank.

WORLD BANK (1995), *World development report 1995: Workers in an integrated world*, Washington, DC: World Bank.

WORLD BANK (1997), *The state in a changing world*, New York: Oxford University Press.

WYRLEY-BIRCH, E.A., I.P. ANDERSON, W.J.R. COX, M. EARINGTON & S.H. WALTER (1982), 'Land suitability and feasability study for oil palm and rubber plantations in South-West Cameroon', Surbiton, Surrey: Land Resources Development Centre.

ZEILIG, L., ed. (2002), *Class struggle and resistance in Africa*, Cheltenham: New Clarion Press.

# Index